BEETHOVEN'S QUARTETS

Joseph de Marliave

Introduction and Notes by
Jean Escarra

Preface by
Gabriel Fauré

Translated by
Hilda Andrews

DOVER PUBLICATIONS, INC.
Mineola, New York

Bibliographical Note

This Dover edition, first published in 1961 and reprinted in 2004, is an unabridged and unaltered republication of the English translation first published in 1928. It is republished by special arrangement with Oxford University Press.

This work was first published in French by the Librairie Félix Alcan, Paris, and the text is that of 1925.

International Standard Book Number: 0-486-43965-8

Manufactured in the United States of America
Dover Publications, Inc., 31 East 2nd Street, Mineola, N.Y. 11501

PREFACE

THE splendid memorial that Joseph de Marliave was to erect in honour of Beethoven and his immortal quartets was destined to become the shrine in which is entombed his own precious memory, a memorial over which might well be inscribed the words : ' Pendent interrupta opera ! '—too significant of his brief and glorious life. In the request to set my name also upon this memorial I have received a sad and honoured privilege. Those who pass by will at least read my name and know my sorrow, and should they stay to examine this fine work, the labour of loving and skilful hands, they will share too the realization of my grief.

It has long been a source of surprise that so important a work as the Beethoven quartets has not had its historian or critic to do it special honour, and the scanty reviews now lost to sight in the mass of musical literature are far from satisfying this long-felt need, indeed only emphasize it. Even German critics, who have written—well or ill—upon every conceivable subject, have not to this day produced a standard study of these quartets. Certainly it was a tremendous undertaking, fascinating though it may be, needing years of work and critical gifts of the most versatile order. It would entail first of all the tracing of the genre back to its source and through its slow evolution from the unaccompanied madrigal to the first quartets of Haydn ; only from a study of its growth and form could rules of structure be disentangled and formulated. Again, it would entail research into the art of Haydn and Mozart, Beethoven's predecessors and his early models, before the art of Beethoven himself could be touched. Finally there looms ahead the study and analysis of this colossal work, the like of which future generations will never see. Each of these quartets is in itself an achievement of art and genius, and has a right to respect and consideration, demands the closest attention to detail, and, on the part of a conscientious critic, a proper understanding of the spirit that gave it birth, of its form, whether classical or re-created anew, or entirely novel, of its technique and of its style. He must realize the promise of the first quartets and how it materialized in those that followed, the musician's favourite methods, how they appear in the early movements and then later on in this long series of pieces, all different, but cast in a mould of almost unchanging form ; then must be defined the slow but uninterrupted upward progress of the inner consciousness, of the inspiration, style, technique, from voluntary imitation to free creation. And finally the material provided in the Beethoven quartets demands a critical knowledge of the technique of string instruments.

Joseph de Marliave has given us this titanic work. The summons of a noble death prevented him from revising the task that occupied so much of his life, but reverent and skilled hands have rescued it from obscurity to give it to us now in the unspoilt freshness of its youthful force and conviction.

When he left Saint-Cyr, sent to the East with a garrison, Joseph de Marliave used to collect every week four instrumentalists to come to his rooms and play the Beethoven quartets. This young sub-lieutenant was cultured and educated enough to have written a thesis on the ' Retreat of the Ten Thousand ', or the ' French War ', or in the disturbing atmosphere of the East to have studied ' German Customs '. All this he may have done—we do not know. But we do know that in his exile he heard and experienced to the full the joy of these *allegros* and the tenderness of these *andantes*. In those secret meetings he penetrated the depths of the charm and the elusive mystery of the Beethoven quartets. One wonders if he would have modified any of his views or tempered his wholehearted admiration if he had lived to make his own revision. But it was surely a more satisfying thing to have undertaken a work and carried it out to the end in the spirit of single-minded love. Even if he had wished it, could the unforgettable impressions of absolute beauty first awakened in his soul ever have faded ? In the study of the last quartets he might have moderated, with a pen grown wiser, the undivided praise he devoted to the first. But he did not ; we must accept his work, a doubly sacred charge, as he left it to us. It is further impressed with two qualities rarely allied, a careful and indefatigable zeal for facts, and the grace of a genuine enthusiasm which infuses the work with sincerity and life. Rare indeed, Joseph de Marliave was not only an incisive critic but a passionate lover of music. None better or in greater degree than he could lose himself in the wonder of the art. Opera, symphony, or quartet meant to him a refuge where he could escape from material existence. Music possessed his entire being, and once back at home he found in it his only delight and pleasure ; he loved it before he understood it ; he felt its enchantment before he studied its science. His acute critical faculty waited upon his aesthetic enjoyment. I hesitate to speak of the *Études musicales*. But I cannot conclude without confessing how dear it is to the soul of an artist to know his work loved and understood.

GABRIEL FAURÉ.

April 1924.

PUBLISHER'S NOTE

THE attention of the Publisher has been directed by Professor Martin Bernstein of New York University to the fact that certain passages which originally appeared in a German study of Beethoven's Quartets by T. Helm (published in 1885) are to be found un-acknowledged in this volume. These passages, trans-lated into French, occurred among the unfinished manuscripts and notes of Joseph de Marliave, who, had he lived to see the work through the press, would doubtless have made the proper acknowledgement of their source. In the preparation of the manuscript for the press they naturally passed as original matter, and the Publisher is glad to be able to make this belated acknowledgement.

INTRODUCTION

JOSEPH DE MARLIAVE wrote the *Essai sur les Quatuors de Beethoven*, included in the *Études musicales*,[1] as an introduction to this book ; it would have seemed natural to reproduce it here together with other unpublished notes, but on examination it was found that the fact of its separate publication made it too complete in itself to be incorporated here as it stood. Yet the necessity for some statement of explanation concerning the manuscript, left as we know in a fragmentary state, and the desirability of presenting some general points of view on certain aspects of so wide a subject, have led me to collect and form into a new introduction all that will help to determine the scope of the work and so heighten its significance.[2]

* *

The manuscript that Mme de Marliave has put into my hands for the purpose of publication consists of some finished studies, some partly finished, some only sketched out, and many rough drafts and notes. I have arranged the whole matter in due order and completed it with additions, especially in the detail of analysis of the last quartets, in order to prepare as unified a text as possible for the press.

In regard to the essential matter of the book, I have of course been prompted by the ordinary demands of good faith to respect unfalteringly the critical dicta of J. de Marliave. I have only allowed myself the task of developing according to my own knowledge the elements of objective analysis contained in the notes

[1] J. de Marliave, *Études musicales*, Paris, Alcan, 1917, pp. 216 onwards.

[2] Several passages in this introduction contain fragments, not published in 1917, of the *Essai sur les Quatuors*.

and of making some additions of my own. It is almost inevitable that there should be gaps in the continuity of so big an undertaking, but the conditions of its publication must be remembered and any imperfections that may still remain in this fine work must be laid to my charge.[1]

*
**

Beethoven did not embark upon the string quartet form until after much consideration. In 1795 Count Apponyi commissioned him to write two quartets, and two string pieces, the trio, Op. 3, and the quintet, Op. 4, were the result of the commission, written in 1796. One can trace in the *andante* of this trio, in E flat, for violin, viola, and 'cello, the outline of the slow movement for the Op. 18 quartet, No. 4. As for the quintet, also in E flat, its third movement,

---

[1] The general works consulted are mentioned in footnotes in the course of the work. A complete list can be found in the various Beethoven bibliographies, of which one of the most recent is Kastner's *Bibliotheca Beethoveniana. Versuch einer Beethoven-Bibliographie enthaltend alle vom Jahre 1827 bis 1913 erschienenen Werke über den grossen Tondichter*, Leipzig, 1913, 4to. Excellent *résumés* are to be found in Riemann's Dictionary; in the French edition of von Lenz's book (1909), *Beethoven et ses trois styles*, p. 491; in M. J. Chantavoine's *Beethoven*, Alcan, 1907, p. 257, &c. One may also add Kerst's *Die Erinnerungen an Beethoven*, Stuttgart, 1913, 2 vols., 8vo, and Leitzmann's *Beethoven's Persönlichkeit im Urteile der Zeitgenossen*, Leipzig, 1914, 2 vols., 8vo. All these are to be found at the Bibliothèque Nationale. Works relating especially to the quartets are few in number, with the exception of reviews and monographs: several chapters of A.-B. Marx's *L. v. Beethoven's Leben und Schaffen*, Berlin, 1863, 8vo; K. Bargeer, *Beethoven's letzte Streichquartette*, 1883; T. Helm, *Beethoven's Streichquartette*, Leipzig, W. Fritzsch, 1885. These are fully annotated and contain complete thematic analyses, but little critical discussion; on the other hand, they include endless commentaries and programmes whose fancy savours often of irrelevance. In his *Cours de composition musicale* (Paris, A. Durand & Son, p. 476) M. Vincent d'Indy stated in 1909 that he intended to devote the second part of Vol. II to an analysis of the Beethoven quartets. M. P. Coindreau published in 1910 an abstract of the lectures on the quartets by M. d'Indy at the Schola Cantorum.

Menuetto quasi allegretto, is remarkable for its scherzo form, a ' new idiom ', as von Lenz comments.[1]

But without making too much of these first ensemble works, certainly the Serenade, Op. 8 (1798) and the Op. 9 trios particularly (also 1798) are landmarks in the artist's career. One critic—T. Helm—assesses them above the quartets of Op. 18, and one is tempted to subscribe to this opinion when one hears the third of these trios, in C minor. From beginning to end this work is marked with an inherent nobility of conception : the first theme of the *allegro* is one of the greatest inspirations that ever came from Beethoven's pen, and the 6/8 *scherzo* is only rivalled by the great *scherzi* of Op. 59.

This trio, in a greater degree, perhaps, than the Op. 18, foretells the lines on which Beethoven was to develop the quartet form.

*
* *

The development of the Beethoven quartet evolved through a series of sixteen works, composed between the years 1800 and 1826, during the second half of the artist's life.[2]

W. von Lenz finds three distinct periods in the creative work of the musician, in his famous *Beethoven et ses trois styles* : the first a period of imitation, the next a phase in which traditional forms are recreated from within in a progressive freedom of style leading to the third period, in which new forms are created and moulded by the force of his imaginative vitality.

I have conformed to this distinction in dividing this

---

[1] W. von Lenz, *Beethoven et ses trois styles*, Paris, 1909 edition, p. 342. Among the posthumous works of Beethoven is an octet for two clarinets, two oboes, two bassoons, and two horns (Artaria) identical, except for a few details, with the Op. 4 quintet. As to which of these two works is the original see von Lenz, op. cit., p. 449.

[2] Actually there are only sixteen complete quartets, as the Grand Fugue, Op. 133, sometimes considered as a XVIIth quartet, is only the original *Finale* to the XIIIth quartet, as will be seen.

work into chapters, since it is particularly convenient in dealing with the quartets. But it is my own conviction, and I have Liszt's authority in support of it, that it would be truer, from both psychological and aesthetic aspects, to divide Beethoven's life of artistic creation into two phases only.[1]

Von Lenz's triple division implies in the second phase only an extension, though considerable, of the manner of the first. The first purely imitative stage, a necessary period in the development of all artists, is mainly interesting because Beethoven there employs the technique of traditional art as he sees it. Its intrinsic value lies in the first glimpses that are to be seen in it of the latent individuality of the musician. Apart from certain instances like the Op. 9 trio, No. 3, and parts of the Op. 18 quartets, Nos. 4 and 6, the *allegretto* of the Op. 10 sonata, No. 2, the Op. 13 sonata, and the Op. 22 sonata, the fact remains that the bulk of the work in Beethoven's first manner, a period ending about 1802, is generally inferior to the best work of the composers of the preceding epoch, Haydn and Mozart.

If one is to follow this idea, it will be apparent that in the first two periods of the artist there is a single underlying motive. This creative period includes, among other works revealing the individual character first anticipated in the instances mentioned above, the symphonies Nos. 3–8; the quartets of Op. 59, Op. 74, Op. 95 (a transition work marked with the style of the last period); the B flat trio, Op. 97; the piano sonatas from Op. 26 to Op. 90; the piano and violin sonatas Op. 30, Nos. 1–3, Op. 47, Op. 96, &c.

These compositions date up to 1817 roughly, and are marked by the following peculiarities:

(*a*) The essential idea of the work is objective and exterior. In this tradition is followed, and the inner imaginative life of Beethoven is not, with rare excep-

[1] *Franz Liszt's Briefe*, published by La Mara, Breitkopf, Leipzig, Book I, p. 124. See below, Chap. II, p. 184, note 1.

tions, the direct motive of inspiration; the artist is still detached, as it were, and if the force of his individuality impels emotions that spring up in his art, it is not yet the sole purpose and function of his art.

He does not express himself, or very little; he is merely recording the impressions he receives of life itself, and from the exterior world. The Op. 59 quartets are the culminating point of this objective art, as J. de Marliave acutely observes.

(*b*) The form of this art is still mainly the traditional style, freely extended. This extension is evident in a range of technical idioms of which our age thinks nothing, but which were at that time a lawless revolt against the academicism of Fuchs and Albrechtsberger. Such technical points are: the use of duple time, usually reserved till the finale, in the first *allegro* (symphonies in C minor and Pastorale); the substitution of the *allegretto*, a new Beethoven form, instead of the *andante* with repetitions (Op. 95 quartet); the changing of the *menuet* into the *scherzo*, which was an essential factor of Beethoven's art, and the disregard of classical rules of key relations and traditional rhythms, &c. The resulting form was an infinitely flexible mould, peculiarly fitted for the reception of Beethoven's immense lyrical power, and which contained the essence of his musical imagination, a creature of leaping impetuosity, violent contrasts, riotous joy obscured in mists of melancholy. It is impossible to imagine a greater constraint for such a temperament than the measured precision of the Mozart form, with its ' trio ' in the correct tonality and careful triple tempo. Consequently one notices[1] that the third part of the *scherzo* in F from the VIIth symphony in A major, is written in D ; that the *scherzo* of the quartet Op. 74 is of unusual proportions and longer than the other movements ; the combined duple and triple rhythms in the C minor symphony ; the introduction of duple measure

[1] Von Lenz, op. cit., p. 63.

episodes in the *scherzo* of the Eroica; the entire *scherzo* written in this rhythm in the Op. 31 sonata, No. 3; all free idiomatic devices that are to abound in the last period (sonata Op. 110, quartets Op. 127, Op. 132, the episode in four time in the *scherzo* of the IXth symphony).

Finally, even the sonata form is to be modified in the style of this period, as von Lenz remarks. Already the method of uninterrupted development appears, which characterizes the last phase (Op. 90). The slow movements become long unbroken melodies (quartets Op. 59, Nos. 1 and 2), linked on to the finale (Op. 59, No. 1): the finales contain the concentrated essence of the whole work.

In summary, by the creative work of the first half of his life, considered as a continuous whole, Beethoven is still involved in the classical tradition of Haydn and Mozart. Yet both in form and in meaning there are many tokens of the imminent change and of the creation of a new art with which his later years are to be filled.

* *
*

It was about 1818 that these new tendencies began to crystallize. The characteristic works of the second manner—the third according to von Lenz—are: the piano sonatas Nos. 28–32, Op. 101 to Op. 111, from 1818 to 1822; the two 'cello and piano sonatas, Op. 102, 1818; the Mass in D, Op. 123, completed in 1822; the overture in C, Op. 124, 1822; the IXth symphony, Op. 125, 1822; and the last quartets, Nos. 12–16, Op. 127–35, written from 1825 to 1827.

Von Lenz has the following comment to make: 'One can compare the third period of Beethoven with the second part of Goethe's *Faust*.[1] The ideas now expressed in a purely individual style of self-revelation are always complex; they are the manifestations of a spirit living in a world of its own outside the bounds of

[1] Von Lenz, op. cit., p. 259.

material existence. Total deafness isolated the composer so completely from external impressions that he
no longer attempted to express the spirit of humanity
or of the world as it is, but as his ideal of it might be.
. . . The third manner of Beethoven, as the outcome of
an inner concentration of unparalleled intensity, has no
longer the freshness of the first two periods, but it
does and always will compel interest as the revelation
of a genius at close grips with reality. Originating in
the same imaginative sphere as our own, Beethoven's
inspiration swells and flows beyond the limits of which
we are conscious. . . . A certain quality of studied care,
in which always the hand of genius is apparent, replaces
the first impulse of imagination ; a deliberate contemplative scrutiny of the impressions of youthful vitality.' [1]
In its particular aspect the expression of this conception
involves strange tonalities (quartet in C sharp minor,
Op. 131), frequent transitions (Gloria of the Mass in
D), curious combinations, ideas which seem to sink
within themselves. 'From this point onwards the
broadening of interest in the episodes overwhelms the
original theme ; the old clarity of idea has gone . . . to
give place to a more complex development of the technical resources of the art.' [2]

Concerning the quartet particularly there are several
characteristics of the last manner pointed out in a
thesis by Sauzay, dedicated to Ingres : [3]

1. The equal importance of all four parts in the
structure of the work, so that interest is equally divided
between all the instruments.

2. Thematic development much further extended
in every technical aspect, i. e. harmony, rhythm, division of the beat, &c.

3. The preparation rather than the resolution of the
melodic phrase.

[1] Von Lenz, op. cit., pp. 66–7. [2] Von Lenz, op. cit., p. 63.
[3] E. Sauzay, *Haydn, Mozart, Beethoven, Études sur le quatuor*, Paris,
1861.

4. The succession of similar movements linked together one after the other in the same time.

5. Much indication of accent, expression marks, explanatory phrases, precautions taken by the artist to ensure a variety of tonal colour expressive of his own ideas.

According to a statement of M. V. d'Indy [1] the various technical innovations of Beethoven in string quartet form may be tabulated thus:

I. *Form of movements.*

(*a*) Sonata form : In five movements, the first theme is not in the dominant nor in the relative of the main key ; in three it is in the key of a major third below, and in two in the key of a major third above the principal key.

(*b*) *Andante* : Beethoven often casts the slow movement in sonata form, a method he never adopts in the piano sonatas. He never resorts to the binary slow movement form ; and only once to sonata form without development. One slow movement is made of a single phrase.

(*c*) *Scherzo* : That of the VIIth quartet, Op. 59, No. 1, is a new type, to be found again in the VIIth and IXth symphonies and in the Op. 97 trio.

(*d*) Rondo form : this is encountered in five pieces, where the rondo is three or four times repeated.

II. *Cyclic Form.*

1. Melodic relations : These are implied in the use of Introductions out of which the work evolves (XIVth quartet).

2. Harmonic relations : The key plan is very carefully thought out and usually based on the *arpeggio* of

[1] Analysis of the seventeen Beethoven quartets, according to notes taken at the Schola Cantorum in Paris, in the lectures on composition given by M. Vincent d'Indy, collected and arranged by M. P. Coindreau (pp. 14–16).

the common chord. The movements following the first are often in the key of a third below, the relative or the subdominant of the main key. (See I (*a*).)

The use of the subdominant of the main key is justified on the plea that this disturbing tonality melts away in the cumulative effect of the other movements. The dominant is never the principal tonality of a piece, whereby monotony is avoided.

3. Rhythmic relations : They lead to the creation of an intermediary movement whose form may vary.

(*a*) A sonata form (VIIth quartet).

(*b*) A variation form (Alla danza tedesca, XIIIth quartet).

(*c*) A suite form (No. 2 of the XIVth quartet, Alla marcia, XVth quartet).

(*d*) A return to the *scherzo* achieved by suppressing the 'trio' and introducing, in a new key, a new element which is not a second theme.

Three quartets have two intermediary movements: the XIIIth, XIVth, and XVth.

The slow movement is placed second in nine quartets, third in five. Three quartets have two slow movements : the VIth, XIIIth, and XIVth. The rondo, disregarded during many years, reappears in the quartets of the last period (XIth and XVth, see the piano sonata Op. 90).

From the technical aspect, the art of the last quartets is dominated by the method of ' grand variation '. The merits of this form are demonstrated by its adaptability to every shade of emotion that modern art must express.[1] But when all has been said, the formula is in itself of little significance : all forms are transient, art is eternal ; and in binding the latter too closely to the former one risks having periodically to discount the creative work of an entire epoch.

Though it is a form of infinite flexibility when forming

[1] See Vincent d'Indy, *Cours de composition musicale*, Book II, part 1, chap. 4, pp. 473 and onwards.

a basis for continuous melody, the grand variation can nevertheless sometimes lead to an over-stereotyped technique. The last quartets present examples of both results.

Beethoven's technique in his last works is often laboured and the music occasionally seems written rather for the eye than for the ear. Contemporary critics reproached him for discords that in no way offend modern ears, but it is a different matter with the effects of dissonance in the Op. 133 Fugue, where the construction is harsh and strained. One may prefer the treatment of the first *allegro* in the VIIth quartet Op. 59, No. 1, whose structure is that of a free divertimento and which is perhaps the highest point that Beethoven ever reached in fluent technique from a purely academic point of view. Fresh technical devices were rarely met with earlier than Op. 127 but increase in number in the works that follow. The XIIIth quartet, Op. 130, has many fine examples which will be pointed out in due course. Above all, in a surprisingly modern way, Beethoven used rhythm with the perfect mastery of genius. All his compositions contain a movement of *scherzo* derivation, in which the most elaborately varied rhythmic effects are to be found; in this he anticipates the developments of the contemporary Russian and Spanish schools. And this essential and inherent element in the music is associated with a relatively less advanced and less intricate technical style than that which accompanies harmonic innovations.

* *

In a word, it is adaptation of the form to the thought, intensity, and intimacy of imaginative power, that are the dominating qualities of the last quartets.[1]

Debussy wrote of Beethoven:[2] 'He had not a grain of " literary " imagination, at least not in the modern

[1] These tendencies reached a culminating point in the third movement of the C sharp minor quartet, Op. 131.

[2] *Revue Blanche*, 1 May 1901.

sense of the word. He was passionately devoted to music and for him it provided his sole consolation and the joy so lamentably lacking in his material life. . . . His unwearying care and the purely musical investigation that filled his thought are proved by the evidence of a certain note-book where no less than two hundred different forms of the main theme of the *Finale* to the IXth symphony are sketched out.' This comment is worthy of attention as a protest against the practice of mutilating a composition with explanatory notes, against the critics who substitute their own conception of a piece for that of the artist, and insist on attaching a ' programme ' at all costs. But to uphold these views as the final criticism of a complex work seems to me to risk being involved in a grave mistake. At least one must understand what is implied in the phrases ' literary musician ' and ' musical investigation '.

Beethoven is a literary musician in so far as he is a romantic, for the former is implicit in the latter. But what is one to understand by romantic ? If one is to accept a phrase beloved of Rémy de Gourmont, who saw in romanticism the ' predominance of emotion over reason ', certainly many of Beethoven's works, even before his later manner, reveal this quality as he explains the spiritual phases through which he passes, and sometimes seems even to explain his explanation. . . . The Op. 127, for example, clearly forecasts another work of undeniably romantic character : Schumann's quartet, Op. 41, No. 3.[1]

---

[1] See also the VIth quartet, Op. 18 (*Finale*), the XIIIth, Op. 130, of which the *scherzo* is full of romanticism, Op. 132, Op. 135 (*Finale*). An instance of the same tendency in a lesser degree is to be seen in various examples of ' programme music ', notably in the XVth quartet. There exists here a conception that needs to be very clearly understood, and which excludes the commonly accepted idea of ' descriptive music ' except in one or two places. For lack of appreciation of this difference certain critics have involved themselves in commentaries of an extravagant nature, like those of Helm and Marx on the XIth and XVth quartets, for instance.

This predominance of emotion in the last Beethoven quartets is the more worthy of notice because Beethoven's own emotional existence at the time was influenced by particular circumstances.

First of all it is manifested in a reaction against crises of unhappiness, all too frequent in the years between Op. 127 and 135. With Beethoven all sorrow begot creative inspiration and often happy inspiration. It is as if his emotion was aroused by suffering to react in a triumphant expression of his power, and phases of gloom and misery were always followed by a burst of leaping energy. In these hours of despair, a few weeks only before his death, he wrote his last work, the *Finale* of the XIIIth quartet, Op. 130, full of the exuberance and swing of a country fair.

Secondly, it is revealed in the intimate and concentrated depth of this emotional power, henceforward to realize only rarely the brilliant objectivity of the works of the first period (Op. 59, for example), and to conceal itself in a deep reticence which had an obvious effect on the technique and style of the last quartets. In this period spontaneous inspirations of joy and grief are to be an exceptional thing (the *Cavatina* of the XIIIth quartet, Op. 130 ; the *Finale* of the same work ; the *Finale* of the XIVth quartet, Op. 131) ; in their place a profound reserve, a long hesitation before revealing his inmost emotion distinguishes many pieces (the *Adagio* of the XIIth quartet, Op. 127 ; *Andante* of the XIIIth ; the fourth movement of the XIVth ; the *Adagio* of the XVth, Op. 132) ; and their profound melancholy is to be slowly, reluctantly lifted from its obscurity, only through the infinite expressive resource of the 'grand variation' form: these pieces divine and express, as it were, an incommunicable sorrow only known in the silent tear trembling upon the lash. We must remember what suffering the artist endured during the last years of his life.

His natural inclination to reserve was strengthened

by his infirmity, and his suffering and irritability, the distress of heart, loving yet never loved, all helped to foster in him an inner life of the spirit almost to the heights of pure ecstasy. Early in life he shut himself up within the confines of a rugged fortress, where he lived through illusions, memories, and regrets. Ceasing to believe in love after the bitterness of his first love affairs, ceasing to believe in the gospel of freedom for humanity after his hero became a despot, he built up a world of the spirit to take the place of a real world in which he could not or would not take part. And for the expression of the beauty contained in this inner world he created a new language of sound whose smallest inflections possess an expressive force never before realized in music, except perhaps in the dramatic art of Mozart.

So in this endless search after the final form of a theme through its various stages of growth—and this search extends to the second section and to details of composition—one need not necessarily see, I think, as Debussy sees, an artist guided by the impulse of purely musical investigation ; it is the effort of an artist in whom anxiety to perfect technical detail in a work results from the desire above all to reveal its main outlines more precisely.

The idea of 'purely musical investigation' perhaps arises in the fact that the art of the last quartets, in which an intricate form is closely bound up with a complex psychological meaning, seems on the surface often to lack the human element that nevertheless throbs within it. One reaches a point where it is no longer possible to dissociate form from meaning. It is an art in which tenderness and all trace of sensuousness is lost in the expression of mind, an art in which there is something ascetic and superhuman, a unique art that breaks the chain of musical evolution. This unparalleled achievement, conceived within the agony of a soul thrust back upon itself, misses perhaps that breath of life which a divine happiness gives. For happiness makes self-knowledge fuller and more complete than is possible even through suffering. The poet said truly: [1] ' C' insegna che il piacere è il più certo mezzo di conoscimento offertoci dalla natura, e che colui il quale molto ha sofferto è men sapiente di colui il quale molto ha godito.'

J. E.

[1] Gabriele d'Annunzio, *Il Fuoco*, p. 101. On this point one might observe that a comparison between Mozart and Beethoven taken as representing two different aspects of musical imagination would involve interesting definitions in the study of the subtle qualities that separate the art of the last quartets from purely classical art.

CONTENTS

CHAPTER I

THE EARLY QUARTETS. (Op. 18, Nos. 1–6.)

ON 29th October 1792, when Beethoven left Bonn for Vienna, where he was to study with Haydn, he received the following letter from his patron Count E. Gabriel Waldstein,[1] who had gained permission from the Elector Maximilian for him to make the journey:

DEAR BEETHOVEN,

In leaving for Vienna to-day you are on the point of realizing a long-cherished desire. The wandering genius of Mozart still grieves for his passing; with Haydn's unquenchable spirit it has found shelter but no home, and longs to find some lasting habitation. Work hard, and the spirit of Mozart's genius will come to you from Haydn's hands.

Always your friend,
WALDSTEIN.

Bonn, 29 *Oct.* 1792.

It was as the incarnate spirit of Mozart, moulded by Haydn's virile talent,[2] that Beethoven was to appear to the musical world when the six quartets of Op. 18, following close upon the 1st symphony, were published in two uniform series nine years later. In these works of Beethoven's youth the clarity and freshness of Haydn are found linked with the grace of Mozart, but so far from being a slavish imitation of these two masters, they form, as it were, the crowning achieve-

---

[1] L. Ernst-Gabriel, Count Waldstein-Wartenburg, Baron Münchengrätz, &c., Counsellor and Chamberlain to the Austrian Emperor, lieutenant-colonel in the army. He was born in 1764, and was therefore six years older than Beethoven.

[2] Yet it is known that Beethoven always refused to be called Haydn's 'pupil'. According to Ries, Haydn himself wished Beethoven to put on the title-page of his works the words: 'pupil of Joseph Haydn'. Beethoven was unwilling, because, as he said, he had taken a few lessons from Haydn but had never really been his pupil.

ment of their art. In this wise Count Waldstein's prediction was justified, but at the same time there are,
even in these first works, traits of a stronger quality, the
stamp of an original genius, unmistakable signs that
this early ambition for him was soon to be transcended.
This was in 1801. Already the shadow of sorrow had
fallen upon the artist, a darkness that was never to lift.[1]
Between the years of 1796 and 1800 deafness had
begun its fatal work, and with an agony of throbbing
ear-drums, Beethoven's hearing grew daily weaker. A
sort of ashamed reserve had kept him from revealing
his malady even to his intimate friends, and it was
during these years of suffering, made worse by the
effort to hide it, that Op. 18 was written; truly the
first of the ' splendid lies ' of which his life was full.
For, in spite of all, he instils into these six quartets all
the energy and confidence of a youthful vitality. ' They
might be called his *Sposalizio*,' remarked von Lenz of
the string trios, Op. 1. And the phrase fits the quartets
too. They have all the grace and brilliant charm of a
painting by Raphael, yet, hidden beneath the sweet
untroubled smile a shade of sadness lingers, where one
thought to see nothing but the tender emotion of
another Mozart. But joyous or sad, this music breathed
so living a vitality, and a melodic power so abundant,
that already it was obvious that Beethoven must soon
find the traditional form a constraint. In this respect
the Op. 18 quartets are inferior to the six great quartets
of Mozart, which witness the subordination of technique to musical idea in a manner inspired by true
genius; and, in spite of certain conventions, these works
reveal a freedom and flexibility, a harmonic freshness,
that perfectly reflect the play of a supple imagination.
They give an impression of smooth and adequate perfection that one misses in the Op. 18. One feels that
Beethoven must create a new musical form in which to
express the world of new ideas surging in his troubled

[1] Romain Rolland, *Beethoven*, p. 17.

soul, and this end is not to be reached without some conflict between form and inspiration.

These six quartets, composed almost at the same time, are grouped under the same opus number. The date given by the note-books shows that they were composed during the years of 1798-9 and 1800. They were not written in the order in which they were finally published; this is clear both from the sequence of notes in the sketch-books and further from a statement by Ries that 'the third string quartet (Op. 18), in D major, is the first quartet Beethoven composed; the one in F which now precedes it was originally the third'.[1] Nevertheless Ries is wrong, or rather his statement is only half true: the quartet in F is not the third but the second in order of composition. On 1st (?) June 1800 Beethoven wrote to his friend Carl Amenda: 'Do not allow your quartet to be played any longer as it is; I have altered it a great deal, for now I have learnt how to write quartets properly—as you will see when you get it.'[2]

Now L. Nohl in his *Neue Zeitschriften für Musik* [3] tells how he was fortunate enough to discover in Russia (Amenda was a clergyman in Courland) the copy of the quartet mentioned in this letter; this work, dated June 25th, 1799, is none other than the quartet in F, and bears the title *Quartetto No. II.*[4]

Moreover, in a note-book of 1799 there are two discarded sketches numbered *Quartet 3*, following several pages devoted to the outline of the quartet in F. It is therefore certain that at the time of composing the quartet in F Beethoven had not yet written a note of the one which was to follow, numbered third by the composer.

[1] Ries-Legentil, p. 136.
[2] *Correspondance de Beethoven*, translated from German into French by J. Chantavoine, p. 19.
[3] Jan. 19, 1872.
[4] The outline of these revisions is found in a note-book of 1800 (Berlin Library). Herr Wilhelm Altmann has published in *Die Musik* (*Drittes Beethovenheft*) one movement of the first version of the quartet.

In his *Beethoveniana* Nottebohm assigns the following chronological order to the works written between January and December 1799:

Song: *The Kiss*, Op. 128 (in its original form).
Rondo in G major for piano, Op. 51, No. 2.
Quartet in D major, Op. 18, No. 3.
Variations for piano on *La Stessa, la Stessissima*.
Quartet in F, Op. 18, No. 1.
Variations for four hands in D.
Quartet in G, Op. 18, No. 2 (with the exception of the second movement, which was revised later).
Quartet in A, Op. 18, No. 5.
2nd, 3rd, and 4th movements of the Septet, Op. 20.

This puts the quartets in the following order : 3, 1, 2, 5 ...

Be that as it may, the work appeared in Vienna in 1801, published by the firm of T. Mollo, in two volumes, the first coming out in June, the second in October; each contained three quartets in their present order, with the title: *Six quatuors pour deux violons, alto et violoncelle, composés et dédiés à S. A. Mgr. le Prince régnant de Lobkowitz,*[1] *etc., par Louis van Beethoven. Op. 18; 1re (2e) livraison. A Vienne, chez T. Mollo et Cie.*

Quartet No. I, Op. 18, No. 1 (in F major).

This has the usual four movements :
Allegro con brio (3/4 $\downarrow \cdot$ = 54).[2]
Adagio affettuoso ed appassionnato (9/8 $\flat$ = 138).
Scherzo (3/4 $\downarrow \cdot$ = 112).
Allegro (2/4 $\downarrow$ = 120).

---

[1] Prince Lobkowitz, Duke of Raudnitz, was one of the gentlemen ushers of Baron van Swieten, the son of the famous Dutch physician, whom Maria Theresa had taken into her service and loaded with honours. Lobkowitz was a little younger than Beethoven, and one of his great admirers and friends. He was himself an excellent violinist, and spent fortunes in satisfying his passion for music.

[2] These metronome numbers are taken from two sources :

1. A thematic catalogue of Beethoven's instrumental works, published by F. Hofmeister, in Leipzig, in 1819, and therefore in Bee-

I. The *Allegro con brio* is an interesting example of Beethoven's technical brilliance of style, and of his skill in 'working' a theme, a device carried to perfection by his predecessors. A very short *motif* of barely a bar's length is developed to exhaustion point:

Allegro con brio

Ex. 1.

According to the note-books, this *motif* underwent many changes before reaching its ultimate shape. On few themes—not even the 'Joy' *motif* in the IXth symphony—was so much trouble spent in working out. Five complete pages of one of the 1798–9 note-books and eleven pages of another are entirely devoted to it, and later in 1800, when Beethoven revised the quartet, it is one of the themes he is found retouching yet again. From its original statement, fairly long and without any

thoven's lifetime. The title of this pamphlet states it to contain certain ' tempo indications according to Mälzel's Metronome '; in it are found those relating to the quartets of Op. 18, 59, 74, and 95.

2. A similar work published the same year by Steiner & Co., in Vienna, entitled : *Bestimmung des musikalischen Zeitmasses nach Mälzel's Metronom., zweite Lieferung. Beethoven: Sämmtliche Quartetten von dem Author selbst bezeichnet.* Wien, bei A. Steiner u. Co. (' Musical *tempo* indications according to Mälzel's Metronome, 2nd Book. The Quartets of Beethoven, with tempo indications by the composer himself.' Vienna, Steiner & Co.). Nevertheless, it must be observed that, according to Schindler, Beethoven only put *tempo* numbers to the VIIth and IXth symphonies and to the last four piano sonatas ; and would certainly not have countenanced the immediate publication of these several *tempo* indications that had been thus extracted from him. W. von Lenz, *Beethoven et ses trois styles*, pp. 308 and 325–6.

clearly defined rhythm, it undergoes a gradual process of contraction to its final truncated form. No particular significance attaches to it, beyond its agile and vivid energy, as it bounds to and fro like a ball among the four instruments. It appears no less than a hundred and two times in the three hundred and three bars of the *Allegro*, treated sometimes as accompanied melody, sometimes in imitation, sometimes woven into the web of counterpoint.

Stated at the outset in unison, the theme passes from one part to another, and lends itself to every possible trick of technique, twisting and changing with extraordinary flexibility, in further contraction or expansion, sparkling with countless nuances and reflecting countless fleeting emotions. At one time sombre and heavy, at another gay and insouciant, a mood of serene contemplation slips into one of unabated vigour—as, for example, in the interesting development of the second section of the movement (following the seventeenth bar after the double bar). At the thirtieth bar a second theme appears, derived from the first, which is used as a bass :

Ex. 2.

This pleasing *motif* shows that already Beethoven knew how to evolve a second characteristic theme out of an original idea of the utmost simplicity, like the first theme here. The thematic development follows, an excellent example of the working out of an idea ; even when the first violin dominates the ensemble, the interplay of question and answer is perfectly sustained and balanced. This *Allegro con brio* astonished contemporary musicians on its appearance, and several years later Spohr still declared that it was the artist's masterpiece and the summit of possible achievement in the quartet genre.

Time has changed this sweeping opinion, and the movement is now considered a fluent but not remarkably interesting work ; it is brilliant but superficial, and one may well believe that the passing emotions to which reference has already been made were the true inspiration of its varied tonality and modulation. Yet at the same time the movement contains signs of Beethoven's individual style.

It can be felt, for instance, in the *pianissimo* viola passage after the exposition (bar 41 and onwards), where the viola shares the theme, in A flat, which the first violin develops in imitation above sustained notes on the second violin and 'cello ; again a little later, when an elegant design unfolds its graces upon the instruments in turn, and again in the second section (bar 37 and onwards), where the theme has a curious unbroken descent in rhythmic periods of four bars, through the successive tonalities of B flat minor, G flat major, F minor, and D flat major. The four-bar periods in the minor are in each case given to the first violin, the corresponding periods in the major to the second violin. The modulation is unprepared but falls upon the ear serene and smooth. During the passages in the major the 'cello moves down through the intervals of the chords of G flat and D flat ; a last modulation leads back to C major, the dominant of F, and this key persists for a long time ; one is not sure for a space of twelve bars whether the tonality of C is established, or whether it is to resolve upon F. This strange sequence of keys, followed by the sustained wait upon a chord that demands resolution, reveals Beethoven's art in creating in the listener a sense both of suspense and of longing for finality, that one can listen for in vain in the music of Haydn and Mozart.

The *Allegro con brio* has its weak points, having too many passages of unison and harmonic padding, in lack of unity between several of the *motifs* and the principal theme, in too glib or too superficial a technique, especially towards the end. One is conscious of the young musician's mastery over form, and at the same time of a certain failure of real inspiration; the movement as a whole affords a better example of 'quartet' composition than of Beethoven's own individual style.

II. The *Adagio* is a different matter; nothing so deeply felt had hitherto (1800) ever come from the composer's pen.[1] Using a method that is to reappear in the XIIth and XVIth quartets, he solidly defines the tonality in the very first bar; the sombre key thus established is D minor, in a slow rhythmic figure, *pp*, on the second violin, viola, and 'cello. At once the first violin gives out the melody, sad and sweet, heavy with tears, above dreary minor harmonies. This phrase is to recur in the *Andante* of the IInd symphony. After the exposition the two violins at the octave have a descending figure:

Ex. 3.

<hr />

[1] According to Amenda, Beethoven was inspired to write this movement by the scene of the tomb in *Romeo and Juliet*. A sketch dated 1799, used at the end of this *Adagio*, bears the words 'Les derniers soupirs', which seems to confirm this interpretation.

The phrase is each time composed of the same notes, and it is the rhythmic change (notice the difference in value of the two A's) that so wonderfully creates the impression of deep resignation, soon followed, on a *sforzando* B flat, by a poignant melody :

Ex. 4.

bringing back *pianissimo* the first notes of the original theme on the 'cello.   Rocked upon an expressive accompaniment on the viola, a second theme in F breathes consolation. But soon fragments of the principal theme return in an advancing wave of emotion, overwhelmed by sparkling demisemiquaver flights. Four bars of arresting pause ensue, in which single chords are struck on each first beat, moving by a simple modulation to the final dominant, *ppp*, out of which the original melody emerges above a stormy accompaniment in unison semiquavers and demisemiquavers on the second violin and viola. The theme of consolation reappears in the key of D major, with greater clarity than before, but after a tentative effort it slips listlessly away into silence. Great depth of tone marks a final statement of the original theme, and with a last *fortissimo* chord of the diminished seventh, the movement seems to shiver asunder. . . . A light breath still flutters in the triplets of the first violin in the last four bars, and then the song dies into a sombre gloom where one feels the weight of an endless grief.

Among Beethoven slow movements, this has only one precursor, the *largo* of the sonata in D, Op. 10, No. 3; later movements, born of a similar inspiration (the slow movements of the quartet in F major, Op. 59, and of the quartet in E flat, Op. 74), are to crystallize its memory.

III. *Scherzo*. The *scherzo* section:

Ex. 5.

passes without comment; the second half is full of pleasing modulations, and ends on a note of whimsical humour.

The *Trio*:

Ex. 6.

carries a more personal quality. Even yet, this is not the true Beethoven *scherzo*, but although still simple and like the *menuet* of Haydn in style, it is among those *scherzi* of Beethoven's first manner which hint at the sparkling tonal audacities that the artist is later to mould into this form.

IV. The first *motif* of the finale (*Allegro*) leaps upon the ear without warning or preparation : [1]

Ex. 7.

At the end of the phrase a vigorous second theme appears :

Ex. 8.

The development is built up on these two *motifs*, and contains passages of great charm ; the following is an example :

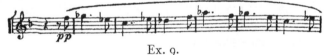

Ex. 9.

The phrase is introduced by four bars of the reiterated chord of D flat ; seven bars of the same beating rhythm follow, modulating almost imperceptibly to C, in which key the figure is repeated ; another example occurs later in a charming episode where the rhythm of the principal theme is given to the two elements of the second theme ; two contrary ideas are now linked together, now opposed, in a passage that leads with growing agitation to the conclusion of the work.

In the first and last movements of the quartet in F Beethoven's mastery over rhythm is remarkable. This

[1] It sprang spontaneously in this same way from the mind of the artist ; at a very early stage in the sketches it approximates to its final form, which is remarkable for its curious rhythm : 3.3.2.2.

thematic development, which seems as if it must demand long and exacting labour, is for him a natural outlet for imaginative vigour, spent without effort.

Quartet No. II, Op. 18, No. 2 (in G major).

Allegro   (2/4 ♩ = 96).
{ *Adagio*   (3/4 ♪ = 72).
{ *Allegro*   (2/4 ♩ = 69).
Allegro   (3/4 ♩. = 52).
Allegro molto (2/4 ♩ = 92).

According to the note-books, much time was spent in the working out of the G major quartet. One comes across ideas for it in several of the books, and in one they occupy no less than thirty-two pages.[1] The principal subject takes practically its final form from the beginning, but curiously enough the sketches for the *Adagio* (in 3/4) are all written in common time. In his final version Beethoven merely modified the rhythm of the original theme, and altered the original duple time to triple time. There is not a single sketch for the *intermezzo* (in 2/4) of the *Adagio*. And finally the last movement in 2/4 is also written in common time in the preliminary sketches.

I. The *Allegro* is modelled on the style of Haydn and Mozart, and embodies all the unerring technical grace of the latter, combined with the freshness of inspiration found in the early works of the former, a freshness that here is almost excessive; sometimes an impassioned note is struck (as in Ex. 11), but no sooner is it felt than it gives place at once to a mood of irresponsible gaiety. This *Allegro* has given the G major quartet the name 'The Compliment Quartet' (Compliments-Quartett) in Germany. Helm's description of it is rather fantastic:

The principal subject—or, better expressed, the group of the three principal themes A, B, and C:

----

[1] Nottebohm, *Zweite Beethoveniana*, Leipzig, 1887, p. 487.

Ex. 10.

brings before one's imagination a brilliant scene in some
eighteenth-century *salon*, with all the ceremonious display and
flourish of courtesy typical of the period. The doors of the
drawing-room swing open to usher in the arriving guests, met
with bows and gracious words of greeting. The master of cere-
monies, the host of the evening, looks upon the gaiety with
a smouldering passion in his eyes, felt in the theme in B minor:

Ex. 11.

but he cannot resist the impulse of the moment, and his lips
curve into a smile; the festivity moves on its exquisite way, and
the guests acknowledge each other's advances with all the formal
elegance of bow and curtsy.

The theme C, describing a graceful turn at the end of this
first phrase, is the fundamental element of the development and
of the third section of the movement. The hum of conversation gains more and more animation and brilliance; hilarious
gentlemen arrive with slightly dishevelled peruke; only the
stern demands of etiquette keep them from breaking the bounds
of good taste. It is like an amusing scene depicted in some old
engraving (notice the unprepared entry of the theme A in E
minor, and later in E major); and apart from some passages
where the inspiration rises to the level of Beethoven's own
individuality, it is instinct with the spirit of Haydn.[1]

[1] T. Helm, *Beethoven's Streichquartette*, pp. 12–13.

It will be noticed that the two ideas in this first movement have an identical conclusion.

II. *Adagio.* Here Beethoven breaks away from tradition. He experiences already that need for a new medium of expression that irked him all his life. The grave beauty of this *Adagio*, reminiscent of the slow movement in the piano sonata, Op. 27, no. 1, is broken by a vigorous *Allegro* in 2/4 time developed at considerable length. Its two repeated sections are followed by several bars of episode in which the original theme is skilfully reintroduced with more elaborate figuration and florid accompaniment on the first violin; the movement is brought to an unexpected conclusion by the *pianissimo* return of the *Allegro* motif. The whole movement is graceful and pleasing, after the manner of Haydn. ' One seems to see in the *Allegro*', Helm goes on to say, ' a troop of irresponsible youths making hits at their old master, the wise philosopher to whom they listened in patience only for a time.' The picture becomes even more vivid when at the repeat of the *Adagio* the 'cello seems to pronounce a solemn exhortation. . . .

The slow movement is in C major, the *Allegro* in F. Beethoven was fond of such contrasts in tonality, especially in his first period; in the VIth quartet, Op. 18, in B flat, and also in the quintet in C, still more surprising instances are to be found.

III. *Allegro.* This *Allegro* is a form of *menuet* after the style of Haydn:

Ex. 12.

One must point out as characteristic of Beethoven the unprepared entry of the key of B major at the beginning of the second section, and the modulation from C major to G major which takes place a bar or two later.

The *Trio* in C major has more originality:

Ex. 13.

The reiterated notes in this theme stamp it as particularly characteristic of Beethoven. In the second section the same theme is stated by the first violin with increased emphasis, and combined with a triplet figure given alternately to the second violin and 'cello, with a monotonous accompaniment on the viola. The whole passage is interestingly and ingeniously written. But in the *Coda* of the *Trio* is found the most individual element of the entire work; the 'cello moves slowly down the diatonic scale of G, producing in its descent an extraordinary harmonic effect, and coming to rest on D, the dominant of the key, to reintroduce the *menuet*.

Ex. 14.

IV. *Allegro molto*. In the finale the gaiety of the first *Allegro* is recaptured, though with less ceremony, and as if the formal flourishes have been set aside. Helm, still picturesque, remarks, ' The champagne has been round '; it is infused with greater warmth and intimacy, an added vigour of movement. Beethoven himself described it as ' aufgeknöpft '.

The theme is very vigorous and gay :

Ex. 15.

and is treated by the 'cello in so comic a fashion that one imagines ' the grave host ' of this gay company to be unable to repress a sigh at the frolics of his guests :

Ex. 16.

In another place, as though to hide as much as possible the offending *motif*, he encircles it with figuration on the first violin, cast around it like gossamer drapery ; but his efforts are in vain, and as the veil lifts the shape of the theme is revealed, and finally emerges once more (second section, after the return of the theme in A flat).

The theme is bubbling with comic gaiety, and Beethoven makes almost inexhaustible use of it, to the

unfailing delight of quartet players. He obtains curious
little effects by the inversion of the three notes :

Ex. 17.

He sets the two figures of the *motif* against each other
with infinitely varied effect, in diminutions, augmenta-
tions, and unexpected turns of harmony, like the
modulation from G minor to A flat major, after the
momentary lull in the sustained chords of the second
section ; endless variety of mood and technique con-
tributes to a brilliant musical *tour de force*.

Quartet No. III, Op. 18, No. 3 (in D major).

Allegro   (¢ ♩ = 120).
Andante   (2/4 ♪ = 92).
Allegro   (3/4 ♩· = 100).
Presto   (6/8 ♩· = 96).

The note-books in which the composer sketched out
the original outlines of this quartet are no longer in
existence. Fifty-eight pages of a 1798 note-book are
devoted to sketches for each of the various movements,
but their advanced state of development indicates that
they are not the original designs. Nearly all are in their
final shape, and any further modifications were of the
slightest.

Remembering that this was the first quartet Beethoven wrote, one is not surprised to find more traces
here than in the five others of Op. 18 of the direct
influence of Haydn and Mozart. Rigid adherence to
form, correct balance of movement with movement,
traditional conventions of *tempo* and rhythm, all the
rules of classical art are perfectly observed. Marx was

right in saying that this work was the most perfect achievement within Beethoven's capacity in the old quartet style. The first violin part dominates the ensemble throughout, especially in the first movement, and the other instruments provide little more than an accompaniment; the 'cello part is still treated in the main merely as a harmonic basis, though it acquires in the finale a certain freedom and independent movement; and in this insistence on a character of its own, apparent here though still unformed, can be recognized one of the few novel traits in which Beethoven's individuality forces its way through the conventional context.[1]

I. *Allegro*. The tenderly moving principal theme, dominating the first part, imparts a lyrical quality to the whole movement:[2]

Ex. 18.

A second subject appears in due course on the first violin:

[1] This work recalls in a different form the D major quartet of Mozart, the first of the quartets dedicated to Frederick William, King of Prussia.

[2] The beginning of this *Allegro*, with the theme opening on the dominant of the key, was considered very audacious. The usual practice of the period, elevated to a definite rule by certain theorists, was to begin a work in ' sonata form ' on the tonic.

Ex. 19.

Bringing with it an atmosphere of uneasy disquietude, this theme gives birth to a *staccato* figure in
the bass, which persists to the end of the exposition ; the
theme then passes to the second violin and viola, and
the first violin takes the 'cello figure, substituting for
the *staccato* a *legato* leading to an episode of quiet and
untroubled serenity.

The development is simple, and chiefly interesting
for the ingeniously contrived re-entry of the original
theme ; the development closes in the tonality of C
sharp major, and while the viola and 'cello still sustain
the C sharp, the second violin sounds the A natural
with which the original theme opens : [1]

Ex. 20.

[1] The same harmonic effect is to be found in the entry of the principal theme in the second section of the *Allegro* in the IInd symphony.

II. *Andante.* This slow movement, in B flat major, is much longer than any *Adagio* of Mozart's and than most of Haydn's. By an innovation of his own Beethoven thus makes the slow movement with its extended development the central point of the whole work. The second violin gives out the following theme, *piano*, on the fourth string:

Ex. 21.

Immediately afterwards, this pensive melody passes to the first violin an octave higher, heard against graceful counter melodies on the viola and second violin. But the promise of these lovely opening bars is not to be fulfilled; the development is built upon two main themes accompanied by two secondary *motifs*, and is quite finely and clearly worked out, but the movement has little real depth of feeling, in spite of its obvious sincerity. Much is sacrificed to symmetry of design. Nevertheless, towards the end, the breath of a stronger inspiration stirs the formality of style. The return of the second *motif* to the principal theme is full of movement and feeling, and the impress of the artist's individual style is felt in the unexpected appearance of rapidly beating sextuplets and in the mystery of the concluding bars, anticipating the end of the slow movement from the Xth quartet.

III. *Allegro.* This third movement might be called 'Menuet'. It bears unmistakable traces of Mozart's influence, and it follows almost exactly the classical form, with its alternating major (*Menuet*) and minor (*Trio*) sections. Otherwise the piece has a veiled grace of distinctly original cast, and in the *Trio* whimsical little figures appear alternately on the violins above held chords on the other instruments.

At the repeat of the *Menuet*, Beethoven makes his instinct for innovation felt, and sets the second repetition of the theme at the octave.

IV. *Presto*. This forms the logical conclusion to the work and the climax of the spirit of *joie de vivre* which flows through the second movement and inspires the intimate contentment of the other two. The four instruments vie with each other throughout in light-hearted gaiety, whether it is in the principal theme or in the triumphant second subject—akin to the finale of the Kreutzer sonata—appearing first on the violin and then on the 'cello :

Ex. 22.

A vigorous rhythm—the same as that of the first subject of the Vth symphony, and one of the most characteristic that Beethoven ever wrote—comes to control this flood of gaiety and to inspire it with new strength :

Ex. 23.

The development flows on with an unfettered freedom of movement. Despite its correct and academic form, it has a certain individual quality, especially from the opening of the second section to the return of the principal theme, curiously introduced by a long *smorzando*. In this finale, which has several points of resemblance with that of the Op. 9 trio in G major, Beethoven rises to the level of his greatest models.

Quartet No. IV., Op. 18, No. 4 (in C minor).

Allegro ma non tanto   (𝄴 ♩ = 84).
Scherzo (Andante scherzo)   (3/8 ♩. = 56).
Menuetto (Allegretto)   (3/4 ♩. = 84).
{ *Allegro*   (𝄵 ○ = 66).
{ *Prestissimo*   (𝄵 ○ = 84).

Nottebohm mentions no preliminary sketches relating to this quartet. Knowing Beethoven's method of work, it is curious that one can find nothing whatever bearing on the working out of themes for the C minor quartet, even supposing one of the note-books to have been lost. It leads one to the conclusion that the composer wrote it at a single stroke, and at express speed, and that it has no connexion whatever with the other works of the same period.

This quartet is the most polished work of Op. 18, and one of the most advanced in style of Beethoven's early manner. It possesses the depth of lyrical feeling and the dramatic power of another work of contemporary date, the Op. 13 piano sonata, also written in the tonality of C minor. Like that it might also be called the 'Pathétique'. Strictly speaking, it is more uneven than the *Sonata Pathétique*, and the *Andante scherzo* and the *Menuet* are of a simplicity which, though charming and graceful, keeps them in the same plane as the corresponding movements of the other quartets. But the first *Allegro* and the finale alone are enough to lift it to the high level of achievement it as a whole attains.

I. *Allegro.* From the lowest note of the first violin a *motif* rises by mournful intervals to the upper register, the *motif* A, resolute and full of movement, beneath the unremitting beats of a 'cello accompaniment:

Ex. 24.

Charged with infinite longing and burning energy, it seems to well up from the depths of the soul in an urgent prayer for deliverance. . . . So Beethoven once wrote :

Alas! If I were only freed (from the curse of deafness) I could conquer the whole world. I feel indeed that my youth is only now beginning ; have I not always had wretched health ? And now for some time my physical strength has been improving, and with it my mental powers. Each day I feel an indescribable sense of being nearer to some end I have in view, in the realization of which alone can your Beethoven live. There is little rest for me! I know of none but sleep, and it irks me to have to give more time to that than I used. If I were but half cured of this infirmity, I would come to you in health and strength to revive our old intimacy. You shall only see me when I am as happy as I am destined to be in this life. Unhappiness I could not endure. I will seize Destiny by the throat, and it shall not overwhelm me utterly. Oh! it would be splendid to live one's life a thousand times over! I feel that a life of silence is not to be my fate.[1]

The passionate voice rises from bar to bar, pausing once as though to take breath ; then swept away with irresistible force (B), soaring on the wings of one of the secondary elements of the theme, in which all the longings of this tortured soul seem pent up, to a mighty climax of triumphant chords. This opening passage is one of the first examples of Beethoven's melodic gift, broad and powerful, expressive and yet uncomplex. Neither in Haydn nor in Mozart could a period so virile be found, so profoundly imaginative and emotional. In Mozart's G minor quintet the opening bars are of similar cast, but less moving and less intense.

An episode of curious rhythmic interest follows, where, above a *staccato* on the 'cello, the first violin states a little *motif* in which surprise and query seem to be mingled. The second violin murmurs the second theme, a suave and consoling melody based on the second phrase (B) of the first theme :

Ex. 25.

[1] Beethoven to Wegeler, Vienna, 16th Nov. 1800 (Chantavoine, *Correspondance de Beethoven*, pp. 30–1).

In this passage the *Allegro* thus gains a unity of inspiration. Through a rapid quaver figure the new theme passes to the first violin for repetition on broad lines. A second decisive, resolute episode in E flat follows, leading to the simple concluding bars of the section.

The second section repeats the elements of the exposition. The main theme echoes in G minor like the lament of a broken spirit; and the four bars of relentless chords that conclude its development resound like the clanging of gates that shut out hope for ever.

But now with unclouded serenity the 'cello in its highest register announces the theme of consolation, and the first violin answers in response. A serenity short-lived, for the theme is twisted into a dreary chromatic descent which loses itself in muffled *tremoli*, quivering *pianissimo* on the viola and second violin.[1] There, in the shadow of a dim obscurity, slow modulations develop; the passage is heavy with a suspense from which the first violin breaks away in a figure of flying quavers; finally the tonality of C minor emerges from the gloom, and the principal theme is heard again. . . . This return of the subject anticipates the massive re-entry of the *Allegro* in the XIth quartet.

The repetition follows traditional rules, and is mainly the same as the exposition. It must be admitted that this formality seems the weak point of a magnificent movement, where a freedom of form, justified by the imaginative meaning of the work, would have been more compatible with the inspiration of the whole than an exact symmetry. However, there are several points of difference between the two sections: the vigorous

---

[1] These *tremoli* are among the first evidences of the symphonic style in the quartet genre. Mendelssohn was later to use the idiom to excess. Already it had appeared on rare occasions, in slow movements of Haydn (XXXth quartet in G minor, bar 49 of the *Largo*), but from the period beginning with the VIIth quartet, Op. 59, No. 1, Beethoven was to make much use of the device to the last.

chords that follow the exposition of the principal theme
extend further and with increased force; and the first
violin, instead of the second, sings the theme of consolation, leading this time to a broad unison of the same
theme on the viola and second violin, sustained by the
'cello, beneath trills on the first violin; the whole passage throbs with joyous fervour.

The emotional inspiration of the movement reaches
its culmination at a point where the principal theme
returns, *fortissimo*, in the key of D flat major; the weak
beat is stressed by the viola and 'cello, with a syncopated figure on the second violin which stresses the
second half of each strong beat, imparting an air of
breathless haste to the ascending curve of the theme.
The pace quickens; and the last bars run aground, as
one might say, on the tonic chord of C minor. Already
we have a glimpse of the heroic inspiration of the
Coriolanus Overture.

II. *Andante* (*Scherzo*). The pleasant principal theme
of the *Andante scherzoso* is, both in rhythm and design, extraordinarily like that of the *Andante* of the
Ist symphony, which belongs to the same period as
Op. 18:

Ex. 26.

The theme is worked out in canon with many beautiful effects. Marx finds in this movement a quality
of serious decision hidden behind a superficial animation and gaiety. The interpretation is purely arbitrary
and has no real basis in the structure of the movement.
On the contrary, it is much more likely that the
musician would have preferred here a movement that
frankly contrasted with the force and profundity of the
Allegro. Beethoven was particularly fond of such contrasting effects; after an agony of desolation, his ardent

spirit would rise again in vivid reaction against despair
and melancholy.

In the *Andante scherzoso* the artist hides his sorrow
under a mask of lively good humour, easing his spirit
in the solution of rather trivial academic problems of
canon and triple counterpoint. It seems at first conceived as a purely mechanical exercise, but not for long.
The artist prevails over the technician, and almost all
the development section reveals his delight in his
creative power, especially the last entry of the theme
before the conclusion, which is pure Beethoven. The
passage evokes a hint of Schumann's *The Poet Speaks*
('Der Dichter spricht').[1] The development offers many
instances of Beethoven's characteristic modulations,
enclosed in a symmetrical sequence of chords : [2]

Ex. 27.

No composer has made more frequent use than
Beethoven of this technical device of chord progressions at points where the imaginative force lies for a
moment passive, awaiting fresh inspiration.

III. *Menuetto.* The *Menuetto*, or *Allegretto*, paints a
fresh contrast with the *Andante scherzoso*, though less
brilliant than that between the first two movements.
It opens with the identical notes that open the *Allegro*,
thus at once adding to the sense of unity in conception
of the work, in recalling a train of thought forgotten for

[1] Schumann, *Scenes of Childhood.*   [2] Cf. the *Adagio* of the Septet.

a moment in the light-heartedness of the *Andante*. It is written in the old minuet form upon a stately theme:

Ex. 28.

The movement is full of an atmosphere of courtly grace, so often found in the third movement of Mozart quartets and symphonies. Its emotion is veiled and controlled, as though the musician were half ashamed to let its existence be felt. This again is typical of Mozart.

The *Trio*, in A flat, is slight in conception. Triplets on the first violin encircle a short theme resembling an inverted Mozart *motif*, repeated first by the second violin, and then in turn by the viola and 'cello.

At the point where the *Menuet* returns, Beethoven has written in the text, *la seconda volta si prende il tempo più allegro*, as if he were suddenly animated by the breathless frenzy that inspires the short and restless periods of the finale. With this increase in pace, usually twice as fast as before, the *Menuet* already becomes itself a spirited *Allegro*.

IV. *Allegro*. By the side of the heroic character of the first movement the *motif* of the finale sometimes seems a little unworthy of the lofty conception of the quartet:

Allegro

Ex. 29.

But one must know it to realize its emotional capacity; it is as full of it as the *Rondo* of the sonata in C minor, Op. 13, which it resembles in manner. After the attempt in the *Andante* at emotional distraction, after the restraint and control of the *Menuet*, imaginative power is given a free rein in a movement full of passionate vigour.

T. Helm offers the following description of the movement, couched in his usual extravagant metaphor :

One imagines four combatants battling against each other, clad in shining armour, armed with sword and shield. At the outset the first violin, the *primus inter pares* among the knightly company, is alone in the arena, a young hero trying his strength with supple limb and sinew; but soon the three other champions enter the lists and the jousting commences. (Notice the exquisite imitations in the third section.) There is a momentary halt, and in the musical interlude (first in A flat, then in C) one seems to see on the rostrum wreathed with flowery garlands a glimpse of a lovely lady waving encouragement and signalling her favours.[1]

Generally speaking, the structure of the finale is essentially in the manner of Mozart.

Its rhythmic eight-bar form [2] reminds the hearer of one of this master's best-known works, the finale of the symphony in G minor. But if the form is similar, the inspiration is totally different. The finale of the

[1] T. Helm, *Beethoven's Streichquartette*, pp. 24–5.

[2] In the first bar of the second phrase there are two consecutive fifths in the accompaniment, to which Ries refers in the following anecdote : 'One day as I was out walking with him (Beethoven) I mentioned the instance in one of the first quartets (that in C minor) where two perfect fifths are used with striking beauty and effect. Beethoven did not remember the passage, and thought that I was wrong, and that they could not have been fifths. As he usually carried ruled paper with him, I asked him for some, and noted down the phrase in four parts. Realizing that I was right after all, Beethoven remarked : " Ah ! Well ! Who is it who says perfect fifths are wrong ? " I was not sure how to take the question, but he insisted, until I replied at length, quite disconcerted, " They are forbidden by the first fundamental rules of harmony ". The question was repeated again, and I added, " It is Marpurg, Kirnberger, Fuchs, and all the theorists, who forbid the use of consecutive fifths. . . ." " Very well," replied Beethoven, " *I* allow the use of them ! " '

The argument that Ries put forward here was that of a schoolboy, for the fifths in this passage proceed in contrary movement, and are separated by rests, so that they are only apparent on reading the score.

symphony, that Mozart thought to make so impassioned and restless, seems full of a discreet reserve by the side of the irresistible force of Beethoven's emotion. This emotional force reaches a climax in the episode in C major :

Ex. 30.

and rises to further heights as the movement approaches its conclusion. At the return of the principal theme in C major the fever is lulled to a calm ; the 'cello, which a moment before had been interrupting the conflict of the other voices with cracking *pizzicati*, drops to a *pianissimo*, *arco*, with a tentative little design, while the theme is shared between the two violins in response. The uncertainty dies as quickly as it came, and the pace tightens up to a more concentrated energy, quickening to a climax and a sudden halt. . . . There are two moving bars of suspense, and, suddenly, the principal theme bursts into a furious *prestissimo*. The pace and tone are almost doubled, and a change of accent on to the weak beat gives an increased sense of emotional intensity. This episode works up to a fiery climax, modulating from the minor to the brilliance of C major ; and three fierce unisons conclude the movement in this tonality.

The emotion of the first *Allegro* and the unrestrained passion of the finale form together the most expressive contrast possible. Instances of similar conclusions, always of striking effect, are to be found in Beethoven's work. The sonata in C minor, Op. 13, and the violin and piano sonata Op. 30, also in C minor, offer beautiful examples.

Quartet No. V, Op. 18, No. 5 (in A major).

Allegro (6/8 ♩· = 104).
Menuetto (3/4 ♩· = 76).
{ *Andante cantabile* (2/4 ♪ = 100).
{ *Poco adagio* (*Coda*) (2/4 ♪ = 88).
Allegro (𝄴 o = 76).

The quartet in A is exactly contemporary with the quartet in G, No. II, and with the septet, Op. 20. If there were further need to prove the unity of inspiration of these three works, evidence is available in a certain note-book of 1799, where outlines of all their themes are found intimately intermingled. Most of them are already in a form very like their final shape, as one noticed in the study of Op. 18, No. 2. They spring up in delightful confusion and spontaneity; and it is as though Beethoven had picked a flower here and there, to make three posies of the same colour and scent. The quartet in A is a veritable act of homage to the spirit of Mozart, as von Lenz remarks, like that in G and the septet, yet more so than these sister works, for in the finale can be found at least one passage where it seems as if a deliberate imitation is intended of a Mozart quartet in the same tonality.[1]

The principal theme of the *Allegro* reveals its showy and effective character in the phrase of the first three bars, which took their final form almost at the first stroke. This first phrase of the theme is simply the ascending scale of A major. Beethoven often employs

[1] For this reason the quartet in A is one of those rare works of Beethoven to find favour in Ulibishev's eyes, since his admiration for Mozart has made him unjust to every other composer. In another chamber music composition of the same period, the quintet in E flat, for piano and wind instruments, Op. 16, Beethoven has again modelled his work on Mozart's piece written for the same instruments and in the same key.

a very simple thematic element as the basis of his melody, especially in his early period, using a scale, or a fragment of a scale, or a common chord, broken or inverted, and many of his most celebrated themes can be traced back to this simple source. But the subtle art of the Master teaches him how to embellish and transform these thematic elements into expressive polished phrases, in which no trace of technical trick or academic manner can be discovered.

In the original sketch of the *Allegro* theme, the ascending figure of the melody stops after three bars, and the *motif* returns upon itself with a heavy, even awkward, effect. In the next sketch Beethoven finds the solution of the problem ; the rising scale of A major continues its upward flight, in the same form, with the first note of each group of three repeated, but without the turns which at first accompany it ; it rises to the submediant, and from this point the phrase falls smoothly in a flexible six-eight figure that ends on the dominant and finally moves to the tonic ; this forms, without any other modification, the principal theme of the first *Allegro*.

The same comment could be made on the theme of the *Andante cantabile* (with variations). That also is composed from a fragment of a descending scale, and from the first outline of the *motif* to the form it finally reached, Beethoven seems to have been continually working for an effect of greater restraint in the descending curve of the theme. A comparison of the first two bars of the phrase in its first and in its final shape shows how simply the result is attained :

First sketch   Second sketch

Ex. 31.

In the note-book there are some barely legible explanatory words, written above the theme, of which

only the word ' pastoral ' can be deciphered, a fragmentary but unmistakable indication of the composer's
intention for the movement.

The sketches for the *Finale* are all written in common
time, instead of in their final form—₵.

I. *Allegro*. The original theme, just analysed above :

Ex. 32.

is followed by a semiquaver figure, rather lacking in
expressive force, in which both design and development
conspire from the start to confirm the suggestion of
Mozart's style. But an individual note is struck in the
secondary theme in E minor :

Ex. 33.

In this contemplative theme, and even in the choice
of tonality—E minor instead of the expected E major,
for the semiquaver figure had finally ended in the
dominant key—Beethoven's own idiom is unmistakable ; the impression persists throughout the lovely
passage that follows, where the four voices are blended
in contrary movement, interrupted by the entry of the
semiquaver figure and a return to the manner of
Mozart, as the exposition section concludes.

The development and the third section, both to be
repeated, contain nothing more than the first ; yet a

certain change of character is observed, felt most in the semiquaver figure—especially in the A minor passage, where it assumes a vigour more characteristic of Beethoven's individual manner than of Mozart's.

A short *Coda* ends the movement: the scale of A major, split up among the parts, forms its sole basis, and recalls the design of the principal theme.

II. *Menuetto.* This movement breathes an atmosphere of sweet, untroubled tenderness, again inspired by the contemplative spirit of Mozart. The trio *motif* is both expressive and individual :

Ex. 34.

It belongs to a type of melody of which Beethoven was very fond, and constantly made use : the theme for variations in the A flat sonata, Op. 26, and one phrase from the third movement of the E flat trio, Op. 70, are of the same class.

III. *Andante cantabile*, a theme and variations. Variation-form was very fashionable at the time when Beethoven began his career, and contemporary musicians used or abused it one and all.[1] Mozart and Haydn had produced marvellous compositions in the style, and

---

[1] The fashion had many admirers, among them the famous Abbé Gelinek, to whom Weber later wrote this pithy epigram :
  Kein Thema in der Welt verschönte dein Genie,
    Das simpelste allein, dich selbst, variirst du nie . . .
(No theme on earth escaped your genius. But the simplest of all, yourself, you never vary.)

Beethoven was not long in following their example. Even during the year in which the quartet in A was composed he wrote many variations, among them a set for piano duet in D minor upon the theme of '*Nähe des Geliebten*', for piano solo on a theme from Salieri's *Falstaff*, ' *la Stessa, la Stessissima* ', on P. Winter's theme ' *Kind, willst du ruhig schlafen* ', and finally the variations in the septet on a Rhineland folk tune.[1]

In all these works he takes as a model the variation-form of Haydn and Mozart. The variation is simply the natural development of the melodic phrase, altered in rhythm and tonality, adorned with fresh figuration, and subject to every possible inflexion of detail. The melody reveals its expressive capacity in passages of joy and sadness, and even, as in the last variation on ' *la Stessa, Alla Austriacca* ', forms a basis for a dance rhythm. But in spite of the florid ornament that encircles it, the theme is always fundamentally the same.

In the *Andante cantabile* of the quartet in A, Beethoven raises the character of variation-form to a higher level ; a certain harmonic basis only is retained, upon which to erect a new melodic structure ; thus each variation is a new creation with an individual rhythm, melody, and expressive power.[2]

Later on, in the last quartets, the variation-form is to assume a still broader aspect, re-created and extended in scope by the free genius of the artist : it would be interesting to trace in detail the sequence of the Beethoven variations, from the simple varied melody for piano up to the IXth symphony and the last quartets—that is to say, up to the creation of the cyclic and synthetic form which gave birth to the drama of Wagner and the symphony of César Franck.[3]

---

[1] See Kretzschmer, *Deutsche Volkslieder, mit ihren Originalweisen*, Berlin, 1838, p. 181.

[2] See Sauzay, *Haydn–Mozart–Beethoven*.

[3] See the comments of M. Vincent d'Indy on this point in his *Cours de composition musicale*, p. 473.

However interesting the variations of the quartet in
A may be, they only represent one of the early stages
in this tremendous development.[1] In writing them
Beethoven obviously took as his model the variations
in Mozart's quartet in A and in Haydn's Emperor
quartet, but he reaches no higher level than Mozart.
Indeed, these three works all reveal so fluent a technique
that it is difficult to choose between them. Perhaps
Mozart's art is most spontaneous and delicate : the
variations in D minor have the limpid purity of a
Raphael Madonna. Haydn reaches the same degree of
clarity with added depth of feeling ; and though sometimes rhythmically weak, his variations have an extraordinarily advanced harmonic interest. Beethoven is at
once more assertive and more virile ; with him a certain
whimsical element touches the serenity of inspiration.
This element is apparent in the first variation, where
the spirited dialogue between the instruments provides
a vivid contrast with the meditative simplicity of the
theme, and in the second, with its delicate sylph-like
figure on the first violin, and in the third, where the
whispering movement of the violins seems to bestow
a curious lyrical quality upon the melody of the basses.
A comparison of the original theme and the fourth
variation :

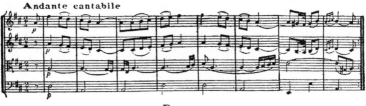

Ex. 35.

[1] These are on an original theme. In the sonata and the quartet, it was
customary to base the variations on an original theme ; but exceptions to
this rule are the Trio by Beethoven for piano, clarinet, and 'cello, Op. 11
(where an air from Martini's *L'Arbore di Diana, Pria che l'impegno*, is
used), the Haydn quartet in which the Austrian national anthem is used,
and later the VIIth Beethoven quartet with its Russian theme, &c.

Ex. 36.

brings out in relief the deepening of emotion and intimacy [1] as the movement extends; the path of the melody on the first violin is the same in both cases, except for the significant alteration of A to A sharp. A heroic inspiration stirs the fifth variation: between the sustained trill on the first violin and the emphatic beat of the 'cello the strains of an orchestra seem to resound, gradually diminishing in tone till the original theme steals back again through a delicately wrought texture of sound. Here are anticipated the brilliant variations of Schubert's D minor quartet on the 'Death and the Maiden' theme.

What further remains to be said by four instruments upon an already much-exploited theme is contained in the *Coda* (*poco adagio*, in D major). Here the influence of Haydn is perceptible. The first section of the theme falls in a slow *pianissimo*, rises tentatively on the first violin, then on the second; the viola and 'cello take it again and the *motif* is obliterated in two *pianissimo* chords.

IV. *Allegro*. The finale opens in an insouciant careless manner which conforms neither to Beethoven's artistic style nor to his imaginative character. The principal theme lacks expressive power, but is a splendid quartet *motif*, and, by reason of its conciseness and animation, developed in the manner of Haydn, lends

---

[1] In this fourth variation occurs a series of perfect fifths which would have disturbed Ries far more than those of the IVth quartet (third and fourth bars in the 'cello and second violin parts: A, E, F♯, and C♯).

itself perfectly to the rapid intricacies of question and imitative response that primarily constitute 'quartet' technique.

The second theme is of an entirely different type. At other times it has been noticed as a peculiarity of these early works of Beethoven that the secondary themes are almost invariably more expressive than the first. Here it seems almost as though the artist experiences a sort of shame at the expense of his inspiration on a work of purely superficial and exterior brilliance, and he recovers himself at this point to breathe emotional life into this fluent and trivial diversion. In deep organ chords on the four instruments the second theme interrupts the animation of the opening passage:

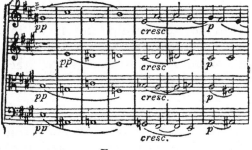

Ex. 37 *a*.

This sudden lull is followed by a statement of the melody, first by the first violin, and later by the 'cello, broad and sustained like a *canto firmo*, above the other voices; these pursue a passage of falling thirds, divide, cross, and overlap in graceful contrary movement, interwoven with the expressive phrase of the violin.

The remarkable point in this passage is that, at the moment when Beethoven seems to be giving full expression to his own robust individuality, the passage is actually a mere imitation, a copy even, of Mozart. In the latter's quartet in A, after having worked out a fluent *motif* for some time, as Beethoven does here, he also interrupts his development with a second theme in chords, in all the parts. The two passages are here quoted in comparison, the one with Beethoven's theme, the other with Mozart's:

Ex. 37 *b*.

Ex. 37 *c*.

After the exposition of the theme in chords, Mozart also places the melody on the first violin above an accompaniment on the other voices, and their movement is again the same as in Beethoven's development, except that it is in quavers instead of crotchets. The close resemblance between the two passages cannot be denied.

The contrast between the two themes is perhaps more marked in the Mozart quartet; there the second *motif* is like a prayer from another world. But Beethoven probes more deeply into the inner possibilities of his *motif*, and thus gains greater effect. His finale is constructed in sonata form, like all the early *Allegros*, and the second theme fills the capacity of the cantilena. After its exposition in the first section, it reappears in the development, closely linked with the principal theme; episodes follow in which the secondary *motif* resounds like the strains of a distant organ, swelling and dying amid the restless animation of the first theme, before reaching the third section or recapitulation.

This much resembles the first; the chord *motif* returns in the principal key of A major, and after it follows the intricate part-writing noticed earlier. The conclusion is anticipated after the manner of Mozart, but as it is about to materialize, the principal theme returns in the subdominant key, as though indefinitely to defer the expected consummation. But the principal key is re-established, and with it the first *motif*, shorn of its banal insouciance, and now invested with eloquent meaning. With this theme the first violin sings a ' farewell ' *motif*, supported by fragments of the same *motif* on the other instruments. The first four notes of the theme slip from voice to voice—first on the violins and then on the 'cello—to the final chord, fading away into the distance in a long last adieu.

Quartet No. VI, Op. 18, No. 6 (in B flat).

Allegro con brio   (𝄵 ○ = 80).
Adagio ma non troppo   (3/4 ♪ = 80).
Scherzo-Allegro   (3/4 ♩· = 63).
⎧ La Malinconia *Adagio*   (3/4 ♪ = 58).
⎨ *Allegretto quasi allegro*   (3/8 ♩·   88).
⎩ *Prestissimo*   (3/8 ♩· = 112).

The only existing sketches of this quartet relate to the finale. The principal theme of this movement was originally harsh and crude, quite unlike the sparkling *motif* that Beethoven finally evolved; and the *Malinconia* section, already associated with the early sketches, provided there a less vivid contrast than in its final context. The final form of the *motif* was developed later, and the note-books reveal two preliminary outlines of similar design.

These sketches are mingled with many others, notably those for the sonata, Op. 22, and the IInd quartet in G. One gathers from this an idea of the artist's methods; he must always have had several works in hand, and the beginning of one is bound up with the continuation or completion of another.

I. *Allegro con brio.* The ease and breadth of the finale in the preceding quartet flows on into the first movement of this ; the gay principal theme, so true to ' quartet ' style, recalls Haydn :

Ex. 38.

while the bridge passage recalls Mozart, especially in the following figure :

Ex. 39.

The two short phrases contained in this passage constitute, with the principal theme, all the elements of the development, in which the melancholy second theme plays a very subordinate part. This first section concludes with a re-exposition of the principal theme. It is important to notice, at the end of the second section, how this same theme returns in a *decrescendo* where the four voices, two by two, join in a dialogue, finishing on a long united pause, *pianissimo*. The passage is characteristic both in rhythm and effect, and anticipates the composer's second period.

The third section is identical with the first, except for

a short and interesting bridge passage (E flat major to E flat minor). This passive acceptance of the classical form is the weak point of the *Allegro con brio*; the working out of repeats according to rule involves the recurrence of the first theme four times in succession, almost without modification, with an inevitably monotonous effect.

II. *Adagio ma non troppo*, in E flat major. At the moment of writing this slow movement, Beethoven must have been enjoying one of the periods of relaxation that he was so rarely to experience during his life.

The first theme is unfolded, sinuous and fluent, with a supple grace:

Ex. 40.

It is first heard on the first violin alone, then split up among the other parts beneath a florid counterpoint. At the entry of the second theme in E flat minor, in a unison of the first violin and 'cello, the movement deepens in meaning, though without any tinge of bitterness. A development of this theme follows the exposition; four times the 'cello attempts the opening phrase of the theme, to abandon the effort at last in a tentative pause. But this is only a passing shadow; the first violin, in a series of springing figures, derived from the first *motif*, detaches itself from this indecision, and re-establishes the original theme. Its two elements (bars one and three of Ex. 40) are developed in contrapuntal opposition. The second element, being the more sprightly, gains the ascendancy, and the movement seems on the point of conclusion in a delicate fluttering of wings. But first the second theme makes a reappearance in C minor, and subsequently, by an unprepared modulation, in C major. The conclusion of this polished composition is built upon elements of the principal theme.

III. *Scherzo.* After the exercise of serene restraint in the foregoing movement, Beethoven gives his imagination free rein. The *Scherzo* opens with the distant sound of horns, and widens to an exuberant outburst of joy. Here the musician's individuality is all-pervasive, felt in the persistent accent on the weak beat, in the regularly alternating *staccato* and *legato*, in the ebullient rhythmic vigour. Of all the quartets of Op. 18, this *Scherzo* is undoubtedly the most original movement.

The feature of the *Trio* is a design for the first violin, evoking by contrast the spirit of Haydn. The little *Coda fortissimo* in the key of B flat minor, based on the *scherzo* theme, reintroduces the *Scherzo* with a curiously naïve effect; it is like an excited cry of consternation from a child at play, an anticipation of Schumann's ' Knecht-Ruprecht '.[1]

IV. *Finale.* This movement is the climax of the B flat quartet, and, according to Ulibishev, its weak point, on account of the programme attached to it. Earlier musical art contains nothing at all like this famous *Malinconia*, flawless example of symbolism in music : here is mirrored the spirit of the artist, with every shade of joy and sorrow manifested in his creative gift.

An *Adagio* opens, bearing the superscription, *La Malinconia*, and the note in Italian : ' *Questo pezzo si deve trattare colla più gran delicatezza.*' (This movement must be played with the greatest subtlety.)

Ex. 40 *a.*

[1] R. Schumann, *Forty-three Piano Pieces for the Young.*

The forty-three bars of the theme ' move like a wander-ing thought without any apparent end '. Sad and sweet, the lament rises several times, as though groping after a hidden clarity, a peace that may never be attained. It lingers without resolution, till stirred by the breath of a sudden bitter wind that touches each note as though with frost. *Forte* follows *piano* in quick succes-sion, in a troubled agony of spirit, to be obscured again in melancholy, as the bass moves slowly up the chromatic scale, labouring beneath an infinite burden of grief.

These tears and sighs, this sinking back upon him-self, intermingled with the emotion of a tender in-spiration, is unlike the virile strength and fortitude that Beethoven was to express in his later works. It is rather the lonely melancholy of an immature spirit already overtaken by the sorrows of the world, longing hopelessly for joy and love, and shut in upon itself in trembling fear of adversity; the sorrow of a tender heart feeling a nameless distress of mind and spirit, knowing the years of youth to be slipping by joyless and desolate; the dispirited listlessness of a child tired of life before it has lived at all.

This, too, is a melancholy that paralyses action. But in spite of all, the world lies in front of the young artist, in eternal hope. ' Take heart, the sun is shining through the clouds! Away with repinings and on with the dance!' After a last pause on the dominant of B flat, the *Malin-conia* gives way to the lively and vivid inspiration of the *Allegretto quasi allegro*, and we are whirled into the gay measure of a country dance, in an irresistible rhythm where 'cello *sforzandi* mark the accented weak beat.

A return of the introspective mood cuts this outburst short; the *Malinconia* reappears, to last only ten bars, for joy is at hand, so near and so alluring, stifling sorrow, and bringing back the gaiety of the dance; nevertheless, the dance is less light-hearted than before, obscured in the sombre shadow of melancholy, and cast in a minor tonality. An abrupt halt is followed by a

long pause ; and for the third and last time the desolate
theme of the *Malinconia* is heard, but the exuberance
of youth and high spirits once more sweeps gloom aside,
and the dance is resumed ; now its overflowing joy
rises to a paean of thanksgiving. A passage in which
the first notes of the *motif* are tossed from part to part
is followed by a very short *poco adagio*, in which the
dance *motif* is twice repeated after pauses. Here one
discerns no hint of returning gloom, but an arresting
moment of self-analysis. Beethoven seems to doubt for
a second whether he can abandon himself to so care-
free a mood. In the wild *Prestissimo* one reads the
answer ; the dance whirls on in a mad riot to the two
decisive chords of the concluding bars. One feels, in
this conflict between a contemplative and melancholy
mood and a wild Elf dance, ending in the triumph of
gaiety, rather the clash of immature emotions experienced in youth, like Goethe's Mignon, for example,
than the stern struggle against adversity in the soul of
the Master of Bonn. Yet it is possible to read into this
moving finale of the B flat quartet—which is also the
conclusion of Op. 18—both an expression of the first
phase of Beethoven's life and a foreknowledge of the
last ; troubled here by the first presentiment of sorrow
in store, as clouds darken a spring morning, at the same
time the artist glances back at the pure joy and tenderness of boyhood, before sinking into the desolation of
a melancholy that he is powerless to resist, and which
is soon to engulf his spirit like the tomb.

* *

The first private performances of the Op. 18 quartets
took place at the house of Prince Lichnowsky. Charles,
Prince Lichnowsky, Count Werdenberg, Lord Gran-
son, Beethoven's friend and patron, was a keen musical
amateur. Every Friday morning four fine *virtuosi* used
to come regularly to his house, artists who were also
connected, after 1797, with the musical circle of Count
A. Rasoumowsky, Russian ambassador in Vienna, to

whom Beethoven dedicated the three Op. 59 quartets. They were Schuppanzigh,[1] first violin, Sina,[2] second violin, Weiss, viola, and Kraft, 'cello. When one or other was absent his place would be taken either by the prince himself, or by Zmeskall von Domanovecz, one of Beethoven's best friends, or Linke the 'cellist, also a member of Rasoumowsky's circle. Though naturally rather intolerant, Beethoven would accept his friends' suggestions in good faith, and even follow them out when the proposed change did not affect the musical idea. According to Wegeler, it was Kraft who got him to alter a passage in the finale of the third trio, Op. 1.

It was in this musical coterie that the new works from the Master's pen were performed for the first time. Great musicians and cultivated amateurs used to come to these friendly gatherings, and Wegeler, who attended regularly, tells how in the presence of the veteran Haydn Beethoven played there for the first time the three sonatas dedicated to him.

At one of the meetings there in 1795 Count Apponyi commissioned Beethoven to compose a quartet, in return for a definite fee ; one knows the outcome of this commission (see the Introduction). But four or five years later, when the artist wrote the Op. 18, he kept the first of his work for the faithful quartet. As he finished a work he explained it to those who were to interpret it : according to Seyfried,[3] 'he told them his ideas and

---

[1] Ignaz Schuppanzigh was born in Vienna in 1776 and died on March 2, 1830 ; he was Mayseder's master, a gifted virtuoso and a wonderful quartettist ; he also founded and directed the *Augarten* orchestra in Vienna. Even in his youth Schuppanzigh was very stout, and his figure was the subject of continuous jokes from Beethoven, among others a comic chorus, seventeen bars long, called 'Praise of the fat one', never published ; it was dedicated by Beethoven to his friend and faithful interpreter ' milord Falstaff', and written on the phrase ' Schuppanzigh est un gredin' (1801). (See Nottebohm and Thayer.)

[2] Sina finally went to settle in France, after having been a member of the two chamber music societies of Lichnowsky and Rasoumowsky. He died in France in 1857. (See Ernouf, *Compositeurs célèbres*, p. 17.)

[3] See Seyfried, *Vie de Beethoven* (tr. from German into French).

inspiration about the piece, and fired the performers with his own spirit'. It was commonly said in Vienna that ' if one wished to understand and appreciate to the full any chamber music of Beethoven's one should hear it played by these fine artists'.

It was this famous group of players, so entirely devoted to Beethoven as even to be called the ' Beethoven Quartet', that gave the first public performances in Vienna of Op. 18, in the years of 1801 and 1802.

The appearance of the six works, published by Mollo, was the signal at first for a concentrated attack : very few critics recognized in them the coming of a new musical era. The *Allgemeine Musikalische Zeitung* of Leipzig, ' like an old broody hen scratching away in the dust of pedantry ', made the following comment upon the appearance of the first series :

Among new works are some fine compositions by L. van Beethoven; his three quartets evidence genuine talent, but they need to be often played, as they are difficult to grasp and not at all popular.[1]

The *Zeitung* did not change its tone when the three following quartets appeared. But public opinion did not confirm this criticism, and in a short time the six quartets met with unqualified success. In the following year, 1802, Mollo published a second edition of Op.18. Beethoven writes to Hofmeister on the 4th April 1802 : ' M. X. . . . has got out a second edition of my quartets, but it is full of mistakes and errata : they seem to swarm like fish in the sea, indefinitely. *Questo è un piacere per un autore*, that is what I call engraving with a vengeance ; my skin is simply covered with scratches from these fine editions of my quartets.'[2] Composers

---

[1] *Leipziger Allgemeine Musikalische Zeitung*, 1801, p. 800. This journal had already appraised the first Trios of Op. 1, with calm contempt, as the ' confused outpourings of a young man's arrogant imagination ', and the first symphony, dubbed 'a ridiculous caricature of Haydn '.

[2] *Correspondance de Beethoven*, translated from German into French by J. Chantavoine, p. 41.

alone reserved their judgment. Carpani tells that Haydn found no originality in the works, although quite approving, and only saw in them a fusion of his own style with Mozart's.

In 1806 the continued success of the Op. 18 encouraged Simrock of Bonn to publish the six quartets arranged as piano sonatas with violin *obbligato* and 'cello *ad lib.* The outrageous *Leipziger Zeitung* pursues its comment:

It must be remarked that these sonatas are really the much-talked-of quartets of which one scarcely tires, in spite of their harsh and rugged style. Pianists who wish to make a mark as technicians will do well not to choose them.[1]

In spite of this derisive criticism, public opinion remained faithful to the original works, and the first six quartets were for a long time thought superior even to those that followed. It is known that Spohr thought the first quartet reached the highest point possible in the quartet genre.

The Op. 18 was soon discovered in certain French musical circles, but little understood. Habeneck, then a violin student at the Conservatoire, played them in 1802 'with his friends, Philipp and others'. He told Schindler in 1840 that of all the artists who heard them play the works Méhul alone realized their worth.[2]

French musical circles generally, less willing to listen to chamber music than the German public, refused for a long time to take up these quartets, and Ries, when travelling in France in 1809, wrote to Beethoven from Paris saying that musical taste was generally inferior there, and that his works were little known or played, least of all the quartets.[3] The famous violinist Baillot appreciated the beauty of the works, and was the self-constituted champion both of the first and of the

---

[1] *Leipziger Allgemeine Musikalische Zeitung*, 1806, p. 670.

[2] Schindler, *Beethoven in Paris*, p. 3.

[3] In his enthusiasm for Beethoven, Ries was anxious to acquaint Paris not only with the compositions but with the artist himself. He

later quartets ; but he was forced by public indifference and general lack of comprehension to abandon performance of them for a time.[1]

From 1830 to 1834 not once did the programmes of these fine concerts include any of the Beethoven quartets.[2] After 1834 they were at last included in the repertoire of various chamber-music societies, and regularly played. In the winter of 1847–8 the violinist Tilmant founded a chamber-music club called the Société de musique classique. Its membership included T. Tilmant, Guerreau, Casimir Ney, A. Tilmant, and Gouffé, string players ; Dorus, Klosé, Rousselot, S. and D. Verroust, wind players ; and Mme Wartel, a pianist. Among performances of Mozart and Haydn quartets, quintets by Reicha, Onslow, and Hummel, this society played, at irregular intervals, several Beethoven quartets, especially those of Op. 18. In the programme of its opening concert in 1849 one observes the quartet in F, Op. 18, where, according to the *Revue et Gazette musicale de Paris*, ' the originality of the great symphonic writer already breaks through the influence and manner of Mozart in brilliant flashes ; the work was performed with fine ensemble and subtlety of feeling by MM. T. Tilmant, Guerreau, A. Tilmant, and C. Ney ' (Feb. 11th, 1849).

asked Beethoven in this letter to send him the date of his birth and other biographical details. Beethoven was offended at the news from Ries about the general disregard for his work in Paris. We know from other sources that he was anxious to conceal his age. He wrote the following letter to his pupil : ' My dear Ries, Your friends have given you very bad advice, on every count, but I know all about them. They are the same from whom you got all the fine news about me in Paris that you sent, the same who are inquiring about my age, information that you could give so well, the same who have so often lowered you in my esteem, and this time permanently. Farewell. Beethoven.' (1809.) The master's resentment was, however, short-lived.

[1] The Baillot Quartet in 1827 was composed of Baillot, Vidal, Urhan, and Norblin. They played most of the Op. 18 quartets during the winter of 1826–7. (See the *Revue musicale*, 1827.)

[2] See the *Gazette musicale* and the *Revue musicale*, 1830–4.

About the same time several concert promoters made a timid trial of these first quartets, evidently a risky matter, but the pill was administered furtively among *bravura* pieces by Goria, Prudent, or Thalberg ! In the *Gazette musicale*, L. Kreutzer sings the praises of M. Massart, who performed the VIth quartet in his concert-rooms with MM. Reynier, Chéri, and Jacquard ; ' it is a noble and serious work,' M. Kreutzer continues, ' one of those works where imagination and technical skill, depth of feeling, and delicacy of treatment strive for the ascendancy. This sixth quartet is delightful; the exquisitely contemplative reverie, named by the composer *la Malinconia*, forms a perfect foil for the sparkling rhythm of the *Finale*; it falls upon the ear like the passionate pleading of a faithful lover whose despair is mocked by a coquette's heartless mirth.'

After such a favourable reception the early Beethoven quartets could not fail to gain the attention of the fashionable public. As we shall see later, the second quartets and the last particularly were at this time very far from being accorded so much praise. Their moment had not then arrived.

English musicians were quick to discover the Beethoven quartets, and the Philharmonic Society expressed the greatest admiration for them.[1] The Society's generosity towards the artist in the last years of his life is a matter of common knowledge. But it was not till 1840 that these masterpieces of chamber music gained the approval of the amateur world and were generally accepted. Alsager, one of the editors of *The Times*, and a man of wide interests and sympathies, had the initiative to form a society for the performance of the Beethoven quartets, and after his death the distinguished 'cellist-composer Rousselot, one of the members of the Society, continued this splendid effort.

[1] The *Musical Review* reports in February 1828 the first concert of the Philharmonic Society, directed by Cramer : ' Beethoven's fifth quartet, Op. 18, was performed with fine feeling. M. Oury, who has not before appeared as first violin at these concerts, gave much pleasure. . . .' The C minor quartet was played at the second concert.

CHAPTER II

THE QUARTETS OF THE SECOND PERIOD
(Op. 59, Nos. 1–3; Op. 74; Op. 95.)

NOWHERE in the whole series of sonatas and symphonies does there exist so striking a contrast as between the quartets of Op. 18 and those of Op. 59. The sonatas and symphonies, distributed evenly throughout Beethoven's life of creative work, form, as it were, landmarks showing the sure progression of the artist towards a freer, more spacious, more perfect medium of expression, and passing from one to another one can quite easily follow the phases of this growth. With the quartets it is far from being the case. Between the sixth and the seventh the continuity breaks abruptly and without warning.

One finds in this interval of six years one work only for strings, the Op. 29 quintet, written in 1802, a beautiful work, but belonging to Beethoven's early period. Indeed, without going so far as T. Helm, who calls this only a reflection of the quartet in F (Op. 18, No. 1),[1] one can say that for all its originality this quintet is really a continuation of the manner of Op. 18, with an extended range of treatment.[2]

The first six quartets are the work of a young composer in the full enthusiasm of youth, eager to imitate the models he loves and admires; those to come are the work of an acknowledged master already famous for many triumphs,[3] of a great spirit strengthened and purified by the experience of a life of struggle and suffering. After having constrained the full tide of his

[1] T. Helm, *Beethoven's Streichquartette*, p. 39.

[2] See note at end of chapter, p. 193.

[3] The principal works are : the first three symphonies ; the Op. 20 septet and the Op. 29 quintet ; three piano concertos (including the Op. 37, in C minor) ; thirteen piano sonatas, among which were the Op. 26, containing the 'marche funèbre', the C♯ minor Op. 27, No. 2, Op. 53, and Op. 57 (the Appassionnata), &c. ; six sonatas for violin and piano, among others those dedicated to the Emperor Alexander,

inspiration within the limits of his medium for expression, his genius now widens the extent of that medium almost to breaking-point.

Between 1800 and 1806, through seasons of gloom and passion, joy and sorrow, tenderness and the bitterness of despair, the soul of Beethoven reached maturity. He had loved in vain Giulietta Guicciardi, spoilt child and selfish coquette, unworthy of the great love he had to give, and upon whom the passion and longing expressed in the C minor sonata (Op. 27, No. 2) was lavished and thrown away. In an access of despair he had even contemplated putting an end to his life, and written in poignant farewell the ' Heiligenstadt Will ' (6 Oct. 1802). Increasing deafness made him still further isolated from the rest of the world, and shut up in loneliness a heart made for love and tenderness. The ideals of liberty, independence, and brotherhood, brought to Vienna by the victorious Revolution, fired him with new enthusiasm ; a true disciple of Plutarch, he fell to dreaming of the ultimate happiness of the human race ; and discovering all too soon the self-seeking and sordid aims hidden beneath the veneer of disinterested ideals, he suffered a disillusionment that bruised his shy, sincere spirit in its tenderest spot. During this period of maturing thought his expressive medium takes a form at once loftier and more spacious. To it belongs the Concerto in C minor (Op. 37), the Eroica, the Sonata to Kreutzer, the Appassionnata, Fidelio. Then at last love comes to him again ; in May of 1806 Thérèse von Brunswick was betrothed to him, a sweet and charming woman, Beethoven's good angel and the ' Immortal Beloved '.[1]

Op. 30, Nos. 1–3, and to Kreutzer, Op. 47 ; the two romances for violin ; Prometheus, music for the Vigano ballet (Op. 43) ; many variations, bagatelles, &c. ; and lieder, including Adélaïde, Op. 46, on Matthisson's poem, &c.

[1] See *L'Immortelle Bien-Aimée de Beethoven*, by Michel Brenet (Courrier musical, 1 Jan. 1909) ; *Beethoven et Wagner*, by T. de Wyzewa, pp. 72 and 99.

In this wonderful time of joy and blossoming hope Beethoven lives in idyllic happiness, and his soaring ecstasy is now, as Taine described it, as overwhelming as have been and are still to be the sudden desolations of despair : ' Never have I known such exaltation,' he confides to Thérèse ; ' all about me is light and purity. I feel I have been up to now like the child in the fairy tale who picked up the pebbles that lay on the path before her and never saw the wonderful flower that was blooming by the roadside.'

During this period, when he believed he had at last attained real happiness, a veritable harvest of beautiful works sprang up as it were in his footsteps : the B flat Symphony, full of passionate tenderness, the Coriolanus Overture, the second Leonora Overture, and the three quartets of Op. 59.

I. *Op. 59.*

If one may say that Haydn created the string quartet as an art form, Beethoven achieved even greater attainment than his predecessor in the quartets of Op. 59, revealing the expressive capacity latent in the genre to an extent never dreamed of by earlier musicians. It is for this reason primarily that these three quartets have so deep a significance.

Beethoven's mature period of creative work is characterized by two main features, first, the prime importance of the musical idea, secondly, the construction of the development.

Among the conversations recounted by Bettina von Arnim to Goethe, we find these remarks of Beethoven : ' A melody slips from the arms of inspiration ; I hasten in eager pursuit, only to lose it in a riot of surging passions. I recapture it, and abandon myself to an ecstasy of delight ; I follow it up with modulation after modulation to achieve in the end the triumph of the musical idea ! ' The musical idea has for Beethoven become the active force and purpose of the work. It is this that moulds the old conventional form into a free medium for lyrical expression. With this realization comes the unceasing trial and research of which the sketch-books bear witness, and the constant mental effort, out of which inspiration grew, to encompass the new idea. From this time onwards Beethoven's melodies have practically nothing in common either with the perfectly turned phrases of Haydn or with Mozart's perfect balance and symmetry. They are primarily emotional and expressive with a dramatic force that is to be found rather in the work of Bach.[1]

With Mozart and Haydn, the development is nothing more than a skilful play upon the themes based on the principles of imitation and fugue, and with little bearing on the construction and particular character of the piece. One can usually anticipate the form it will take. With Beethoven, while the development is logically and constructively worked out in obedience to laws of tonality as a finely wrought web of sound, it has also a psychological significance. No longer is he bound by a rigid adherence to the old rules ; with the emotional content of the piece as a guide he acquires an amazing diversity of expression, which reaches its climax in the variation form of the later quartets. This new conception of the quartet was no sudden growth in the artist's mind, and in describing Op. 59 as ' three miracles dropped from heaven ', von Lenz is wrong : one must trace the sequence of Beethoven's work from 1799, the date of Op. 18, in the form of the sonata, the overture, and the symphony, and realize that in Op. 59 he was applying to the quartet form ideas conceived before on a broad musical basis. Certain sections of earlier works have already anticipated this development : the *Allegro* of the trio in C minor, Op. 9, the *Adagio* of the quartet

---

[1] Cf. the articles in the *Tribune de Saint-Gervais* (August and September 1899) where M. Vincent d'Indy establishes the relation between J. S. Bach and Beethoven, through Ph. E. Bach and Ph. W. Rust, and considers it incorrect to trace the relation through Mozart and Haydn.

in F, Op. 18, No. 1, the first *Allegro* of the quartet in C minor, the *Malinconia* from the quartet in B flat, the quintet, Op. 29 ; all these rise above the formal limitations of the genre, and herald the coming of that ' third epoch in quartet music, of which Haydn marked the first and Mozart the second '.[1]

The quality underlying the Op. 59 quartets is their psychological objectivity. Although he possessed an inexhaustible source of inspiration within himself, Beethoven here portrays objectively the joys and sorrows of the outside world. If one compares Op. 59 with the Op. 127 quartet from this aspect the contrast is immediately apparent. In Op. 59 he gives to the world a proof of his limitless capacity for expression, within the compass of the four lines of melody ; but in the later quartets he writes in pure introspective revelation, caring little whether the world understands him or not. They are his *apologia pro vita sua*, the priceless casket where lies hidden the great promise for the music of the future.

In the quartets of the second period there is still a flavour of the old sonata style, in spite of the ever-widening thought and altering form ;[2] in the later quartets there is a complete break with earlier conventions. The one depicts a world where the splendid force

[1] Von Lenz, *Beethoven et ses trois styles*, p. 336.

[2] ' The slow movement with repeats and a fixed number of bars in its various sections is discarded ; the Minuet with its inviolable rules has gone ; there is left no rigid form at all, in fact, but in its place a new creation—the Allegretto of Beethoven (sonata in C sharp minor, quartet in F minor, *Appassionnata* . . .). The Scherzo is no longer merely interpolated in the place of the Minuet as in the six first quartets . . . the duple rhythm hitherto almost invariably reserved for the finales is now to be found in the first Allegro. . . . In the " style of the second period " the fixed rules of sonata form are relaxed ; one single movement perhaps contains a whole sonata, and a very beautiful sonata at that (Op. 90). The Adagio may now be an endless lament (VIIth quartet) ; or a vision of Paradise where mortal love finds eternal happiness (VIIIth quartet) ; it may lead on to the finale without a break (VIIth quartet). . . .' (von Lenz, pp. 60 ff.)

and power of the composer is omnipotent; in the other Beethoven is himself his own world, and opens his heart to us unfettered by formal limitations; his soul is revealed in the sound-language of his own creation. It is a succession of ' moments ' of emotional intensity, more or less disconnected, while in Op. 59 such effects are linked together and lost in a masterly conception of the outside world.

The quartets of Op. 59 should more properly be called quartet-symphonies. In them all, and especially in the third in C major, one has the sense that the composer is striving after the symphonic idiom, with orchestral effects that sometimes seem to burst the slender framework of the quartet genre; the instruments seem too frail, the bows too slight to bear the burden of sound laid upon them. And this orchestral quality distinguishes these quartets from those that are to follow, more contemplative, subtler, and more finely drawn, whose exquisite song 'les voix rassemblées au sein du bois concave . . .' are perfectly adequate to express.

The three quartets were written one after another almost without a break. The first rough sketches go back to 1804, and are found scattered, without dates, in various note-books belonging to the next two years, here two loose leaves slipped in among the notes for *Leonora* (a book belonging to Ernst Mendelssohn-Bartholdy in Berlin,[1] which also contains the end of a draft, begun elsewhere, of the last three movements of the VIIth quartet in F), there several odd leaves crumpled and creased with folds (in the records of the *Gesellschaft der Musikfreunde* at Vienna), covered with scratched-out notes and sketches for the VIIIth and IXth quartets.

The studies for the quartets of Op. 18 reveal the spontaneous charm and facility of youth; a *motif* comes into being at one stroke, or a swift sketch of an entire

[1] Nottebohm, *Zweite Beethoveniana*, p. 79.

piece, sometimes a piece almost complete with its tonality, rhythm, development, and form practically the same as in its final shape. But later all this is changed. 'Beethoven's conception of the meaning of music underwent a fundamental change between 1800 and his death; in the early days he saw it, with the eyes of all the eighteenth century, as a delightful art which he was to use as the expression of poetic thought; slowly he came to realize in it a meaning so sublime that he himself could barely compass it.' [1] His actual method of work suffered a similar change, and 'the early facility gave place to a period where the birth of the musical thought came of long and painful mental torment. Music was wrung from his very soul; as if inspired by superhuman forces he wrought into his work a burning frenzy of song'. Zelter writes to Goethe: 'His compositions seem almost to fill him with a secret horror.' Indeed, within his seething imagination a riot of ideas would grow and mature for years before being brought forth in final form.

Even the shape of his note-books was changed. Beethoven now used books of smaller size, carrying them always with him, under his arm or in his pocket, where they got crumpled and worn. He no longer left them behind on his table where he could not get to them to record momentary impressions that might occur to him. [2] He used continually to quote a phrase from Schiller's *Joan of Arc* : 'I dare not go out without my banner!' He was never seen without his scraps of ruled paper on which, as inspiration came to him on his walks or while visiting, he would scribble down his ideas. And with the altered size of his note-books even the character of his sketches was modified. One would imagine that as his genius matured and strengthened an artist could work with an ease that grew daily more fluent, but with Beethoven the reverse was the case. While in 1800 he would dash down more than a hundred bars of music upon the paper almost

[1] J. Chantavoine, *Beethoven*, p. 76.
[2] Outlines of the VIIIth and IXth quartets, made out of doors during his walks, written in pencil, and on worn and creased scraps of paper.

without taking breath, year by year the number of preliminary drafts and tentative sketches increased. Developments no longer occurred to him in their completed state; he would constantly correct details, giving minute care and attention, hesitating to put a theme in its final form, adding, taking away a note here and there, making infinitesimal changes that he notes as *meilleur* (a word one finds scribbled so often in the note-books), as the sculptor, to make his study still more perfect, touches and re-touches the clay with infinite pains.'[1]

He is no longer fired by the fresh inspiration of the early years when he was still under Mozart's influence, flashing upon him with lightning speed; this is a patiently awaited inspiration, strikingly defined by Napoleon as ' the sudden solution to a problem long pondered ', born of mature thought and subconscious growth.

So one disentangles the themes of the Op. 59 quartets from a disorderly *mélange* of numerous and hasty notes crossed out and written over time after time. One idea alone seems to have sprung full grown from the mind of the artist, that of the *Adagio* of the VIIth quartet; two sketches, already nearly complete, are all he gives, and written against them without explanation are the words—' *Eine Trauer-weide oder Akazien-Baum aufs Grab meines Bruders* ' (A weeping willow or an acacia on the grave of my brother). Which brother could this be? At this time Beethoven had lost only one brother, who would have been a year older than himself; he was born on April 2nd, 1769, and had lived only a week. . . . Is this magnificent work of serene resignation a lament over the death of a child? Other sentences with no obvious bearing on the themes are scribbled here and there on the worn pages; the words *Schrann Mantel* are found in the middle of an outline of the *Allegretto vivace* of the VIIth quartet.[2]

---

[1] J. Chantavoine, *Beethoven*, pp. 77–8.

[2] Nottebohm says that *Schrann*, written lower down as *Schramm*, was the name of a tailor in Vienna to whom Beethoven had sent his

There are dozens of sketches for the finale of the VIIIth and of all the IXth quartet; the tonality is vague, and the theme for the *Menuet* of the IXth is begun in pencil, and finally written out in ink in one of its many phases, after being much worked on. It is later used in the *Allegretto* of the VIIth symphony, and was evidently originally intended for the second movement of the quartet in C (IXth), but was soon replaced by another. On an odd page at the end, torn and creased by constant rubbing in his pocket, Beethoven writes, after an interrupted sketch of the theme of the fugue : ' Eben so wie du dich hier in den Strudel der Gesellschaft stürzest, eben so möglich ist's Opern trotz allen gesellschaftlichen Hindernissen zu schreiben. Kein Geheimniss sey dein Nichthören mehr auch bei der Kunst.' (Even as you are to-day being drawn into the stream of society, so it is possible, in spite of social hindrances, to continue your work. Let your deafness be no longer a secret—not even in art.) Here is self-revelation like the Heiligenstadt Will. The love of ' The Immortal Beloved ' gave Beethoven confidence in his own powers ; with a love like that he need not fear the world's pity ; putting aside his physical weakness, he takes up the struggle for self-expression with renewed courage, even as he throws himself into the ' stream of society ', sustained by a tireless energy burning to find an outlet. His first great song of victory is the magnificent fugue of the quartet in C.

The three quartets, linked under one opus number, appeared in January 1808 with the following title :

' *Trois quatuors pour deux violons, alto et violoncelle.* Composés par Louis van Beethoven. Œuvre 59ᵉ. Livraison à Vienne au Magasin de J. Riedl, 582, Hohenmarkt.' [1]

---

cloak to be repaired. Thayer, who reads it as *Schwann* (swan), imagines it to be the name of a tavern where Beethoven might have left something behind.

[1] Nottebohm gives as the publisher : ' Kunst- und Industrie-Comptoir

In its third impression the edition had the following dedication :

'Trois Quatuors très humblement dédiés à son Excellence Monsieur le Comte de Rasoumoffsky, Conseiller privé actuel de Sa Majesté l'Empereur de Toutes les Russies, Sénateur, Chevalier des ordres de St. André, de St. Alexandre-Newsky, et Grand-Croix de celui de St. Wladimir de la 1ʳᵉ Classe, etc., etc., par Louis van Beethoven.' [1]

in Wien ; Schreyvogel und Co. in Pest'. The edition that he had was not the first, however. The firm of J. Riedl went out of existence about this time, and his publications were taken up by various other firms, Schreyvogel among them. (See *Ergänzungsband zum Handbuch der musikalischen Literatur*, &c., C. F. Whistling of Leipzig (1824), pp. 1241–2.)

[1] Rasoumowsky was the Russian ambassador in Vienna. 'This wealthy prince had had a magnificent palace built on the banks of the Danube, and gathering together artistic treasures of priceless value, loved to invite the *élite* of Viennese society to his house, with all its display of pomp and magnificence. At these brilliant parties, music always held the place of honour, for Rasoumowsky loved it with a passion not unmixed with a certain sense that he owed to it part of the prosperity he enjoyed. His family came from the Ukraine, and was of low half-Cossack extraction. His uncle, Alexis Gregoriewitch Rasum, was born at Lemeschi in 1709, and became a humble member of the Imperial Choir at St. Petersburg, never dreaming of the good fortune destined to come to him, when one day during a service the Tsarina Elizabeth desired him to be presented to her, struck by his exquisite voice. Liking his manner as much as his voice she fell in love with him, and some little time afterwards secretly married her favourite at a tiny village church near the gates of Moscow. By an extraordinary trick of fate the brother of Alexis Gregoriewitch, Cyrille Rasum, younger by twenty years, was to enjoy similar good fortune. Received at the Russian court, his personality and wit enabled him to rise to a position where he came into contact with ladies in the highest circles ; his beauty made the same impression on Catherine the Great as his elder brother's had upon Elizabeth. With honours and titles showered upon him, though he never made a royal marriage, he rose to the highest dignities of the State. Cyrille Rasoumowsky, field-marshal and general of Little Russia, left four sons to inherit his good fortune and brilliant attainments ; we find the youngest now at Vienna. Andreas Cyrillowitch Rasoumowsky had received with the Grand Duke Paul at the Russian Court a deep and varied education, from which his

The first two of Op. 59 are often called the ' Russian Quartets ', and Beethoven actually makes use in them of two Russian folk melodies. Through Rasoumowsky, probably, Beethoven first became aware of the wealth of beauty in Russian folk-song, but was it at his patron's request that Beethoven chose these themes for the *Finale* of the quartet in F major, and for the *Scherzo* of the E minor, or through desire to please him, or just because he was fascinated by their originality? In any case it is of no importance; it is not here that one will find the clue to the essential meaning of the works.

nimble and receptive brain had profited far more than that of his imperial fellow-student. When his education was finished, his father wished him to enter the Imperial Navy. Rasoumowsky took his training and reached the rank of captain before he was twenty-five. But he had other ambitions for himself, and felt he was destined for the diplomatic service. After having been through his diplomatic course he was straight away appointed ambassador in Venice, leaving it soon after for Vesuvius. At Naples his manner and personal charm endeared him to Queen Caroline, and had she not already been married, his uncle's romantic story might have been repeated over again. Following the course of his career, he left Italy, and in Scandinavia represented his country at Copenhagen and Stockholm; but ambition urged him to Vienna, and, successful in getting appointed, he went there early in 1792. Rasoumowsky did not wait for his appointment before consolidating his position and making a brilliant marriage into one of the most aristocratic families in Austria; in 1788 he had married the beautiful Countess Elizabeth of Thun, sister-in-law to Prince Lichnowski, whose affection for Beethoven is well known. By this marriage he was introduced straight into a musical circle thronged with all the great composers of the moment. He met Mozart, Haydn, towards whom he was particularly drawn, and, later, Beethoven. From 1805, the date of the composition of the Russian quartets dedicated to Rasoumowsky, the relations between the famous composer and the great diplomat became very intimate. It was at his house, at the Archduke Rudolph's, and at Prince Lichnowski's, that Beethoven's new musical creations were heard for the first time.' (Wilder, *Beethoven*.)

At the time of the Congress of Vienna in 1815, when the Tsar Alexander conferred the title of prince upon his ambassador, Rasoumowsky's intimacy with Beethoven enabled him to introduce him into the *salons* of the Imperial train. It was at Rasoumowsky's house that several royal personages asked to be presented to Beethoven.

Moreover, the use of Russian themes gives no specifically Russian cast to these quartets, in the sense that one finds it in Rubinstein's quartet in C minor, for example, or in the quartets of Borodin ; they are pure Beethoven. The artist took two melodic ideas, and his genius developed them into original works of a character unmistakably his own.

Quartet No. VII, Op. 59, No. 1 (in F major).

Allegro (♩ = 88).
Allegretto vivace e sempre scherzando (♩· = 56).
Adagio molto e mesto (♪ = 88).
⎰ *Allegro* (♩ = 126).
⎬ *Adagio* (♪ = 69).
⎱ *Presto* (♩ = 92).

Of the three quartets of Op. 59, the one in F major is nearest to the early manner ; nevertheless it has a definite freedom from formal tradition and a remarkable novelty of style.

With an assurance and felicity never equalled before or since, Beethoven extracts here from the four instruments every conceivable effect within their capacity. With them he seems literally to tread new paths of sound, and when the full expression of his thought demands a richer colouring he manages to create the effect produced by other instruments, the oboe, the clarinet, even the organ or harp, or, especially in the *Scherzo*, the horn.

I. *Allegro*. A.-B. Marx gives a splendid analysis of this *Allegro*, which may be quoted. But the biographer of Beethoven did not appreciate quite keenly enough the immense importance and technical merit of this first movement, and gaps occur in his analysis which must be filled in. Without any preparation the 'cello gives out the subject, starting on the fifth of the tonic

chord, against a beating accompaniment on the second
violin and viola : [1]

Ex. 41.

The phrase has none of the heavily marked, over-
decisive rhythm that so abrupt an opening might lead
one to expect; on the contrary, it moves on its way
serenely through the unchanging beat of the accompaniment, meditative and sweet, like the calm after a
storm. At the eighth bar the harmony changes, the
first violin takes up the theme with greater warmth,
and, heard above the increasingly sonorous rhythmic
monotone of the other instruments, brings it to a
vigorous conclusion; this in turn fades away into an
uneasy silence, but with the bridge passage another
theme, suave and graceful, makes its appearance :

Ex. 42.

[1] Some 'cellists—A. Franchomme, Delsart—could never resign themselves to the B flat in the third bar, and played instead an ineffective and
insipid B natural !

Given at first on the two violins, then on the viola and 'cello, the melody moves in a sequence of thirds, fifths, and sixths with the effect of horns, and comes to an end in a phrase suggesting the first theme, continued for several bars, taken to a high pitch and finally closing in the key of G major. After this, following a short, quickly moving passage for 'cello solo, important because it contains the germ of a triplet figure to be used later in the development, several bars of modulation bring the episode in truly classical fashion to the key of C major for the entry of the second subject.

At the outset this theme seems to share the contemplative character of the first, but it quickly works up a pulsating enthusiasm, involving all the parts in a vigorous development :

Ex. 43.

The passage concludes with a curious see-sawing effect of chords, where the two bass instruments are as it were balanced against the violins ; the last two bars, *forte* and sonorous, lead to the cadence, which closes the exposition, leading through the chord of C–E–G–B flat to the return of the first section.

With unhesitating precision this wonderful fabric of sound is woven strand by strand before our eyes. Each instrument is a voice singing in turn the poet's joy and strife; from the vibrating of sixteen strings flutters a winged fantasy, now clearly seen, now vanishing in one knows not what shape, flitting away into the mist of darkness or lost in blinding light.

The first section is not repeated—a violation of the rules of rigid sonata form that occurs for the first time in the history of quartet writing.[1]

Instead of a repetition pure and simple, Beethoven is satisfied with a reintroduction of the principal key, and at the fifth bar the 'cello varies the theme with a figure resembling that of the cadence, derived, as the cadence was, from the principal subject:

Ex. 44.

This variation introduces a modulation to the subdominant key, and the first violin plays the first four bars of the theme in B flat; the viola takes it up, and, modulating to G minor, gives the melody in this last key to the second violin; in quick succession all the instruments have the theme in free imitation.

From this point onwards Beethoven makes the logical working out and play of part-writing, as he often did, develop into the expression of an indomitable force. The tranquil mood of the principal subject is invested with an epic power; the parts press on, now together, now separated, with renewed strength; leaving the key of G minor, their restless energy breaks out into a purely orchestral flight, in a unison followed by broken chords, which leads them, with the effect upon the ear of having reached the principal tonality, to the key of

[1] The Beethoven autograph MS. of the VIIth quartet, in the Royal Library, Berlin, bears the following inscription : ' Quartetto primo. La prima parte solamente una volta. Quartett angefangen am 26 May 1806.'

E flat. The ear expects this vigorous tonal climax to form the conclusion of the section in this key, but, on the contrary—in accordance with an idiom of Beethoven's style remarked by Wagner in his monograph on the IXth symphony—having reached its height, the passage does not end on the *fortissimo*, resolving unexpectedly into a *piano*, followed by a *crescendo*.

The epic strain is broken by a return of the curious rocking effect of poised chords in the first section, like a poignant cry of grief, or a voice echoing from another world. In the first section these chords occupy only six bars; here they stretch over eight, and in the last two bars modulate towards the key of F minor; the development here takes a surprising turn: with a distant organ-like sonority the second violin, viola, and 'cello sustain for six bars the *piano* chord of C major (dominant of F minor), then for two bars the chord of F minor, two bars more of D flat, and one bar of G flat major; following these progressions by bar or half-bar, while the 'cello moves up the scale of the dominant, one traces them successively through the keys of E flat minor, A flat, F minor, B flat minor, G flat, D flat, in long sustained chords, while the first violin works through a long modulating scale passage developed out of the quaver figure of the principal subject.

The whole passage is wonderfully effective. No composer ever realized quite as Beethoven did the latent expressive force in a series of long-held *mezzo piano* chords. Voices from an invisible choir seem to float up out of a mysterious gulf to the soul of the artist hovering above.

After these remote harmonies, the second violin, viola, and 'cello pursue the accompaniment with fresh animation, giving out the opening phrase of the principal subject, first in turn, then together, while the first violin continues the quaver figure. Finally, the first violin takes the theme, and the vigour slackens off; the parts seem to be caressingly intertwined, and unite

in a bar of trills. But this effect is shortlived; the
second violin and the viola share the quaver figure from
the cadence, and once more we are plunged into an
atmosphere of darkness and mystery. Above this figure
the second violin lifts a new secondary theme in two
phrases, the one (A) of a melancholy cast, the other
(B) more emphatic :

Ex. 45.

and while the quaver figure of the cadence, mingled
with that from the third bar of the principal subject,
moves from one instrument to another, each in turn
states the new twofold theme. The contemplative strain
of this episode soon gains a rapid increase of energy as
the melody, played *staccato*, passes from part to part.
A short *crescendo* brings the section to its climax; the
first half of the secondary theme alone persists, and the
phrase finally descends the scale in a unison of the four
instruments, falling in broad intervals, to dissipate
the fever of its melancholy in the depths of a sustained
bass.

After a pause of one bar on low G, the scene changes
abruptly for the entry of the third section of the movement. On the first violin soaring triplet figures seem
to fly up with beating wings out of the darkness towards
the light, while the other instruments take a fragment
of the original theme as a basis upon which to build
up the entire concluding section. Borne on the wings
of the ascending triplets it rises higher and higher, until
the first violin reaches C in *altissimo*.

From this point the return to the opening *Allegro*,

for the third section in sonata form, is effected by the following means :

Ex. 46.

A secondary figure, interpolated before in the first section in the development of the principal subject, follows immediately upon the climax attained in that C in *altissimo*. Through a progression of chords of the diminished seventh it presses on up to F in *altissimo* (ninth bar of Ex. 46), with another triumphant climax. At this point all the parts make a headlong rush for the main theme, the 'cello ascending, the others falling, in precipitate haste. We are on it before we are aware, for the 'cello takes it up while the first violin is still continuing its rapid descent to join the second violin, one bar later, in the accompaniment.

This passage for the first violin, with its bold originality and freedom, recalls a similar passage in the first movement of the IXth symphony, also for the first violin. This, however, has an entirely different significance.

The third section is very much like the first, but with many differences of detail, preserving the essentials of sonata form while enjoying perfect freedom. The original contemplative vein of the principal subject is replaced by a lively animation ; before stating the theme, the first violin runs up a rapid scale passage, as though to take it by assault, and in irrepressible abandon plays it first in F major, then in E flat major, until restrained by a *diminuendo, poco ritardando* ; then again we hear the distant sound of horns (Ex. 42) ; it differs from the first section in that the statement of this theme is followed by several bars of vigorous dialogue between the two groups of instruments. A modulation to C major leads to the short rapid passage for the 'cello, doubled here by the viola ; the rest of the repetition is the same as the first section, except that the cadence now introduces the *Coda*. Its entry is marked by the principal subject played *piano* on the first violin, with a substantial harmonic background on the other instruments ; this harmonic sonority gradually increases, with a sustained fifth of the key on the 'cello, and farther away a sustained sixth on the second violin. The theme rises and works up to a powerful culminating point, the climax of the whole movement ; in this passage, as in many others in the Op. 59 quartets, the instruments, while exhausting their resources of tone, seem unequal to the demand upon them. Only a full orchestra, one feels, could find adequate expression for this vast tumult of beauty.

Hovering for a second above the clamour of voices, the imagination of the artist sinks to a calmer level. Linked falling thirds, at first on the violins, then on the viola and 'cello, follow ; a triplet figure, starting on the first violin, flutters across the parts ; through it a little later the principal theme, unrecognizable at first, makes its way. As it approaches, the form of the first phrase of the theme materializes, blended with the triplet figure, and then, urged on by the viola and 'cello (the former reinforcing the chord with a seventh), rises on the violins to the octave to control the ensemble anew. While the first violin sustains C in *altissimo* for five bars (dominant of the principal key), the various main themes of the movement spring up on the other instruments, and disappear as if in flight; the first violin has a *piano* descent to C three octaves lower, where it disappears in a *pianissimo* chord of F; a moment of suspense in a sudden change to the key of D minor leads to a vigorous return of F major with two decisive concluding chords.

From the technical point of view—and this is one of the gaps in Marx's analysis—the first movement of Op. 59, No. 1, is a veritable revelation of Beethoven's perfect command over the academic form, to which his genius gave new life. In the two phrases of the original theme one can see the germ of a development in the form of a fugal *divertissement*. From this standpoint the *Allegro* of the VIIth quartet is of vast significance.

II. *Allegretto vivace e sempre scherzando.* Marx gives the following paragraph to the *Scherzo*, the first of the succession of great movements written by Beethoven in this form:

One can find no defined meaning in this dance, whose outward aspects are ever changing yet always akin; perhaps it is that this light-hearted fantasy finds in itself its own meaning and its own purpose. But it is the fantasy of an eager and sensitive spirit; joy and sorrow are reflected like sunlight and shadow flickering over a vast plain as the clouds move across the sun.

Marx, always precise, notices that these shifting moods, separated by whimsical and unexpected modulations, change ten times. Between this *Scherzo* and the *Allegro* that precedes it there is no apparent psychological link; the *Scherzo* lives in a world of its own. Musically, it is a triumph of rhythmic and melodic originality, with a fullness of inspiration and charm almost beyond belief. It is not extravagant praise to say that the piece has never been equalled in the literature of the string quartet.

It opens with a dialogue between two *motifs*, first on the 'cello and second violin, then on the viola and first violin :

Allegretto vivace e sempre scherzando. ♩.=56

Ex. 47.

The first *motif* consists merely of the rhythmic variation of one note, a figure that any one might have thought of, and that most would have discarded as meaningless.[1] When we hear what Beethoven made of this apparently insignificant figure, we understand Schumann's remark : ' Beethoven picked up his *motifs* in the street, but he re-created them into the most beautiful utterances in the world ' ; and also the parallel established briefly by Wagner between Mozart's method of development from synthesis to analysis, and Beethoven's in the reverse direction : ' In his symphonic works, Mozart always gives first the complete theme, and then dissects it into smaller and smaller fragments ; Beethoven shows his originality by be-

[1] The tale is told how at the first performance of the *Allegretto* at St. Petersburg, where Rasoumowsky had sent it, general amusement and surprise were caused by this entry on the 'cello, and it was thought to be a mistake on the part of the performer. This was early in 1812, at the house of Count Soltykow, and Romberg, the famous 'cellist, declared that the *Scherzo* was a vulgar hoax and quite unplayable. The story goes that he threw his part on the floor and trampled on it (von Lenz, p. 375).

ginning with these fragmentary *motifs* and using them to build up a structure of increasing loftiness and power.'

The dialogue, first in B flat, then in A flat, is interrupted by an energetic statement of the first *motif* in C flat, given out by all four instruments, and modulating smoothly into B flat:

Ex. 48.

in which tonality is cast the following theme (A):

Ex. 49.

coming entirely unforeseen in its tender charm after the gaiety of the opening passage. It appears only for a moment, giving place to the principal subject heard *fortissimo* on all four instruments in a changed form. This ' transformed principal theme' is based on the rhythmic figure of the modulating bar (Ex. 48):

The third bar of the theme leaps from part to part in modulation towards the dominant of D minor, and, while the middle parts keep up the rhythmic design, a new theme (B) appears on the first violin, bringing an atmosphere of longing and passionate melancholy:

Ex. 50.

The plaintive little theme leads into a melody of a more sombre hue:

Ex. 51.

followed by a passage where one seems to hear the mysterious echo of a distant horn:

Ex. 52.

This can be considered as a development either of
the fourth bar of the preceding example (Ex. 51), or
of the principal subject. The imagination of the artist
seems to be concentrated there, and to retire within
itself; the *crescendi* and *diminuendi* give the effect of
quickened gasping breaths, dropping into silence and
dying away on the reiterated D, as the principal subject
is murmured *pianissimo* on all four instruments in
unison. At the fifth bar an unexpected G flat lifts the
oppressive gloom and changes the key; and a return
back to the original tonality re-establishes once more
the gay and whimsical humour of the opening section.

The two *motifs* begin their dialogue over again, with
the difference that here the rhythmic principal figure is
answered by a second *motif* based directly on the original
counter-subject—a ' transformed counter-subject ':

Ex. 53.

This interrupts the dialogue to carry on the theme
alone, to play by itself, as it were, first on the second
violin and viola, then, after a tentative interruption of
the principal *motif*, on the two violins, pursuing its gay
unhurried way, until the principal figure breaks in upon
its frolics with a steady unyielding insistence, and a
regular *mêlée* ensues. The struggle between the two
themes, the first in the two lower parts, the other in the
upper parts, with vigorous alternation from *ff* to *pp*,
seems to epitomize all the irresponsible gaiety of this
first section of the movement, coming to a characteristically vivid conclusion on the dominant of F.
This outburst is followed at once by a broad, sustained

melody in F minor, modulating to C minor, back again
to F minor, and stretching still through another sixteen
bars; the artist lingers over it caressingly, as though
he found there the expression of his inmost thoughts.

The end of the episode leads to a restatement of the
principal subject, and then, in the key of D flat, to
the counter-subject, which modulates in syncopations
through the keys of F and C minor, and comes to an
abrupt stop on F sharp, dominant of B. After a bar's
rest the melody (A) (Ex. 49), languid and sweet,
appears in all four parts. As on its first appearance, the
theme quickly gives way to the principal figure, heard
this time in a graceful *legato*.

Ex. 54.

Whispered delicately, *pianissimo*, it is first divided
between the two violins; then, *piano* (no longer *pp*),
both violins give it in unison, modulating through G
flat and E flat to C, dominant of F major; and in the
key of C major, here taken as the prevailing tonality of
the piece, the 'cello with its utmost sonority intones the
principal figure in octaves, in its original form; at the
same time the first violin rushes in with a brilliant
passage in semiquavers, leading finally to a crashing
entry of the principal theme in all four voices. The
Scherzo here reaches its full height; the little rhythmic
figure, so insignificant at first, has attained an immense
power, 'one of the most wonderful utterances in the
world,' as Schumann described it, built into a majestic

structure of sound that only a full orchestra, with wood-wind, brass, and percussion, could realize in all its massive significance.

Beethoven is *par excellence* the musician of contrasts. Against this wild clamour, which would not be out of place in the Eroica Symphony, is set as a foil the ethereal fairy delicacy of a sort of Elf dance, recalling the fantasy of the *Midsummer-Night's Dream*; for six bars the beating semiquavers are reiterated with gradually decreasing violence; the pitch of the beating rhythm rises higher and higher (the 'cello even up to A in *alt*), and, with a combination of the two main themes—the first freely altered—the development begins *sempre staccato e piano*, with an intensity that increases rapidly to a point where it is arrested *fortissimo* in the key of B flat minor.

One bar of rest, and the principal subject emerges once more in G flat major, with a new counter-subject:

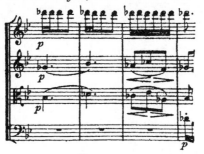

Ex. 55.

Through these modulations and various combined statements of the principal figure and the new theme, we return to the melody (A) (Ex. 49) in the three lowest parts, while the first violin sustains a trill on F for four bars, continuing on G and A, and ending on B flat, where the original figure, with fresh force, bursts into a *fortissimo* four-part ensemble (with double stopping on the violins).

This marks the commencement of a kind of third section of the movement, according to sonata form, but of a very free type. It works through a development similar to that of the first section, but with various interesting changes, as, for instance, the appearance of a new *motif* derived from the last counter-subject (Ex. 55):

Ex. 56.

A little later the *Coda* begins—seventy-three bars before the end of the movement—*staccato, piano*, resembling the fairy-like episode of the second section. The broad melody and the figures developed from it slip away, and *staccato* semiquavers mount from the 'cello to the viola, and from the viola to the violins, as if expressing the unceasing struggles of spirits entombed in darkness, towards the light. So is reached a moving statement of the counter-subject (Ex. 55) above the principal rhythmic figure on the 'cello; Beethoven follows it with yet another exposition of the second principal *motif* (Ex. 53) cunningly distributed among the parts; as the end approaches, the tender melody of the first part is heard twice in succession, in B flat major, then in E minor; it fades sadly away, and the two original themes (transformed) are given out in a *pianissimo* whisper on all four instruments, rising till they are lost in space. But this is not the end—Beethoven prefers to finish on an energetic note; and after a *pizzicato* chord—the first *pizzicato* in the whole work —the original *motif*, minus its last quaver, descends in leaps, *arco* (from G flat on the first violin, to E natural on the second violin, and to F on the viola); and a final *fortissimo* of the transformed principal theme—not the counter-subject—ends with three heavily accented chords of B flat.

And so this elfin fantasy of sound comes to an end, without divisions, trio, or repetitions, a tissue of dreams woven of silk and gold. . . .

III. *Adagio molto e mesto.* As the *Scherzo* is remarkable for the number and surprising variety of its themes and methods of combining them, so is the *Adagio* remarkable for the simplicity and breadth of its construction. Strictly speaking, there are two themes only in the slow movement, but the expressive possibility in these two is literally inexhaustible; it is the spirituality of their inspiration, the profundity of their inner significance, that give this *Adagio* its quickened meaning, rather than their capacity for rhythmic or tonal variety or changes of technical aspect.

The first violin, *sotto voce*, strikes at once a note of timid apprehension in the long-drawn melody [1] that forms the principal theme; for the first bar or two the other instruments merely fill in the harmony.

With the modulation to A flat in the fifth bar the feeling grows in warmth and animation, and already the viola part has assumed a definite melodic form side by side with the violin.

Adagio molto e mesto. ♩=88(♪=44)

[1] M. Vincent d'Indy, in his *Cours de composition musicale*, Book I, p. 37, calls attention to the fact that this melody, composed of four perfectly balanced phrases with weak endings, owes its effect to the expressive phrasing, which counterbalances the monotonous rhythm of the natural accent.

Ex. 57.

Six bars later the 'cello takes up the theme at a high
pitch, seconded by the first violin ; given out with all
the expressive power of the instrument, the melody
hovers, isolated, above the other voices ; the whole
passage affords a beautiful example of the melodic contrapuntal writing in which both Beethoven and Wagner
delighted.

In this melody, one of the most plaintive themes that
he ever wrote, Beethoven gives himself wholly up to
the melancholy side of his imagination, but his
naturally robust temperament quickly reasserts itself,
finding expression in the vigorous figure that follows :

Ex. 58.

yet it falls back almost at once into a melancholy vein,
though of a less gloomy cast, and coloured by a resolute

resignation. The theme that expresses it is first heard
on the 'cello :

Ex. 59.

beneath a demisemiquaver figure on the first violin
evolved from the vigorous preceding phrase (Ex. 58);
there is something impressive in its entire simplicity—
it is actually only the broken common chord of the
tonic; but it grows in intensity of meaning like the
inexorable march of destiny, suggesting the force of
a heroic pessimism as it moves from voice to voice.

A more impassioned flight breaks out to culminate
on the chord of the diminished seventh of G minor;
and the element of tragedy finds its fulfilment in a
phrase that seems to express grief beyond consolation.

Ex. 60.

Even this sorrow spends its forces and makes way as
though exhausted for a return of the second theme
(Ex. 59), introduced by a modulation to A flat in a more

cheerful mood, an effect accentuated by the major
tonality. In its turn it yields again to the plaintive first
tune, given by the 'cello in the key of G minor at a high
pitch. Then follows suddenly an episode of such passionate emotion as neither this nor any other quartet
has ever before displayed ; relieved by the second violin
of the original theme (Ex. 57), the 'cello breaks into
pizzicato demisemiquavers, like thudding heart-beats,
in a stormy *crescendo*, while against it the three other
instruments declaim the first phrase of the theme in a
riot of excitement. *Tristan* itself never scaled greater
emotional heights !

The fury gives place to a profound calm, as the
pent-up emotion of the artist exhausts itself in this
outburst, and now sinks to the depths of weary despair.
Beneath the *pizzicati* of the viola, the first violin, and,
soon, the second violin, the unaltering rhythm of the
tragic little *motif* (Ex. 60) is heard on the 'cello, a
moment later on the first violin, finally, most plaintive
of all, on the viola, trembling like a tear.

But a shining vision of consolation from above approaches in a new and beautiful melody borne on the
first violin, *molto cantabile, piano* ; and, as if the artist
found his own happiness springing from the heart of
sorrow, it is in the grief *motif* that he finds this new
'consolation' theme. The following example shows
how the former phrase (Ex. 59) is transfigured into
a tender melody, soaring up in the key of D flat :

Ex. 61.

Here perfect happiness shines through the despair
of a moment ago. . . . Beethoven often created such
contrasts, but never one more striking than this. The
weary spirit is possessed with a new courage; vigorous
touches give life to the theme (in bars 8, p. 41, and 1,
p. 42, in the complete Eulenburg edition, 1911, the
expression mark *sfp* to the last quaver gives the effect
of an almost boastful self-confidence !). . . . But it is an
evanescent happiness, quickly passing, and already the
atmosphere of sorrow creeps back again; in the lower
register the viola murmurs the *motif* of despair to a
sestuplet accompaniment on the second violin; the first
violin drops from the heights, modulating to F minor,
to return to the opening section of the movement with
a statement of the principal theme.

In accordance with the rules of sonata form, the
Adagio follows from this point the same course as the
first section, as far as the return of the second theme
(Ex. 59). But it is modified, and gains by the use of
various technical devices a new breadth of meaning and
emphasis. The long-drawn-out melody of the opening
section, given out by the first violin, is here sustained
by an intricate accompaniment (by the fluttering ses-
tuplets of the last episode continued on the second
violin, by a continuous *staccato* demisemiquaver C on
the viola, and by energetic *pizzicati* on the 'cello). The
theme itself is ornamented by the extension of the semi-

quaver phrases into demisemiquavers (bars 4 and 7 of
Ex. 57). The vigorous *motif* (Ex. 58) comes this time
in the key of C major, to dispel the prevailing melancholy mood ; the first violin modulates to F minor, and
in this key the 'cello unfolds the heroic theme of
Ex. 59. The next sixteen bars from this point are
identical with the sixteen corresponding bars in the
first section, except for differing tonality; in the concluding bars, however, out of the heartache of the grief
motif emerges, not the heroic ecstasy of the second
principal theme, nor the serene ' consolation ' theme,
but the first principal subject (Ex. 57) persisting on
the second violin, more closely knit than before, and
accompanied by imitations in canon on the first violin ;
it is finally taken by both instruments to the octave,
with redoubled intensity of expressive power.

Then with the *Coda* peace comes again ; the sun
shines at last through the clouds of gloom.

It will have been noticed that at the seventeenth-
eighteenth bar from the beginning of the movement,
following the *morendo* conclusion to the second long
melodic phrase of eight bars, the 'cello part has a little
upward leap of a minor sixth—F–D flat—impelling
upwards the vigorous *motif* in C minor that follows four
bars later (Ex. 58); in the *Coda* this leap of a sixth
occurs on the two violins, and prepares the entry of
a serene *cantabile* melody, leading at once back to the
principal subject :

Ex. 62.

Here the principal subject is heard in a new form
for the last time, with both rhythm and harmony so
much altered that it assumes a new aspect of prophetic
questioning :

Ex. 63.

to which the reply is found in the bold return to the
tonality of C major; one recalls the earlier occasion
when it expressed a burst of self-confidence (bars 8,
p. 41, and 1, p. 42, Eulenburg edition; see p. 82);
but the mood, then only felt for a second, seems here
to materialize.

The question is reiterated; and then the lower voices
are arrested, sustaining the dominant chord of C major,
while on this harmonic basis a *recitativo* melody is
unfolded by the first violin in a long hemidemisemi-

quaver passage, adorned towards the end with florid decorations on the other instruments, in the form of descending scales of C major. Here Beethoven reveals two new characteristic idioms ; we find on the one hand an eloquent spiritual meaning, a musical significance, given to an effect of brilliant virtuosity—a trait more frequently found in his later works ; on the other, a long-held significant pause on a sustained chord of which the ear is expecting the resolution. The latter effect was employed, before Op. 59, in the third Leonora Overture (at the beginning of the *Allegro*).

IV. *Finale*. The passage for the first violin comes to an end on a trilled C ; this C is taken as the dominant of F major, and beneath the still persisting trill the 'cello gives out, in the key of F, the Russian [1] melody in 2/4, upon which the final *Allegro* is based. There is therefore no break between the third movement and the last. In developing the brilliant musical structure that straightway begins here, Beethoven seems to find again the joy of living and of creative power, centred, as he so often found it, in the heart of sorrow.

The Russian melody chosen for the theme of this movement is curiously suggestive. It seems to reflect all the melancholy bitter-sweetness that flows out of Russian temperament in joy and sadness alike, and moulds the natural idiom of Slav folk-song ; Beethoven builds his finale on this twofold characteristic ; the movement sparkles with life and gaiety, but it is a gaiety touched

---

[1] The Slav element in Beethoven's music goes a long way back. The passionate melody in the *trio* in A minor of the second piano sonata is a typically Russian theme (see von Lenz, op. cit., p. 148). Yet it is just possible that in this case Beethoven *unconsciously* caught this spirit. In 1796, the year when Beethoven, aged twenty-six, wrote this sonata, the number of Russian tunes known in Germany was probably very limited. In 1794 we find the piano variations on a Russian theme. The melodies of the VIIth and VIIIth quartets were supplied by Count Rasoumowsky, to whom the *opus* was dedicated.

with underlying gloom. ' To realize the full force of this brilliant finale one should have actually seen one of these national festivals held in Asiatic Russia ; when the first breath of spring melts the snow, and the steppe casts off its icy cloak and reappears in its sweet-scented garment of flowers.' [1]

Yet one cannot say that this Russian theme is as significant as an original Beethoven tune—as, for instance, the theme of the first *Allegro* of this quartet ; if it has this depth of meaning, it is the genius of the composer that evokes it. The finale is one of the most instructive and interesting movements that Beethoven ever wrote ; it recalls and even surpasses the finale of the IVth symphony (in B flat) in originality and vigour, in ingenuity of device, and in perfect grasp of form.

Starting in F major and modulating to D minor, the theme passes from the 'cello to the first violin (Marx finds the return to the C in the eighth bar rather unusual). The two violins take it up next, developing it in imitation, and investing it with a rising energy, until the first violin interrupts with a *fortissimo* ascending figure in semiquavers ; a modulation to C major brings a second theme on the second violin, resembling the first, but contemplative and serene, accompanied by a figure of leaping octaves on the first violin, and by syncopated *non legato* quavers on the viola and 'cello :

[1] See Ippolito Valetta, *I Quartetti di Beethoven*.

Ex. 64.

Filling the atmosphere with uneasy disquiet, the first
violin, and below it the 'cello at the sixth, give the
melody in the minor, linking to it a new *pianissimo*
melody, questioning and timid, based on the Russian
theme, and in the key of C minor :

Ex. 65.

This hesitant anxiety is abruptly broken by a *fortissimo* chord of C major ; it is followed by a series of
scale passages on all four instruments on the dominant
of C, and four dominant chords ; then once more, *poco
ritenuto*, echoes the question, to be answered at once
by a third theme, vigorous and assertive :

Ex. 66.

It is first heard on the viola and 'cello, then on the two

violins, above a clamour of syncopation, in a passage
recalling the second Leonora Overture. With this climax,
gradually fading away to a *pianissimo*, the end of the
first section is reached; the first violin takes up its C
major trill, and the Russian melody opens the repetition, which is given complete.

The second section is an admirable piece of thematic
development, in which all the points are so easily recognizable, and the construction is so clear, that examples
are unnecessary. The climax reached at the end of the
first section recurs here in the key of D minor with
a powerful orchestral effect, sinking to a calm with the
return of the principal subject, as the third section of
the movement begins. The development is very much
the same as that of the first section, with the modifications necessitated by sonata form (entry of the secondary theme in the key of F, &c.). In the last few bars
before the *Coda* all the pent-up forces of the finale
break out in an exultant *fanfare* on the chord of the
seventh, on C; it is the trumpet-call of the Leonora
Overture. In it is embodied, in all its intensity, the contrast between the gloom of the *Adagio* and the song of
victory that follows the agonizing struggle against fate.

Into this song of victory the *Coda* breaks, to translate
it into spheres of celestial rapture.

An imitative figure—the principal theme inverted—
is distributed among the parts, and blossoms into a
delicate flowing theme (bringing to mind one of Wagner's melodies in the ' Mastersingers ').

Ex. 67.

The *motif* at once develops in the rhythm ♪ ♪
♪ ♪ ♪ | ♪ ♪ . . . changing later to ♪♪♪ ♪♪♪ . . . ;
overwhelmed with trills, interrupted by cries of triumph,
it works up to the tremendous climax of the final *fortissimo* chord ; an abrupt transition and an interrupted
cadence cut short its flight, and a short *Adagio* (*ma non
troppo*) begins, in which the principal theme, hiding its
aspect of melancholy, reveals only its light-hearted
optimism, and the last notes of the first phrase of the
subject become the composer's words of farewell :

Ex. 68.

An eloquent farewell, uttered by each voice in turn,
slipping away into the distance. . . . A little *pianissimo*
rustling seems to silence it altogether ; and suddenly
a crashing *presto* of nine bars hurls itself *fortissimo* upon
the F major chords of the conclusion.

Quartet No. VIII, Op. 59, No. 2 (in E minor).

Allegro (♩. = 84).
Molto adagio (♩ = 60).
Allegretto (♩. = 69).
Presto (𝅝 = 88).

The IInd quartet of Op. 59, in E minor, is cast in
quite a different mould from the quartet in F. A comparison of the first movements of the two works reveals
the contrast most clearly, for by the side of the *Allegro*
of the VIIth, so full of an inspired spirituality, the

first movement of the quartet in E minor seems extraordinarily realistic. The *Allegro* of the VIIth, calm and unfaltering, lays bare the depths of the dark mystery of music ; in the *Allegro* of the VIIIth a bitter and unavailing struggle with a hostile fate is pictured ; it is as if a giant's hand were outstretched to pluck back the rebel spirit when on the very point of surmounting the final obstacle. A mighty wrath, stubborn, impotent, seems to break out at the beginning of this work, presented in the symmetrical form of tradition—a new point of contrast with the *Allegro* of the VIIth, and one more precisely definable. In place of the great lyrical movement of the *Allegro* in F, unified and free in spite of certain concessions to classical form, moving step by step to an irresistible end, we find here the three distinct sections proper to strict first-movement form, with a concluding *Coda* ; in other words, the old academic style of Haydn and Mozart, though here more flexible and supple, infinitely more expressive. . . . As a wonderful portrayal of a troubled, suffering spirit, beset by hostile influences, this first movement of the quartet in E minor is perhaps more self-revealing than any.

I. *Allegro*. It is Beethoven himself that one seems to see flinging down a challenge, in the vigorous upward leap of a fifth that opens the quartet :

Ex. 69.

After a bar of silence, the principal subject, composed
of two flexible phrases, slips in *pianissimo*, almost apprehensive. . . . Another bar of silence,[1] and the principal
subject, this time in F major, is heard again, still *pianissimo*, but with growing determination. A third expressive pause—a silence as full of significance as sound,
Wagner described it—as expressive as the plaintive little
motif A of the principal theme that follows immediately
after it, passing from the viola to the first violin. Given
out by the two violins and the 'cello, the *motif* seems
like a question, to which the answer comes, plaintive
too, but resigned, in a beautiful period of melodic part-
writing :

Ex. 70.

With an air of melancholy the two violins and the
viola each sing their individual themes : the viola part
recalls the mournful melody from the *Adagio* of the
quartet in F ; the first violin has a figure based on
the inverted principal subject, which it extends into a
semiquaver passage, followed by the second violin and
the viola : for the first time the latent emotion makes
an effort to break its bonds and to escape, but the

[1] Ulibishev (*Beethoven, ses critiques et ses glossateurs*, p. 261) considers the transition from the chord of E-G-E to the unison of F, in
spite of the bar's rest in between, ' one of the weakest and emptiest
progressions in the whole realm of consecutive octaves '.

passage comes to an abrupt stop on two chords that
take one back to the introductory opening bars. Once
more comes one of those expressive pauses characteristic of the movement; the plaintive response is
heard, but with a modified contrapuntal design: the
melancholy viola phrase is lifted to the first violin as
a principal *motif*, and the rapid semiquaver passage that
extends it, as though to set free an outburst of passion,
modulates through C major to the key of G minor:

Ex. 71.

and followed in its soaring flight by a *tremolo* passage
on the lower voices (derived from Ex. 70), comes to
an end on the dominant of G. A calmer phase ensues,
and the second subject (also derived imitatively from
Ex. 70) brings an atmosphere of tender intimacy:

Ex. 72.

and after the final statement of the theme on the 'cello,
another lovely melody flows from the first violin:

Ex. 73.

While this melody persists, the mood of intimate calm prevails; the parts move in similar or in contrary motion in free counterpoint. A phrase on the first violin calls to mind in a characteristic way the point near the beginning of the movement, where an emotional outburst is cut short by a sudden modulation:

Ex. 74.

Here the passage reaches a different conclusion:

Ex. 75.

The force hitherto suppressed seems to come to the surface. A new quality springs up, expressed in the rhythmic form of the second theme, played *forte* with heavily marked accent.

The atmosphere changes, now unperturbed and

calm, now full of regained force; for a moment the scene recedes into the distance in a syncopated passage with sustained chromatic harmonies, gradually quickening in intensity. Like the sun at last shining through a bank of scudding clouds dispersed by heavy winds, here the tonality of G major triumphantly asserts itself:

Ex. 76.

A modulation to E minor brings back the leap of a fifth of the introductory bars, and the first section is now repeated in its entirety. At the *seconda volta* the modulation to E minor is followed by a modulation to G flat, the tonality of the two final chords.

The development section has at first a tender, contemplative character. The brief, questioning chords of the introduction become the underlying *motif*, repeated three times, followed each time by a bar's rest, moving smoothly from E flat major to B minor. Twice whispered *sotto voce*, the third time the *motif* hurls itself *fortissimo*, as if fired by a sudden resolution, upon the dominant of B minor, and beneath this sustained F sharp on the first violin, the 'cello insinuates *pianissimo* the first phrase (A) of the principal subject, and in reply the held F sharp merges into the second phrase (B) of the same theme, coming to a tentative stop on a chord of G. After another pause, the two phrases (A) and (B) re-enter in the key of C minor, and modulate to A flat;

ver twice as many bars as before, gaining in
power.

ar-cut phrase of the final passage (*prima volta*)
to E flat major and leads on to the repetition
ire second and third sections. One cannot
Beethoven conformed so closely to the tradi-
n; a repeat at this point only weakens the
ted hitherto, and consequently is usually left
formance. At the *seconda volta* the modula-
esses through E minor to C minor, and the
eap of a fifth of the introduction opens the

oda reveals an artist who was still a respecter
It corresponds, as a sort of fourth section, to
art of the development, and what was vainly
here here reaches fulfilment. Here are the
stioning chords, heard three times after suc-
uses (modulating here from C minor through
G sharp minor); the same sudden resolution,
rte and sustained by the first violin, this time
the 'cello. But here, under this doubly held
motif A is repeated alternately by the second
d the viola in response; and from this en-
rise a host of mystic harmonies. Leaving the
ained D sharp, the first violin begins a slow
of the scale, while the 'cello slowly ascends;
hese two voices come nearer together, they en-
re and more narrowly fluent imitative phrases
iddle parts. Reuniting as the syncopated figure
s, the four voices work up an increasing inten-
finally burst into a veritable cry of fury!
tranquil response of violin and viola (Ex. 70)
to lull the storm, but the semiquaver figure flies
arrying all before it. At the emotional apex of
sage the principal subject (*motif* A) reappears,
er apprehensive as at first, but *fortissimo*, with
defiance. The artist triumphs; 'taking Fate
hroat' he defies the sorrow and heart-break of

this A flat in logical sequence would be taken as the
dominant of D flat, and one expects a further development in the latter tonality. But it does not materialize;
the key of A flat persists, and makes way for a short
episode embodying the twofold principal subject. In
spite of striking modulations this is really no more than
an ingenious play upon the themes after the manner of
Haydn. The inspiration gains in intensity and individuality, as the rising *crescendo* established in the chromatic syncopated passage—similar to that in the first
section—bursts into the tonality of C major.

Fortissimo, the challenging *motif* of leaping fifths is
vigorously given out, first in the lower voices (the viola
in octaves), then in the upper, accompanied by a rushing semiquaver figure in the other two parts in thirds
and sixths. The four bars of this phrase are repeated
in the key of A minor. A period of calm supervenes
after these eight bars of stormy agitation, momentarily
disturbed by the semiquaver figure of the first section,
which comes to an end in a sighing, plaintive *ritardando*: [1]

Ex. 77.

The calm is shortlived: beneath the languor of grief
burns an overpowering resentment against opposing
fate. With redoubled vigour the semiquaver figure
springs up in unison on the four instruments and

[1] There is a similar *ritardando* in the famous oboe cadence passage
in the first movement of the C minor symphony. Schumann used the
same idiom in the first movement of his Trio in D minor.

broadens to a climax, again as though to set free an outburst of emotion. The first violin rises up to this climax, modulating from A minor to B flat major, E flat major, D minor, and E minor, to a final triumphant unison of trills : the culminating point of the whole movement, crowning the triumph of the artist's power.

The last three bars of brings back the introdu section of the movement. the ease with which the confines itself within th repeated section, necessi form, seems the natural that inspires it), has not g ciated as one of the most si genius. In such moments, over matter is made mani been noticed in the quartet truth of A.-B. Marx's state into the world not to breal

The third section follow It only differs from it i modulation required by s final section in E major, &c alterations that Beethoven n his thought new interest. theme is considerably lengt

Ex. 7

stretches o expressive

The cle modulates of the en guess why tional for effect crea out in pe tion prog fortissimo Coda.

This C of forms. the first p awaited same que cessive pa A flat to hurled f joined b note, the violin ar semble a long-sus descent and as t close mo of the m reappea sity and

The returns away, the pas no long ringing by the

a hostile destiny. . . . At this transcendent climax the *motif* A of the principal theme bears an almost colossal significance; *diminuendo*, the *motif* B slips in for the last time and firmly establishes the tonic; two *piano* chords mark the conclusion.

II. *Adagio*. The impassioned *Allegro* is followed by a slow movement breathing an inspired idealism, profoundly spiritual yet deeply human : ' a vision of Paradise where mortal love finds eternal happiness '.[1] It is an unbroken stream of melody, with its various phrases bound together by connecting chords, not split up and set one against the other in the working out of the counterpoint—an unending melodic line often found in the later Beethoven quartets, and developed to perfection by R. Wagner.

Holtz the violinist, an intimate friend of Beethoven's, and a member of the famous Schuppanzigh Quartet, tells how the composer conceived the idea of this movement one night, at Baden, near Vienna, as he gazed up at the stars, contemplating the harmony of the spheres.[2]

Another critic, W. Thayer, writing from a purely intellectual standpoint, dissects the most deeply inspired works of the composer in the light of cold reason, and ridicules this story of Holtz's. But those who are alive to the imaginative and emotional aspects of the work find the interpretation highly suggestive, and on hearing the movement experience anew the spiritual emotion evoked by the mystery of a starry night.

' *Si tratta questo pezzo con molto sentimento* ' (this piece must be played with much feeling) is the inscription the movement bears. The grave chorale-like opening of the *Adagio*, lasting eight bars, should reflect a mood of calm contemplation. For eight more bars it is repeated on the lower voices, while the theme in florid figuration is heard on the first violin, in a manner

[1] Von Lenz, *Beethoven et ses trois styles*, p. 65.
[2] Also recounted by Carl Czerny, *École du piano*, Part IV, p. 62.

often used by Beethoven in his later works. The second
eight-bar phrase leads to a new *staccato* figure on the
first violin, below which, one bar later, the second violin
works out a sort of variation on the earlier theme, less
gravely serene than before, but with more tenderness
and warmth: it is repeated in turn by the 'cello and
viola. Then the four instruments are reunited in a new
self-assertive melodic figure of marked rhythm, opening
on a *forte* and dropping at once to a *piano*:

Ex. 80.

(It will be noticed how, in the third bar of this example,
a sudden intimacy of feeling is gained by a simple
modulation to the minor on the 'cello, playing in a high
register ; such expressive changes, effected by similarly
simple means, are a feature of Beethoven's style.) The
emotion of this last bar, slightly tinged with melancholy, yields before the firm assurance of another
theme heard two bars later on the lower instruments :

Ex. 81.

while the first violin, in fluent semiquavers, soars heaven-wards, to drop down to earth a second later in a graceful curve of melody, joining the other instruments in an ensemble statement of the vigorous *motif*; which leads after two bars to the following strange episode:

Ex. 82.

The artist seems to fall into a mood of uneasy hesitation ; across the slowly fading spaced chords of the other instruments a single melancholy plaint is lifted up on the viola : a voice from within, a dim figure of mystery in the darkness. It persists beneath a little sighing figure on the violins and slow-falling triplets, high up, on the 'cello. But the mist of uncertainty clears away as the delicate triplet pattern is unfolded, *sempre piano e dolce*, on the first violin, while the lower voices murmur from the shadow a new melody that distantly echoes the principal theme. Rising and falling, the triplet figure flows smoothly on, passing from voice to voice, until the 'cello completes its melodic curve, as another grave chorale-like theme appears on the other instruments. The triplets then pass to the first violin ; above the dominant chord of B major, sustained by the lower parts with sonorous depth of tone, the first violin, as though thrilled with the delight of this *moment musical*, soars enraptured with the triplet figure and hovers over shining heights. After eleven bars the episode closes with a last theme, four bars in length, bringing a sense of repose :

Ex. 83.

Enlivened by a final trill on the first violin, this tranquil *motif* leads on to the principal subject. The tonality of B major continues. But the end is not yet in sight, and the night holds further terrors for the lonely traveller. The principal subject modulates

smoothly from B major to D major, making way for a
fortissimo passage on the first violin, which plunges us
without warning into the depths of darkness.

Yet at first we are greeted by the *motif* of repose
(Ex. 83) in the key of D major, firmly established. The
tonality changes at once to the minor, bringing disquiet ; and with another modulation to B flat, as though
towards G minor, the atmosphere of gloom deepens.
Black clouds bank up (in the shape of a new triplet
figure, uneasy, *pianissimo*, in imitative and chromatic
sequence), while, also in chromatic sequence, the 'cello
rolls out the muffled beats of the principal theme, and
on the upper voices, bar by bar, a little *motif* rises in
semitones, like sighs issuing from the grave.

Ex. 84.

The triplet movement grows in vigour, spreading at
last to the 'cello, and in all four parts scales the heights
to perish in the gloom ; another flight is followed by a
piercing cry, striking fear into the heart like a death-knell.

Ex. 85.

Out of a sudden silence grows the plaintive theme heard a moment since (Ex. 82), now on the 'cello, through the *decrescendo* chords of the other instruments. When at last it seems that all has faded into nothingness, the original chorale theme emerges from the shadows to open the development section in accordance with the free sonata form adopted here. The section that follows develops in the same way as the opening of the *Adagio* before the appearance of the moving triplet figure; but there are, as usually with Beethoven, important alterations. The theme in florid figuration given to the first violin in the second eight-bar phrase, here enters at once on the 'cello, and is more quickly worked out. The triplet figure which comes later forms in this section a continuous melodic line, producing an extraordinary effect at the conclusion, as it wavers as though arrested for want of breath; the triplets stop, and the melodic curve is completed by crotchets slowly falling, to come to rest, not on the tonic, as is anticipated, but on a modulating chord (dominant of A major)—an idiom Wagner often used:

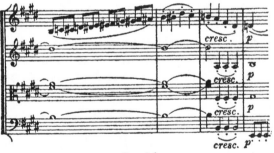

Ex. 86.

The tranquil theme in A major (not in E major), starting from this dominant chord, heightens the effect of repose; for four bars it slips from major to minor, reaching the key of E major in the next four, to establish it. A short *crescendo* introduces a vigorous statement of the principal chorale theme, declaimed *fortissimo* by all four instruments. A descending passage in semi-quavers on the first violin follows, as gay as the phrase that opened the development was melancholy, and brings back for a last time the theme of repose which fills the next six bars (in E, with fluctuating modulations to the seventh of A major). Then the triplet phrase falls like a blessing upon the four instruments, bringing a heavenly peace ; fading away as it passes from one voice to another, the *motif* finally loses itself on the 'cello. . . . With a long *pianissimo* chord of E major, slow and sustained like an organ pedal, the dream dies away into infinite space. . . .

III. *Allegretto*. The type of movement that Beethoven called not *Scherzo* nor *Menuetto*, but simply *Allegretto*, has a character all its own. It is not merely one of those *jeux d'esprit* scintillating with the Master's wit and humour ; it is no longer the expressive dance form of Haydn, or the graceful measure of Mozart. This *Allegretto*, with its emotional nature and romantic bearing, seems to foreshadow the Mazurkas of Chopin.[1]

[1] ' In the old form of sonata,' says von Lenz, ' between the menuet and its trio was a constant interchange of amenities—if the tonality of the menuet was major, the trio was in the minor, and vice versa. . . .

' From the time that he adopted the style of his second manner, Beethoven decided that this close inter-relationship had exhausted its possibilities. . . . The creation of a new rhythmic form, and a definite emancipation from the old style of the menuet involved many innovations : the increasing length and importance of the third movement (quartet Op. 74) . . . the episodes in duple time in the *scherzi* of the quartets of Op. 127 and Op. 132 . . . and similar instances. . . . In turn tender, stern, impassioned, or timid, the *Allegretto* takes every imaginable shape. In the F minor quartet it is like a supplication, passing without a break from a contemplative ecstasy to a section that takes the place of the *Scherzo*—a type of *scherzo* that can only be designated by the title it bears : *Allegro assai vivace ma serioso*, for its vigorous and closely knit style is purely individual, without a parallel or a name among musical forms.

' It was not a question of taking a form of known construction and type, and renaming it *Allegretto* ; the *Allegretto* of Beethoven introduces entirely new ideas in new forms. Constantly varying, it combines both slow movement and *Scherzo* in the piano trio in E flat (Op. 70) ;

It is built up on a curiously constructed rhythm, depending for its effect on an accented second beat of the bar, extended by a dot half its length :

Ex. 87.

The first section is very short, and is repeated in its entirety. The second opens in melancholy mood in the

it becomes the *Andante* in the VIIth and VIIIth symphonies, and in the F minor quartet. In the Vth and VIth symphonies the *Scherzo* changes its name but not its form ; it is no longer content even to portray an imaginative fantasy in a form without fixed rules, like the *Scherzo* of the quartet in F and of the Op. 74 quartet ; it is a continuous movement of increasingly profound inspiration, leading to the finale that it magnificently foreshadows. A new creation rising phoenix-like from

key of G minor, modulating to A minor; gaining
heroic energy with the entry of F major, it reaches a
climax four bars later, when the *motif* is transferred to
the basses, to be given out with furious vigour against
fortissimo chords on the violins, and coming to a stop
finally in the tonality of E minor; at this point the
expressive element, heard in a distant *piano*, gains the
ascendancy, interrupted by a brief return to the heroic,
and a new theme, high up on the 'cello, enters and fades
softly away to a delicate whimsical accompaniment of
the principal *motif* on the first violin:

Ex. 88 *a*.

The *alternativo* (called *Maggiore*, as in Beethoven's
early works) offers a contrast to the principal section,
accentuated by the fact that it is based on a Russian [1]
folk-tune of marked originality and vigour.

In the key of E major in the lower parts, and in
B major in the upper parts, it passes from one to

the ashes of the old outworn form, the *Scherzo* in Beethoven's hands
became a free movement, affording endless scope for creative genius;
to-day one takes it as a matter of course, although at the time it was
one of the most important innovations in the history of chamber
music. . . .

'The *Scherzo* of Beethoven was at first only a tentative attempt
(quintet in C, first trios and quartets), and for a long time he adhered
to the accepted form, before finally evolving the freely constructed
scherzi of the second and third manner.' (Von Lenz, pp. 62–5.)

[1] This Russian theme was used by Rimsky-Korsakov in his opera
The Tsar's Bride (see pp. 43 and 128, ed. Belaieff). There it is sym-
bolical of the majesty of the Tsar. Moussorgsky, in *Boris Godounov*,
introduces it into the musical description of the Kremlin bells.

another, sometimes as accompanied melody, sometimes in canon, with occasionally an almost metallic resonance. But the sadness inherent in all Russian melody touches the picture with melancholy ; the last two bars of the theme end in E minor, and the first section of the *Allegretto* returns. Beethoven gives the following indication for the repetition : *Da capo il minore, ma senza replica, ed allora ancora una volta il trio, e dopo di nuovo da capo il minore senza replica.* (*Da capo* the minor section without repeats ; then the *Trio* once more, followed again by the minor section without repeats.)

As in the first movement of the quartet, formal repetitions are freely employed. From this time onwards Beethoven adopts the following general *scherzo* form—principal section, *Alternativo*, principal section, *Alternativo*, principal section—in *scherzi* or in the movements that take the place of the *scherzo*, as in the B flat and A major symphonies, and the quartets in F minor (Op. 95), and E flat major (Op. 74). Generally speaking, the principal section is at first complete, with all the detailed repeats, appearing later without the repeats, and finally much abridged ; and the *scherzi* of the last period have an unexpected concluding section (VIIth and IXth symphonies, and the quartet in E flat, Op. 127).

R. Schumann used the same *scherzo* form, but with this difference,[1] that between the three repetitions of the principal section are two different *Alternativo* sections (the B flat and C major symphonies and the piano quintet, &c.).

IV. *Finale.* All the splendour of Beethoven's passionate emotion, only glimpsed in the first and third movements, is triumphantly disclosed in this spectacular work, the most brilliant quartet finale that had ever been written.

[1] We find it also in the early works of Beethoven (quintet in E flat, Op. 4), but he subsequently abandoned this form.

From a sudden chord of C major, struck *forte* by the four instruments, springs the melody:

Ex. 88 *b*.

In these ten opening bars are the elements of all the subsequent working out, and a detailed examination of them is necessary in order to appreciate Beethoven's method of developing thematic material. At the seventh bar the placid serenity of the theme is disturbed by a short modulation to E minor, but the major is re-established with a repetition of the melody in the original key. This incessant movement in the tonality of C, foreign to the principal tonality of the quartet, and the persistent effort to foreshadow an effect that never materializes, is one of the features of the movement and the source of much of its characteristic humour.

The last bar of Ex. 88*b* is followed by seven bars

identical with bars 2–8 of the example, but after the eighth bar the episode in E minor is extended and varied :

Ex. 89.

After these bars of delay the principal theme bursts in, impatient of restraint, swept with suppressed emotion.

At the fourth entry of the theme, again after a protracted modulation, the second violin works out an imitative figure from the fifth bar ; at the seventh bar the key of E minor reappears, and the artist lingers in the key as though finding there a shade of emotion that harmonizes with the natural disposition of his thought : the first violin moves in this tonality for five bars, developing the *motif* heard at the seventh bar of the theme in Ex. 88*b* :

Ex. 90.

It is the first of the broad sweeping effects in which this finale abounds. After this flight the movement

broadens into a quaver figure on the first violin, while
the second violin toys with a fluent *motif* derived from
the principal subject, and with a *motif* based on the
ninth bar of Ex. 88*b*:

Ex. 91.

which is at once taken up by the upper parts.

This elaborate working out of the principal theme
comes to a stop with the entry of the second subject
in B minor on the first violin:

Ex. 92.

The melody is typical of the genre in which it is cast, with brilliant play between the parts; its minor tonality makes it dark and disturbed. It stretches over eight bars and is immediately repeated by the lower instruments, then giving place to a short development in an episode based on the *motif* of the fifth bar of Ex. 91. This melodic fragment of three notes only prepares the re-entry of the principal subject; split up among the four parts, it forms a lively eighteen-bar development, in which the tonality of B minor gradually merges into C major, and with the tonic chord of C the principal subject starts again.

It must be observed that this section of the finale contains no new feature, interesting though it may be. It is in just this same facile way that Haydn prepares the re-entry of themes in symphony and quartet (see, for instance, the finale of the symphony in B flat major). At the time when he was writing Op. 59, moreover, Beethoven liked these effective returns of the subject immensely. The first movement of the IVth symphony in B flat, and of the piano sonata in C (Op. 53), afford similar examples.

This return of the principal theme leads to a repetition of the *Presto*; for thirty-eight bars the construction is the same as that of the opening section. At this point the movement reveals a new aspect: the fourth bar of the principal subject is used as a *motif*, and is developed first on the violin, then on the 'cello, against a chorale-like counterpoint in the other parts in semibreves and minims, which lasts for twenty-four bars. Then against a long-held chord of B flat, the original *motif* emerges again, *pianissimo*; after seven bars, its leaping rhythm changes from ♪♪ | ♩ ┐ ♪♪ ┐ ♪ | ♩ . . . . to ♩ ♩ ♩ ♪♪ | ♩ ♩ ♩ ♪♪ . . ., resulting in the following robust figure:

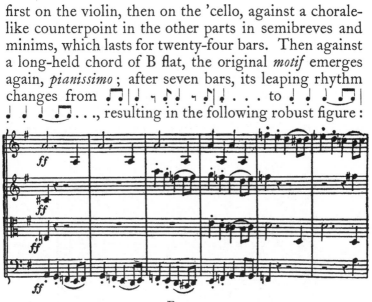

Ex. 93.

The *motif* vigorously cuts a way for itself, first in the bass and then forming a new development with the other voices. This spirited clash of melodies, crowned with intermingling trills, leads to a splendid statement of the *motif* of Ex. 92, this time in E minor, the principal tonality of the quartet. The *motif* now stretches over twice its original sixteen-bar length, extended by a short episode in F minor, where the original form of the theme undergoes a modification that makes of it practically a new figure: (Ex. 94).

Once more the re-entry of the chord of C major and of the principal subject is prepared. This new statement of the theme occupies twenty-eight bars in all, ending with the same impassioned phrase as before (first four bars of Ex. 91). An energetic statement of the *motif* from the principal theme on the second violin moves to the first violin, and is heard in descent, ascending in contrary motion on the 'cello; at the seventh bar it yields to the modified principal *motif* (Ex. 93), and four

bars later—all the changes occur as swiftly as thought
can grasp them—to a figure not hitherto used as a
theme, being merely a phrase contained in the eighth
bar of the principal subject (Ex. 88 *b*). This new figure
fades away and is lost in the lower parts, accompanied
in its fall by a slow chromatic descent in semibreves on
the first violin. The movement seems to have achieved
its climax. . . . But, *pianissimo*, though with marked
rhythm, the principal subject steals back, linked with

Ex. 94.

the modified principal *motif*; out of the blending of
these two an animated third theme is formed. But as
it develops it splits up again into its two elements,
struggling one against the other as they rise to a powerful *fortissimo*. The melodic working out is very condensed : (Ex. 95 *a*).

After an expressive pause, the *motif* from the eighth
bar of Ex. 88 *b* is heard, calm and resigned, in the key
of E minor. The episode is repeated; this time the
motif resolves itself into curious harmonic progressions,
first in semibreves, then in crotchets and quavers (F
major, E flat major, G flat major, &c. . . . for the semibreves, the various chords of E minor for the crotchets
and quavers). A hush falls on the rhythm of this passage, recalling the works of the first manner (finale of

the violin and piano sonata, Op. 23). But a hammering *crescendo* rises to a *fortissimo* statement of the principal theme in C major. The modulation to E minor becomes the starting-point of a sort of *Coda (più presto)* where the fundamental tonality is established. In these

Ex. 95 *a*.

twenty-seven bars the distinctive rhythm of the principal theme soars up in a magnificent flight, and after a B in *altissimo* reiterated for three bars on the first violin, six massive chords bring the movement to an end with a blare of trumpets. Never had the string quartet revealed such an intensity of emotion; the composer here attains an expressive power which the *prestissimo* of the C minor quartet (Op. 18, No. 4) no more than foreshadowed.

Quartet No. IX, Op. 59, No. 3 (in C major).

{ *Introduzione. Andante con moto* ($\flat$ = 69).
{ *Allegro vivace* ($\downarrow$ = 88).
  Andante con moto quasi allegretto ($\flat \cdot$ = 56).
  Menuetto ($\flat$ = 116).
  Allegro molto ($\downarrow$ = 168).

Austrian musicians call this work the Eroica Quartet, by analogy with the IIIrd symphony. Marx compares it with the symphony in C minor, and in his opinion the *Introduction* and the *Andante* were never equalled. For him it is ' one of those works of Beethoven that most perfectly reveal the indomitable spirit of the Master, the courage of a man who did not shrink from probing the very depths of his being, and finding there only darkness and lonely despair, could yet greet his destiny with a cry of defiance '.

Above all, the interest of the IXth quartet lies in showing how between the first and the third of the Op. 59 compositions their quality of psychological objectivity developed. The finale of Op. 59, No. 3, assumes symphonic proportions in pure brilliance of objective conception and expressive power.

The following study embraces Marx's purely technical analysis as far as possible.

I. *Introduction.* The first movement is preceded by twenty-nine introductory bars, in which spaced chords, in tonalities far removed from the principal key of the work, are heard and disappear. The harmony wanders at will as the voices die away into the distance; separated by wide intervals the parts finally unite in a long-sustained chord of B-A♭-D-F, following a bar of silence; at the end of three bars the viola moves down a semitone, and the resulting progression B-G-D-F resolves at once on to the tonic chord of C major, for the commencement of the *Allegro vivace*.

II. *Allegro vivace.* Fluent yet with a timid air the first violin gives out the principal theme :

Ex. 95 *b.*

Repeated in D minor in a form already slightly modified, and instilled with the vigour that underlies its slight and graceful aspect, this theme resounds like a rallying call and reassembles the four voices on the dominant seventh of F major—C-E-G-B♭.

Instead of a resolution on to the tonic chord, a simple modulation brings back the key of C major, and with a decisive statement of the principal theme the tentative doubts of the first bars are triumphantly dispelled : [1]

Ex. 96.

[1] If one compares this opening section with the corresponding passage in Mozart's quartet in C, to which it is superficially akin, one realizes in Beethoven's work an infinitely deeper psychological significance. Mozart's Introduction (the deliberate harshness of which Fétis would have liked to alter) in no sense anticipates the feeling of the *Allegro* that follows ; after so sombre an opening the gaiety of the *Allegro* strikes a wholly unexpected contrast. Beethoven, on the other

An echo of Mozart's quartet in C seems to linger in the easy grace of the bridge passage, bringing a sense of repose, after the vigour of the principal theme :

Ex. 97.

It leads up to the second subject :

Ex. 98.

which springs from the last bar of an ascending semi-quaver scale in broken thirds on the 'cello ; the melody creates an atmosphere at once grave and serene, giving an unexpectedly intimate turn to the character of the movement.

hand, deliberately leads up to the effect of daylight breaking upon the darkness. Still more significant is the relation in the Op. 132 quartet between the Introduction and the principal movement. Yet M. Vincent d'Indy (a note taken by M. Coindreau) remarks that the Introduction of the IXth quartet has no link with the first movement.

The first violin repeats it twice more; the lower
voices take the two notes of its first phrase in persistent
reiteration beneath an energetic semiquaver figure,
heard on the violins, at first in imitation, then together;
this figure leads in turn to another twisting *motif* passing
from part to part:

Ex. 99.

The treatment of these various melodic figures up to
the end of the first section, though here more forceful,
recalls again the quartet in C of Mozart, and Haydn's
Emperor quartet. The section concludes with a characteristic *motif* derived from Ex. 99:

Ex. 100.

Its successive *fugato* entries on the different instruments
give it an air of stubborn determination. Five bars of
development lift it to a decisive statement:

Ex. 101 *a.*

and from this point it falls to the four-bar cadence,

mezza voce, based on the first notes of the second subject:

Ex. 101 *b*.

It will be observed how this technically brilliant conclusion to the first section is ingeniously linked to the opening bars of the movement; returning to the tentative entry of the principal theme, it moves to another plane of emotion without in any way destroying the unity of conception of the piece.

The second section (development) opens in a very high register. The first phrase of the second subject modulates to E flat, and once the tonality is established the principal theme appears as at first, unaccompanied, on the first violin, two bars longer than in the first section. The other voices seize upon its hesitating conclusion, and resolve it decisively; taking the first notes of the main theme, they treat it in lively imitation, modulating through F major to E minor; above a pedal B on the 'cello, chorale-like chords descend, moving towards this tonality. At this point a rushing violin figure in F major breaks in, to merge after two bars into the unruffled calm of the bridge passage.

The return of the second theme is effected in the same way as in Ex. 98, but it is differently worked out. The first notes of the *motif* are given to the basses in imitation, while the violins have a semiquaver figure in the form of *arpeggio* chords of D minor and C minor. Two bars follow, in which the distribution of the *motifs* among the parts is inverted. Then the 'cello takes up the heroic strain again, and all the instruments fall *fortissimo* upon the following theme, a development of the first two notes of the *motif* of Ex. 98.

Ex. 102.

In this passage there is a titanic rhythmic power, surging onwards with an output of energy that quickly exhausts itself, as the *motif* seems to shorten its stride and drops lower and lower, all the time with alternating beat between the upper and lower instruments; out of the depths arises a new melody of haunting tenderness, based on the same *motif* (from the eighth bar of Ex. 102).

The soul of Beethoven seems to rise from this surging theme to meet us, with an echo of unhappy memories in a far-off past. . . . But the rhythm closes up, the pace quickens, and the volume of sound increases to a long trill on G-A♭ on the first violin. Two bars farther on the trill changes to G-A♮, and the storm passes over. On the lower voices appear, *pianissimo*, *fugato* entries of the *motif* formed from the first two notes of the second theme, and the first violin works up a free variation on the principal subject in semiquavers and triplets, in the form of an expressive *recitativo*, a graceful passage occupying twelve bars. The first violin terminates with a trill, first on B♭, then on B♮; the viola and 'cello move in a chromatic descent with the violins to the dominant seventh chord, and finally with the tonic chord of C major the return of the principal subject opens the third section of the movement.

This section is rather different from the first; Beethoven aims at accentuating by every possible means the triumphant character of the theme. Consequently the rhythm is quickened, and the phrase:

Ex. 103.

is altered to :

Ex. 104.

gaining by its altered form a new significance in the
development. All that could possibly detract from the
heroic strain is suppressed. The bridge passage disappears, swept away by a whirlwind energy ; the second
theme follows straight after the figure in contrary motion with which the principal subject ends, gaining
from it a flourish it never possessed before :

Ex. 105 a.

and the course of its rapid development, leaping over
four agitated bars, produces an episode of vigorous
rhythm in which the first two notes of the *motif* are
worked in syncopation, the upper instruments against
the lower.

Up to its conclusion in C major, the rest of the third
section is very much like the first.

It closes with a short *Coda*, which, though unexpected, is the logical parallel to the cadence ending to the first section. The first notes of the second subject form its main element. With its rhythm accentuated on the second violin, and reinforced by 'cello *pizzicati*, it seems to settle down with heavy beats on the tonic of C major. Then it rises to F ; the 'cello—*arco*—twice repeats the two notes in the dominant, *pianissimo e stringendo*, and a brilliant six-bar *stretto* leads through a series of chromatic chords to the conclusion in the fundamental key.

One of the most remarkable features of the thematic construction of this *Allegro* is the frequency with which Beethoven uses the *motif* of the first two notes of the second subject (Ex. 98). Haydn employed a similar figure in the first movement of his last quartet in B flat major, but Beethoven's method of development, equally flexible, is incomparably more varied and expressive.

If we compare the structure of this *Allegro vivace* with that of Beethoven's other quartets, A.-B. Marx declares, and notice in particular how often the two violins are linked together in extended melodic passages, and how often broad ensembles of the four instruments are achieved by the use of the same vigorous rhythmic form, we realize that the quartet in C major, more than any other, embodies the orchestral style.

Cherubini worked on the same lines in his quartet in E flat, but in a far less brilliant way ; Beethoven's attains bigger symphonic proportions. In fact, in the Eroica Quartet, inspiration overflowed the limits of its medium for expression, even though that expressive medium was already extended beyond ordinary bounds. One might well wonder whether the little voice of the string quartet is really entitled to attempt an achievement that would be no easy matter for the hundred voices of the symphony.

III. *Andante con moto quasi allegretto.* This, according to A.-B. Marx, is an ' extraordinarily odd move-

ment '. Above heavy, muffled *pizzicati* on the 'cello
a long-drawn melancholy phrase is unfolded :

Ex. 105 *b*.

expressing, not the keen suffering of a recent grief, but
some old remembered heartache, coming back out of
the past to lie heavy upon the spirit with the dreary
weight of despair. . . . The impassive *pizzicati* of the
'cello bring back the opening phrase of the melody ;
impassive still, in the following section the melody is
divided among the three upper voices and floats forlornly
above them in drifting mists of sadness. An atmosphere
of infinite desolation is created by the use of the ano-
malous modes of :

$$C \mid B \ A \ G\sharp \ F \ E \ D \mid C \ B \ A$$

and

$$F \mid E \ D \ C\sharp \ B\flat \ A \ G \mid F \ E \ D$$

which, as Marx notices, ' have no defined character,
leaving the spirit to wander in a waste of vague melancholy '. The melodic line moves on without break or
accent, except for a brief *crescendo* in the concluding
bars, like a strangled sob, followed by a mood of utter
resignation, in the passage :

Ex. 106.

But the mood quickly passes, as though with the realiza-

tion that nothing can lighten the burden of grief;
against the inexorable beats of the 'cello a desolate voice
rises from the viola, choked with tears; reaching the end of
its plaintive phrase, it is joined by the three other instruments, giving sudden voice to a lament so bitter that one
seems to hear a cry of sorrow from an unseen world:

Ex. 107.

The viola phrase is repeated in turn by the second
violin and the 'cello.

But the second principal subject, a naïve, simple
theme, comes like a joyous memory to lift this bitterness

Ex. 108.

It is only for a moment that a smile breaks through the tears, though the smile lingers in the wistful 'heartache' *motif*, this time given by the 'cello ; losing now the sharpness of grief, the theme merges into a continuous unbroken melody that forms the central point of the development.[1]

Ex. 109.

The gloom fades with the reappearance of the second subject, the ' consolation ' *motif*, heard first in the gay tonality of A major, then again in an access of renewed lightheartedness after a modulation through D minor to E flat.

[1] The *Adagio* of Mozart's quartet in E flat contains a similar development section.

A shadow falls over the spirit of the artist, and darker than ever by contrast, the muffled *pizzicati* of the 'cello sink into the depths of darkness and despair, while the unseen voices, in broad stretches of harmony, seem to cling to the fading beauty of the passing dream. . . . (Ex. 110.)

As the slow beats of the *pizzicati* come to an end on the E from which they started, the modified first subject returns. Beethoven here makes very free use of sonata form. The theme is given to the second violin while the first violin works out a counterpoint above:

Ex. 110.

This third section follows much the same form as the first. Twice the 'resignation' *motif* (Ex. 106) appears, arrested the second time on a sustained A-C in the upper parts, while the 'cello, urged on by a mysterious, irresistible force, pursues its *pizzicati* to a far-away *pianissimo* conclusion where one seems to hear the echo of an inexorable doom. Two light *pizzicati* on the tonic close the movement; and so disappears from sight a tone picture wherein is reflected every nuance of sorrow that the human soul can experience. . . .

This *Andante* is profoundly moving and impressive when given a lyrical, intimate interpretation, free from any trace of emotional insincerity, and in which much is made of its delicate grace—a rare quality in Beethoven's work. Some quartettists interpret the episode of the 'consolation' *motif* (in C major, then in A and

E flat) in a gay, irresponsible vein, at the same time quickening the pace. This is an easy effect to produce, but not that intended by Beethoven. He wrote against the passage: *staccato*, or *piano*, or *dolce*, but never *agitato*, or even *stringendo*. The melody in major tonality is like a flickering brightness, quickly eclipsed; never should it be given a trivial or obvious interpretation, since it typifies in a sense the clear light of day.

IV. *Menuetto*. The spirit in which the two preceding quartets are written would lead one to expect in the quartet in C a *scherzo* movement with a dazzling brilliance of construction, to make it a worthy successor to the others. But Beethoven perhaps felt the incongruity of placing side by side with the profound pessimism of the slow movement a purely lighthearted *jeu d'esprit*. Deliberately, perhaps, he set against the emotional intensity of the *Andante* this unimpassioned movement, in which gradually it was to find relief; such an explanation is justified by his insistence on the psychological conception of music. At all events, the movement that follows bears out its title of *Menuetto grazioso*. Once more Beethoven took his inspiration from the old sonata form; and though less spirited and lively than the *Menuet* of Haydn, this movement has all the polished grace and charm of the old French *Menuet*, to which Mozart returned in *Don Juan*.

The first section is not repeated:

MENUETTO
Grazioso

Ex. 111.

In the second section the parts develop the theme in imitation ; a little before the end a particularly expressive passage occurs :

Ex. 112 *a*.

The fourth and fifth bars of this episode should be noticed for the germ of a formula of ' soaring ecstasy ', an idiom used later by Mendelssohn almost to excess.

The *Trio* has a more sprightly character, and opens with a characteristic figure based on the common chord :

Ex. 112 *b*.

Like the *Menuet*, it includes two sections: the first ends in the key of C, and the second begins in A, by an unprepared transition. This A is taken as the dominant of E minor, and soon afterwards the tonality of F major is re-established, and persists to the end. The second section of the *Trio* is repeated ; a return to the *Menuet* follows, leading on *pianissimo* to a *Coda* based on the original *motif* of the *Menuet*. With growing energy the muffled roll of the bass seems to dispel the last lingering traces of grief. One cannot yet guess where the *Coda* is leading us, but the animated conclusion, broadening to a *crescendo* on the chord of the dominant seventh of C, seems to herald some great achievement.

V. *Finale.* This final *Allegro*, in which the tonal resources of the string quartet genre are strained to their utmost limits, takes the form of a colossal fugue, breaking sometimes strict fugal conventions, but superior in dramatic intensity even to the fugues of Bach. As Hans von Bülow [1] comments:

For Beethoven, the fugue is not an end in itself, but the most perfectly expressive means of obtaining effect, in the same way that R. Wagner conceived the meaning of music in general in relation to his musical dramas. Consequently, the emotional nature of the fugue of Beethoven has nothing in common with the purely formal, objective and classical beauty of the fugue of Bach, which is an end in itself.

Certainly the fugue of the quartet in C has a deeper meaning than that contained in its intrinsic fugal form.

After the passionate and despairing flights of the preceding movements the fire of the Master's inspiration steadies to a clear flame; never before has Beethoven felt so conscious of the strength and imaginative force of his genius. At the very point when he is beginning the outlines of this fugue one finds scrawled in triumph across his note-book the words: 'Never again need you feel ashamed of your deafness, nor others wonder at it. Can anything in the world prevent you from expressing your soul in music?' [2] And it is about this time that Bettina von Arnim writes to Goethe, after seeing Beethoven conduct his orchestra:

O Goethe! No prince or emperor ever felt conscious like Beethoven of the reality of his omnipotence, and the sense that he is the source of all strength and power. He stood there, erect, with an indomitable force flowing from him. . . . His genius seemed to transform everything into a deliberate and conscious

[1] Critical edition of the Beethoven Sonatas.   [2] See p. 59.

activity. . . . One felt that a day must come when, in a new and perfect existence, he would reappear as the Lord of the world.[1]

No musical form could lend itself so well as the fugue to the manifestation of such a force, provided that appreciation of the subtle and intricate formal design of the work was subordinated to the all-important general effect obtained. All Beethoven wished to borrow from the fugue form was its dynamic impulsion, gained by the strengthening of one part with another, the impetus that each successive entry of the subject gives to the musical idea, as each part adds its own to swell the voice of the others, the sudden quickening of interest in *stretto* passages, the surging waves of sound that mingle and overlap—in a word, all possible increase of vitality and energy that the use of fugue could bestow. It was his breath that gave life to these empty forms ; it is of no account whether, in so doing, he disorganized any part of their conventional mechanism. . . . Beethoven may have written music more profound, but never more triumphant. This fugue, soon transformed into double fugue, reminds one of the finale of Mozart's symphony in C major ; though less formally perfect, it rises to greater emotional heights. A technical analysis such as Marx gives is unnecessary ; one need only give a commentary on the lines of Helm.

The ten-bar subject is given out on the viola, answered by the second violin above a counter-subject preceded by several link-bars of the quaver movement on the viola ; the 'cello then enters, and finally the first violin, extending the theme from ten to sixteen bars and concluding with the *Coda* : (Ex. 113).

An answering call in thirds on the second violin and viola brings to mind the clamour and *fanfare* of a battle-field. The *motif* rises, picking up the principal fugue subject in its flight, and gives place to a brilliant play

[1] Goethe's *Briefwechsel mit einem Kinde*, Book II, p. 190.

of imitative figures. . . . Soon the pace quickens, and
the four instruments abandon the imitations, to embark
upon a moving episode in the key of E flat. A pause
of one bar on the dominant of the key cuts the passage

Ex. 113.

short, and the second violin and viola work out the
principal subject in contrary motion for three bars,
uniting at a point where, again in contrary motion, the
'cello enters with the theme. An effective modulation
to F minor brings in the first violin to join the fray.
Other developments follow in D flat and C sharp minor
in a short vigorous *stretto*, while the *fanfare* figure is
sounded on the viola. After another episode, the two
violins give out a modified version of the principal
theme :

Ex. 114.

At the same time occurs a modulation from C sharp
minor to D minor, and with it opens what is perhaps
the most interesting section of the whole movement.

From the noise of battle Beethoven turns to describe
upon the four instruments the fury of the elements;
in the long quaver passage moving from the fourth
string of the first violin to the third string of the
second we hear the howling of the wind; the roar
of the sea in the same passage on the fourth string
of the viola, and especially on the 'cello G string; vivid
flashes of lightning in the principal subject, heard on
the first, and then on the second violin, above *sforzando*
chords on the lower instruments; thunder rolls in a
final crashing unison. It is notable that each of these
eight-bar phrases, in which one or other of the instruments dominates the ensemble, concludes with a
modulation of striking simplicity. . . . And in the course
of each phrase the three accompanying instruments
have an air of choosing their notes at random, as though
careless of the sustaining chords; with the rise and fall
of minor harmonies one seems to see the shadow of
passing clouds, revealing a sudden glimpse of clear sky
in an unexpected modulation to the major!

In the 'lightning' *motif* the first violin works up an
extraordinary rhythmic force:

Ex. 115.

Nothing has ever been written for the quartet to
equal this climax of monumental power; the *sforzando*

chord on the three other instruments bursts like a wild cry in response to each dazzling flash; it brings to mind the song of Orpheus in Gluck's opera, and the relentless interruption of the furies. (Compare also the trumpet-call of the second Leonora Overture, closely akin to this movement.)

The rolling of thunder comes to a stop on the sub-dominant of C; a long pause ensues, followed by a unison of the four instruments on the dominant. With a sudden *piano* the fugue begins again; the parts enter in the same order as in the exposition, but a new counter-subject in minims gives added vigour and movement. The fugue works out as before up to the stormy development section just analysed; the various episodes are repeated in their proper tonalities, and the last is linked to a brilliant *Coda* glittering with trills, which form a dominant pedal on the first violin, second violin, and viola successively for twenty-two bars; beneath it are heard snatches of the principal subject, lacking its first two notes, against the counter-subject in minims. Rising to G in *altissimo*, the first violin falls from that point with the principal theme, against the counter-subject in syncopation on the inner parts. The subject is gradually taken up by all the instruments while a new counter-subject appears on the second violin. Finally, all the voices join in a massive contrary movement, the upper parts against the lower, broaden-ing to a splendid conclusion. A sudden pause is fol-lowed by another three-bar unison, and a *crescendo* of thirty bars begins, leading to the final climax of literally epic grandeur; it seems no longer four instruments but eight that one hears, swept on by resistless force to the *fortissimo* concluding chords. . . . Beethoven achieves at this point the utmost tonal power that the string quartet can produce; at the same time he reaches the limit of its brilliant and purely ' objective ' expressive capacity. His purpose must now be to elevate to the same point the inner significance of his compositions, the subjective aspect. This he achieves in the quartets of the last period, and already in a certain degree in the Xth quartet that follows, Op. 74.

Few works have had a worse reception at the outset than these Op. 59 quartets. Even Beethoven's best friends were doubtful, and the story goes that ' when the members of the Schuppanzigh Quartet, all friends of the Master and well acquainted with his style, first read through the quartet in F, they burst out laughing, convinced that a joke was being played on them '.[1] Brunswick alone was firm in the belief that they were a great work, and borrowed them from Beethoven for closer study.

Adverse criticism did not hinder Beethoven from selling the quartets, not only to his publisher in Vienna, but also to Muzio Clementi, who had recently established a firm in London, for publication in England among several other works. The original contract between the composer and his publisher was drawn up in French : [2]

La convention suivante a été faite entre M. M. Clementi et M. Louis V. Beethoven.

1. M. Louis Beethoven cède à M. Clementi les manuscrits de ses œuvres ci-après énumérées, avec le droit de les publier dans les Royaumes-Unis britanniques, en se réservant la liberté de faire publier ou de vendre pour faire publier ces mêmes ouvrages hors des dits royaumes: (*a*) trois Quatuors, (*b*) une Symphonie, N.B. la quatrième qu'il a composée, (*c*) une ouverture de *Coriolan*, tragédie de M. Collin, (*d*) un concert pour le piano, N.B. le quatrième qu'il a composé, (*e*) un concert pour le violon, N.B. le premier qu'il a composé, (*f*) ce dernier concert arrangé pour le piano avec des notes additionnelles.

[1] One day, when Schuppanzigh was complaining of the difficulty of a certain passage in the VIIth quartet, in F, Beethoven said angrily : ' Do you think I am troubling about a wretched violin when I am inspired by the breath of the Spirit ? ' (Mme Audley, *Louis van Beethoven*, p. 200 ; also Wilder, *Beethoven*, p. 268).

[2] The copy of the agreement was found by Thayer among the papers of Otto Jahn. See Wilder, p. 278.

2. M. M. Clementi fera payer pour ces 6 ouvrages, à M. Louis V. Beethoven, la valeur de deux cents livres sterling au cours de Vienne, par MM. Schuller et C°, aussitôt qu'on aura à Vienne la nouvelle de l'arrivée de ces ouvrages à Londres.

3. Si M. L. V. Beethoven ne pouvait livrer ensemble ces 6 ouvrages, il ne serait payé par MM. Schuller et C° qu'à proportion des pièces livrées, par ex. en livrant la moitié, il recevra la moitié, en livrant le tiers, il recevra le tiers de la somme convenue.

4. M. L. V. Beethoven promet de ne vendre ces ouvrages soit en Allemagne, soit en France, soit ailleurs, qu'avec la condition de ne les publier que quatre mois après leur départ respectif pour l'Angleterre; pour le concert pour le violon et pour la symphonie et l'ouverture, qui viennent de partir pour l'Angleterre, M. L. V. Beethoven promet de ne les vendre qu'à la condition de ne pas les publier avant le 1er septembre 1807.

5. On est convenu de plus que M. L. V. Beethoven compose aux mêmes conditions, dans un temps non déterminé et à son aise, trois sonates ou deux sonates et une fantaisie pour le piano, avec ou sans accompagnement, comme il voudra, et que M. Clementi lui fera payer, de la même manière, soixante livres sterling.

6. M. M. Clementi donnera à M. L. V. Beethoven deux exemplaires de chacun de ces ouvrages.

Fait en double et signé à Vienne, le 20 avril 1807
Muzio Clementi. Louis Van Beethoven.
Comme témoin: J. Gleichenstein.

Urgent need of money led Beethoven to lose no time in fulfilling his side of the contract, and in dispatching the manuscripts to London. The quartets suffered some delay, since the separate parts were in the possession of Count Brunswick, to whom Beethoven wrote at once :

Vienna, *May.*

Dear Brunswick,

This is to tell you that I have come to a very satisfactory arrangement with Clementi; I am to have two hundred pounds, and retain the right to sell the works I am handing over to him, in Germany and France. Clementi has also made other suggestions to me, and in a year or two I ought to be able to reach a position worthy of an artist. But I must have my quartets, dear Brunswick, as it would take too long to have fresh parts copied out from my score. Please send the parts you have by return. I will let you have them back in four or five days at the latest, but please do not keep me waiting for them, as you will cause me serious inconvenience. . . .

Kiss Thérèse for me, and tell her I shall soon be a great man. And don't forget to send the quartets to-morrow without fail! *The quartets! The quar-tets! T-h-e q-u-a-r-t-e-t-s!*
LUDWIG VAN BEETHOVEN.

During 1807 they were played privately in Vienna from the manuscript, and the *Allgemeine Musikalische Zeitung*[1] makes the following reference :

Three new quartets by Beethoven, dedicated to Count Rasoumowsky, the Russian Ambassador, are attracting considerable attention. They are of great length and difficulty; and with the exception of that in C minor (*sic*), which must make an immediate appeal to a cultivated ear for its originality, its melodic interest and harmonic vigour, they will be found perhaps too obscure to find general acceptance, though finely constructed and profoundly conceived.

They finally appeared in Vienna in January 1808, published by Schreivogel, at the *Kunst- und Industrie-Comptoir*, and the first public performance was given in the month following, with no greater success than the year before. It is related how the composer Gyrowets ' seeing a friend ordering one of these much-abused quartets, felt so strongly on the subject as to try and persuade him not to, convinced that he was only throwing his money away ! '[2]

The Abbé Maximilien Stadler, the master of Weber and Meyerbeer, and a fine organist, though a musician of limited imaginative capacity, was another adverse critic; he always made a point of beating a hasty retreat if he chanced to be present at a chamber concert when one or other of the quartets was being performed.

---

[1] *Allg. Mus. Zeit.*, 1807, p. 400. (Quoted by von Lenz, *Beethoven et ses trois styles*, p. 375.)   [2] Wilder, *Beethoven*, p. 269.

But musical circles in Vienna were not long in changing their opinion, and the works attracted the most enthusiastic admirers, among them Rossini. When he was in Vienna in 1822, Mayseder introduced the quartets to his notice as the most remarkable productions of the age, and Rossini expressed the wish to meet the composer of such magnificent works.[1]

They were performed for the first time in Russia at the beginning of 1812, at the house of Marshal Count Soltykow (see p. 71, footnote 1, the story related about Romberg).

The success of Op. 59 in France was no more propitious. For a long time they were not known at all in Paris. The Bohrer Quartet [2] (the brothers Bohrer, Tilmant, and Urhan) included them in their programme for 1831, but no public interest was aroused. Habeneck, an ardent admirer, and anxious to create a wider popularity for the works, conceived the idea of having separate movements performed on a string orchestra at the concerts at the Conservatoire, selecting those likely to make the most general appeal; and in 1832, at the fourth concert on 18th March, the programme included:

1. The Pastoral Symphony—*Beethoven*.

2. Concerto in G—*Beethoven*, played by M. Mendelssohn.

3. *Le Sommeil* from Gluck's *Armide*, sung by M. Ad. Nourrit, followed by a chorus from the same opera: *Poursuivons jusqu'au trépas* . . .

4. Movement from a quartet—*Beethoven*, played by string orchestra.

[1] See p. 201, footnote 1 (relating to the interview with Rossini).
[2] Anton Bohrer, violinist, born at Munich in 1783, was a pupil of Kreutzer; his brother Max, a 'cellist, born in 1785, was a pupil of Schwartz; after many tours they settled in Paris in 1831–2. In 1832 Max became principal 'cellist and leader of the orchestra at Stuttgart, where he died in 1867. In 1834 Anton settled at Hanover as leader of the orchestra there; he died in 1852.

5. Duet from *Medea—Cherubini*, sung by M. Ad. Nourrit and Mlle. Falcon.

6. Overture—*Beethoven*, followed by the final chorus from *Christ on the Mount of Olives*.

Fétis's *Revue musicale*, publishing this programme, comments : 'The movement from the Beethoven quartet, performed on a string orchestra, will be a curious modification of his original conception.' [1]

There were, as a matter of fact, two quartet movements performed at this concert—the *Adagio* from the VIIth, in F, and the fugue from the IXth, in C. In a critique in the *Revue musicale* of March 24, 1832, there is the following comment :

In the *Adagio* the effect was far from satisfying, although the ensemble was perfect. In order to hold attention and sustain unflagging interest, a piece of this type, written throughout in *cantabile* vein, demands an individual reading of each line of melody, impossible when several instruments are playing the same part. . . . One felt it to be no more than an orchestral piece, lacking the variety of colour and phrasing that wind instruments afford.

But if the effect of this piece fell rather short of expectations, it was not so with the fugue : here, the performance was technically perfect and artistically flawless. The vigorous movement of this fugue demands only perfect ensemble, accuracy, and finish, qualities that were here to be found in a superlative degree . . . exact precision and fine balance of bowing that blended all these technical effects into a perfect whole, finally an incomparable zest . . . aroused great enthusiasm from the audience. [2]

The critic of the *Revue musicale* does not vouchsafe a word of criticism of the work itself. The Op. 59 still evoked lively opposition from many quarters, and among its bitterest enemies was one Onslow, a clever amateur, but a musician without genius ; he was himself

[1] *Revue musicale*, March 17, 1832, p. 54.

[2] *Revue musicale*, 1832, p. 59. This fugue is even now quite often performed at the *Philharmonic* in Vienna, with all the string instruments.

a composer of chamber music and even of symphonies, which he esteemed superior to Beethoven's, and he harboured a grievance in the fact that Beethoven's were preferred to his by Habeneck and the Conservatoire orchestra.[1]

Between 1830 and 1850 the Op. 59 quartets several times appeared in programmes of chamber concerts, but never with any regularity. In 1839 the brothers Franco-Mendès performed the C major quartet, and Allard and Chevillard, with Aumont and Armaingaud, played the one in F major at one of their chamber music evenings at the house of M. Petzold, in January of 1840. The *Revue et Gazette musicale* comments:

The finest virtuoso in the world, playing one of the loveliest melodies, could never equal the effect produced by the four instruments in this beautiful quartet, especially in the slow movement, where each successive entry of the exquisitely moving theme in F minor stirred the audience to applause and admiration.

In 1850 Chevillard the 'cellist founded the ' Société des Quatuors de Beethoven '; from that time forward a sustained effort was made to arouse public appreciation of these magnificent works by means of regular performances both in France and in Germany, and it is to the honour of Chevillard that the attempt met with unqualified success.

That year also marked the beginning of a period of keen interest among musical critics in compositions that had not hitherto attracted public recognition. The Russian critic Ulibishev had just published a *Vie de Mozart*, in which he acclaimed the composer of *Don Juan* as the greatest musician the world had ever known. In 1852 we find W. von Lenz disputing the statement, in the preface to his famous work, *Beethoven et ses trois styles*, where he makes a critical, if rather extravagant, study of Beethoven's work, and particularly

[1] See Ernouf, *Compositeurs célèbres, Beethoven*, p. 64.

of the piano sonatas. On the subject of Op. 59, he remarks that ' these quartets are nothing short of miracles ', and in another place :

This work is the very stronghold of chamber music. . . . It throws down a triumphant challenge to the past, the present, and the future. Short of being to Beethoven what Beethoven was to Mozart, and creating by force of genius a whole world of new conceptions and new styles, no one could ever aspire to the achievement of three such masterpieces, uniting to form a perfect whole in an entirely new form. Moreover, mere novelty of form would never ring true unless it were the natural outcome and development of the composer's whole work, not an isolated style applied to one particular genre or instrument. . . . It is only after learning to express musical thought through the medium of many different instruments that one can turn at last to the instrument of one's choice, and find there fullest and deepest expression. The three quartets dedicated to Count Rasoumow-sky are the natural fulfilment of the promise of the symphonies and the piano sonatas, but a greater achievement, since the form of the quartet is less adapted to innovation of style than either the sonata or the symphony. . . . The content of these quartets is as great as the content of the symphonies, only the medium is different.[1]

In response to von Lenz's book, Ulibishev published in 1857 another study on *Beethoven, ses critiques et ses glossateurs*, where the Op. 59 works receive the following comment :

Few people liked them at the time of their first appearance in St. Petersburg. But since then opinion has changed, and contemporary critics place them far above the first six quartets that Beethoven wrote. Some have gone so far as to call them miracles. If I cared at all for public opinion, I should not have the hardihood to confess that for my part the quartets have never much interested me. It has been in vain that I have played them for years, and heard them played by performers of the front rank; I have tried to make myself like what has at last found general acceptance, but I cannot find them interesting. I feel sure that

[1] Von Lenz, *Beethoven et ses trois styles*, Paris, Lavinée, 1855, pp. 144–5 ; 2nd edition, Paris, Legouix, 1909, pp. 175–6.

many others share my opinion, but dare not express it, since in no community is individual opinion so much dominated by prejudice and self-deception, cliques and catchwords, as the world of music. . . . Thanks to the untiring eloquence of the more recent critics of Beethoven since 1848, the Rasoumowsky quartets are now preferred to the first six, I will not say by the general public, but by competent judges. Already we can look forward to the day when the recognition of the last five quartets will leave the Op. 59 as far behind as Op. 59 has left Op. 18. To-day the Op. 59 are called the 'great' Beethoven quartets, soon the Op. 127, 130, 131, 132 and 135 works will be called the 'very great' quartets, and these titles will undoubtedly be quite exact, since the score of the longest Op. 18 quartet is thirty pages in length, the longest in Op. 59 is thirty-eight, and the longest of the last, sixty-two. Certainly one cannot quarrel with their arithmetic.

A minute though not very comprehensive study of Op. 59 follows, of which one passage only need be quoted to show with what little insight he had studied them :

What then is one to expect to find in a quartet or in any elaborately constructed instrumental composition? Melodic and harmonic interest, individuality, feeling, construction, development and scoring, in all of which the excellence depends, so far as a string quartet is concerned, upon the ability to write within the technical capacity of the various instruments, and above all for the violin.

He concludes with the following anecdote :

M. Damcke once did me the honour of inviting me to a *matinée musicale*, at which the artists were M. Maurer and his two sons, and a violist, M. Albrecht, of the Italian orchestra. I had never heard a finer quartet of players in St. Petersburg. The first piece was Beethoven's quartet in F, Op. 59, No. 1. At the conclusion of the work my host asked me my opinion of the last movement; I replied that Beethoven's treatment of this unfortunate little Russian melody, overwhelmed as it was by a veritable flood of German scholarship, gave me the impression of one of our peasants dressed up in a doctor's wig and gown, left with his beard still untrimmed, his hide boots, and his moujik's rough hair showing through the wig. It offended both taste and common sense. Glinka, in *Kamarinskaïa*, showed one how Russian themes should be used. So far from being turned out for this uncompromising criticism, I discovered that both M. L. Maurer, himself a talented composer, M. Damcke, an enlightened critic, and the three virtuosi, M. Albrecht and M. Maurer's two sons, were one and all of the opinion that my remark was perfectly justified! [1]

Ulibishev's prediction of the recognition destined for the last five quartets was to be actually fulfilled, though without its ironical implication. The greatest of the Beethoven quartets were soon to come into their own. The *Revue philosophique et religieuse* of 1st August 1856 contains a remarkable article by J.-B. Sabatier, entitled *Les derniers Quatuors de Beethoven*; unfortunately the author extols them at the expense of the Op. 59:

The opening of the quartet in F is overburdened by the accompaniment (!) and the design seems too involved. The composer has not yet found his final manner; later he simplifies the exposition, as the slow movements of the Op. 127 and 135 quartets testify. Here the theme recurs too frequently, and in the accompanying parts there is still a certain heaviness and lack of individuality which mar the effect; in the later quartets this quality altogether disappears.

In 1860 there was published an article called *Les dernières confidences du génie de Beethoven*. The author was a priest, the Abbé Lacuria, a keen and enlightened amateur musician and an extraordinarily clever executant. In speaking of the Op. 59 he strikes a new note of criticism:

The three quartets of Op. 59 are of the same period as the B flat Symphony (Op. 60), composed at the time when Beethoven was hoping to marry Juliette (*sic*). These Op. 59 quartets

---

[1] Ulibishev, *Beethoven, ses critiques et ses glossateurs*, Paris, Gavelet, 1857, pp. 257–67.

are the most perfect works that exist in the chamber-music genre. As one listens one is inspired by the new life and hope that break out of the music, and fill even his moments of gloom with radiance. One is constantly reminded of his letters to Juliette.

The first quartet of Op. 59, No. VII, in F, recalls this passage: ' My waking thoughts fly to you, my beloved; sometimes in happiness, sometimes in sadness, I await whatever destiny the gods may have in store for us; your love makes me at once the happiest and unhappiest of men.' How vividly this recalls the first movement—' My thoughts fly to you, my beloved.' And could there be found a more perfect picture of changing sun and shadow than the *Allegro scherzando*, upon which the heavy melancholy of the *Adagio* falls like the weariness of deferred hope? ' I have resolved to wander far away, until I can fly back to your arms.' And the Russian theme of the finale rises like a prayer for patience: ' I await whatever destiny the gods may have in store for us ! '

In the second quartet of the group, No. VIII, in E, only the first movement breathes an atmosphere of uneasiness; the *Adagio* is filled with a happiness so serene and pure that the soul wanders at peace in an earthly paradise; figures irradiated by the sunset-glow seem to pass before one, loth to leave, until with the last murmurs of the 'cello they fade away into the distance. . . . One of Beethoven's most remarkable qualities is a wealth of imaginative power, and a unique originality which makes his work not only unlike any other composer's, but even unlike any other from his own hand, with the result that many of his compositions are isolated and incomparable, without even a family likeness. The first movement of the C sharp minor sonata, dedicated to Juliette (Op. 27), is of this type, and the slow movement of the symphony in A.

Another such movement is found in the third quartet of Op. 59, No. IX, in C, the *Allegretto* substituted for the usual slow movement. It is a dream fantasy which carries us away to Elfland on the wings of an autumn night wind.

Above a beating *pizzicato* on the 'cello the violin gives out a melody in the minor, clear and passionless, moonlit. It dies away in the *pizzicati* of the bass, like a flickering sigh borne on the breeze; as one or other of the instruments takes up the song, the other voices rise in little passing gusts of melody, and fade away, while the persistent *pizzicato*, like a far-away fairy harp, casts a shadow of mystery over the scene. A little phrase in the major passes from part to part, thrown hither and thither among the instruments, and finally gives place to the long-drawn minor melody of the opening; it dies into distant silence, lulled to rest on the last fading vibrations of the harp. . . . It is one of those movements that, once heard, leaves an unforgettable impression.

The beautiful finale of the quartet is the only music that rivals the overture to the *Magic Flute*.[1]

II. *Op.* 74.

The Op. 74 quartet was written only two years after the Op. 59; nevertheless, it reveals a fundamental change of thought as well as of form. Here we find none of the outward brilliance of effect, the deliberate objectivity, and pure technical beauty of the three quartets of the earlier group. Here one sees mirrored in the music the dark places of the artist's own soul; here at last Beethoven finds expression for all his pent-up love and sorrow, plumbing the depths of his unsatisfied longings, laying bare the secret beauty of his inmost thoughts. At the same time he evokes a fuller expressive richness from the genre of the quartet than ever hitherto. In the study of Op. 59 it has been remarked how one sometimes feels a sense of constraint imposed upon Beethoven's magnificent imaginative flights, a limitation of tonal capacity, as though the extent of their range could only be realized to the full by the vast resources of an orchestra. In Op. 74 there is so perfect a union between the thought of the artist and its expression through the medium of the string quartet, that one can imagine no other medium to take its place.

The Xth quartet, Op. 74, in E flat, sprang from a twofold inspiration: the intimate consciousness of his tenderest and saddest emotions, and the resolute determination

---

[1] Lacuria, *Les dernières confidences du génie de Beethoven* (reprinted in the *Occident*, October 1903).

to resist the bitter realities of life. But no longer does Beethoven waver between these two guiding influences as though hesitating on the brink of decision; with the realization of what life henceforward has to offer, uncertainty disappears, and at this spiritual crisis he accepts without flinching the inevitable struggle that was always to be his part.

For this reason the Xth quartet is significant as marking a milestone in Beethoven's creative life. Thirteen or fourteen years later, in the Op. 127 quartet, the conflict between these opposing forces is renewed, but never with greater poignancy and bitterness than now.

Quartet No. X, Op. 74 (in E flat major).

$\begin{cases} \textit{Poco adagio} & (\textit{♩} = 60). \\ \textit{Allegro} & (\textit{♩} = 84). \end{cases}$

$\textit{Adagio ma non troppo} \quad (\textit{♪} = 72).$

$\begin{cases} \textit{Presto} & (\textit{♩.} = 100). \\ \textit{Più presto} & (\textit{♩.} = 100). \end{cases}$

$\begin{cases} \textit{Allegro con variazioni} & (\textit{♩} = 100). \\ \textit{Un poco più vivace} & (\textit{♩} = 76). \\ \textit{Allegro} & (\textit{♩} = 84). \end{cases}$

The early sketches for this quartet in E flat date from 1809, and the work was finished in the same year.

The period of untroubled calm in which the Op. 59 quartets were written lasted for several years. Beethoven was secure and happy in the faithful love of his ' Immortal Beloved ', his constant inspiration and talisman against despair; his material prosperity was ensured by satisfactory agreements with the publishers, and by the patronage of his Imperial pupil, the Archduke Rudolph. Not yet quite isolated from the rest of the world by his increasing deafness, as he lay dreaming on the banks of the stream which runs through the valley of Heiligenstadt he could still hear, as he told Schindler, the song of 'the orioles, the quails, the nightingales, and the cuckoos who helped him to compose' the wonderful slow movement of the Pastorale.[1]

In 1809 clouds began to cast their shadow over this pathetic serenity. After the battle of Ratisbon the French army marched towards Vienna, having driven back the Austrian army to the Danube. The Court fled from the city, and Beethoven found himself deserted by his Imperial patrons, stranded penniless and suffering, in the clamour and distress of the siege and final surrender of the town.[2] Hidden in a cellar during the roar of the bombardment, in terror lest it should make his deafness worse, with his head buried in cushions to deaden the noise, Beethoven only left his refuge to remain a prisoner in a town for two months under siege, where food was scarce and dear, and the heat almost unendurable.

Other worries were added to his physical distress, since he was prevented by force of circumstances from seeing Thérèse Brunswick during this time. This year he composed for her the sonata in F sharp major, Op. 78, in which one can sense not only the agony of suspense and separation, but a dim foreboding of the trouble in store for him in the breaking of his engagement. An overwhelming melancholy possessed him. In a letter to Thérèse (7th July 1806) he cries: 'O God, why must one be separated from one so beloved? Yet my life in Vienna now is a wretched existence. . . .'

[1] Schindler, *Biographie von Ludwig van Beethoven, Erster Theil*, p. 154.

[2] It was on the occasion of the departure of the Archduke Rudolph that Beethoven wrote the Op. 81 sonata, *Les Adieux, l'Absence, le Retour*. The words 'The Farewell, Vienna, 4th May, 1809, the date of the departure of H.I.H. my honoured Archduke, Prince Rudolph', are written against the first movement; and against the finale, which must have been written after peace was signed, is written 'The Return of H.I.H. my honoured Archduke, Prince Rudolph, 30 Jan., 1810'.

And when he sent to his friend Gleichenstein the first copy of the sonata for 'cello and piano, Op. 69, which had just been published, he scrawled under the dedication the words: ' *Inter lacrymas et luctum* '—amid sorrow and tears.

It was amid sorrow and tears that he wrote the quartet of Op. 74. The four movements of this work were composed in the order in which they are printed. The preliminary sketches fill thirty pages of his notebook, ten for the first movement alone (pages 65–75), and twenty for the other three (pages 76–95). The first ten pages reveal ideas practically in their final form; it is probable that this complex work was sketched out before in other books now lost, perhaps even before the war, and it was not till after the final surrender of Vienna in July 1809, when the inhabitants were at last allowed to go out of the town, that Beethoven felt able to take up his work again. The sketches are full of passing interruptions in the form of short studies in chord progressions, or personal memoranda, such as ' *Vom 4ten an wird des Bedienten Kostgeld wieder bezahlt* ' (After the 4th the servant's wages are due again), or studies for the *Lied*, Op. 82, No. 2, or the beginning of a movement in florid counterpoint, bearing the words: ' *Denkmal Johann Sebastian Bachs Quintett* ' (Quintet to the memory of J.-S. Bach), showing Beethoven's intention of writing some time a work in honour of Bach; there are outlines of the Sonatina, Op. 79, ideas for a *Concertstück* for the piano in G minor, various unfinished fragments, attempts at a setting of Goethe's song *Freudvoll und leidvoll*, and at a transcription for solo piano of the choral fantasia, and, finally, endless studies for the Sonata in E flat, Op. 81, *Les Adieux*.[1]

In the margin of the page containing these studies Beethoven wrote ' *Beim goldnen Kreutz* ' (At the Golden

[1] It is strange how fond Beethoven was of writing in the heroic tonality of E flat, during this year of war, 1809. Actually, he wrote in

Cross); it was the name of an inn on the outskirts of Vienna where he used often to go, and where he may have stayed to work at his quartet, when at last the people in Vienna were allowed to leave the town.

He decided on the theme for the *Adagio* almost at once, but was evidently uncertain of the working out and development, altering and correcting ten times before it took its final shape. The opening of the third movement was originally to have been thus:

Ex. 115 *b*.

For the middle section, *più presto quasi prestissimo*, two themes (Ex. 116) were outlined, different in form from the final theme, though rhythmically the same. It should be noticed how Beethoven finally employed the opening bars of the second, in a contrary movement:

Ex. 116.

this key a *Trio*, Op. 70, No. 2 (dedicated to Countess Erdoedy), the fifth piano concerto, Op. 73, the Op. 74 quartet, the Op. 81 sonata, and other works.

The theme for the variations was several times altered, though very simple in character. The original study :

Ex. 117.

was entirely different from the final form of the melody, which grew slowly into shape after many corrections ; and many further alterations still were devoted to the variations.

The original manuscript of the E flat quartet belongs to E. Mendelssohn-Bartholdy in Berlin, and is dated 1809 ; [1] on one of the pages in the third movement are written the words : *Partitur von Egmont, gleich* (sic) *an Goethe* (score of music for Goethe's *Egmont*). The music of *Egmont* was not composed until 1810, evidence that Beethoven was already thinking of it while writing the quartet. Certainly, sketches for a setting of Clara's song, *Freudvoll und leidvoll*, are also to be found scattered among these for the Op. 74 quartet, but there is nothing to connect that work, a vocal duet with piano accompaniment, with Beethoven's music for *Egmont*, written in the following year.

Op. 74 appeared in December 1810, under the following title : ' *Quatuor pour deux violons, viola et violoncelle*, composé et dédié à son Altesse le Prince régnant de Lobkowitz, Duc de Raudnitz, par L. V. Beethoven. Propriété des éditeurs. Œuv. 74, à Leipzig chez Breitkopf et Härtel.'

I. *Poco adagio, Allegro.* This is the second time that Beethoven precedes the first movement with an introduction (see the IXth quartet, in C, Op. 59). As a rule,

[1] Between February and October of 1809 Beethoven composed the following works : March in F major (no *opus* number) ; Concerto in E flat, Op. 73 ; Sonata, Op. 81 ; Overture, Op. 116 ; Lied, Op. 82, No. 2 ; Variations in D, Op. 76 ; *Lieder*, Op. 75, Nos. 5 and 6 ; Transcription for solo piano of the Choral Fantasia, Op. 80; first movement of the Sonatina, Op. 79 ; Fantasia, Op. 77.

he leaps at the first bar to the very heart of his theme. The Introduction here is deeply significant and far more closely bound to the *Allegro* that follows than in the IXth quartet. It is a short passage of no defined form, but eloquent of Beethoven's state of emotional ecstasy, his aspirations and desires. For this reason, as well as for its purely musical value, the Introduction is quoted entire. The veil between the spirit of the artist and our understanding is for a moment drawn aside, and we stand on the threshold of a comprehension that will enable us to divine the secret of the later quartets, and to penetrate the mystery of self-revelation that darkens his work from Op. 127 to the end. Op. 74 is the key to the soul of Beethoven.

Ex. 118.

The wistful questioning figure that forms the theme slips through the web of tone again and again, in bars 1, 3, 7, and 8, on the viola in bar 14, then on the first violin, and finally three times on the 'cello, where it rises from A flat to E flat and G flat. A comparison of this deeply-felt Introduction with the brilliant surface cleverness of the first movement of the quartet in F, Op. 18, shows up in sharp relief the complete change of style, the flawless control and use of technique, that Beethoven acquired in maturity for the expression of his deepest inspiration. The passage is extraordinary for its boldly effective modulations, notably in the tenth bar where the A flat is taken as the subdominant, for the individuality of feeling, the effortless linking of phrase with phrase. Its emotional subtlety and its advanced modern technique make this music for all time. Moreover it is rare even in Beethoven's work to find so perfect a unity of design, and so unbroken a continuity as exists here. One is reminded of Schumann's comment on the Introduction to Schubert's symphony in C: ' It leads on without a break to the first movement; one finds oneself there without realizing quite how it happened.'

This short section is so eloquent that Beethoven's own expression-mark—*espressivo*—written against the eleventh and twelfth bars seems hardly necessary; it breathes conviction as a masterpiece of consummate art, above all for its harmonic depths—' harmonic abysses', von Lenz described them—its surging aspirations, which rise out of the music to return time after

time upon an unexpected subdominant, and the tension
of the slow chromatic ascent in the concluding bars.
The *Allegro* is linked to the Introduction by a series
of vigorous chords, in contrast to its heavy melancholy.
'Beethoven has never written anything more characteristic than this passage, with its sudden leap of energy
from a clinging languor; and nothing more charac-

Ex. 119.

teristic than this simple *motif*, which, analysed, is only
a variation of the common chord.' [1]

The figure which these chords form is not to be the
principal subject; this appears at the third bar on the
first violin, bringing back the mood of the Introduction, but calmer and more restrained, a tender little
theme rocking upon an accompaniment in Beethoven's
favourite manner. (The idiomatic return to the subdominant reappears, and at the fifth bar one almost
seems to hear again the theme of the *Adagio*.) The
motif stretches over eight bars, above a statement in
augmentation of the ascending chord figure; in turn
this figure is heard *pizzicato*, first on the viola and 'cello,
then on the two violins, moving freely beneath a persistent accompaniment on the other instruments. The
effect of this part-writing is curiously harp-like, and it

[1] J. Chantavoine, *Beethoven*, p. 143.

is for this reason, and because the passage is repeated
several times in the course of the first movement, that
the Op. 74 is sometimes called the Harp Quartet.

The *pizzicato* passage is broken by an abrupt inter-
jection (Ex. 119), which leads on to the bridge passage,
or rather, to the two bridge passages; of these the first
is thematically derived from the figure that accompanies the principal subject, and the second opens
gaily with :

Ex. 120.

The semiquaver scales in the lower parts pass to the
second violin and then to the first, rising and falling
with increasing vigour to a point where the first violin
gives out the second theme, a suave and tender melody :

Ex. 121.

It floats serenely above the persistent rolling semiquavers of the bass, affording a contrast that typifies
the duality of inspiration in the work, the psychological
clash of intimate emotions against bitter reality. After
a short contemplative episode, the defiant mood gains
the upper hand, expressed in a climax of horn-like
sonority :

Ex. 122.

Almost at once the four voices shrink into themselves,
and are lost in a sudden *diminuendo* conclusion.

This first section is repeated, and the chord figure,
after the conclusion in B flat, breaks out *fortissimo* in
G major, opening the middle section. The principal
theme in G is first divided between the violins, and then
heard in unison, modulating to the tonality of C, and
is worked out in an entirely individual way. As the
inner parts develop a semiquaver accompaniment,
sempre forte, the outer parts give out a fragment of the
second theme (Ex. 123).

The spirit of the artist clouds over with apprehension
and gloom as the chord figure, its rhythmic insistence gone, creeps like a dark shadow upon the scene ;
the first violin moves by intervals from C through a
rising octave, echoed mournfully by the 'cello, while with
unabated vigour the menacing semiquaver figure per-

sists in the inner parts. Dropping down an octave to
the original C, the first violin falters, and twice moves
down a semitone, to C flat and then to B flat, where
it stays for five bars before moving by intervals to B flat
an octave lower; the 'cello makes tentative efforts to
ascend as if to reach the faltering voice above, but
it descends finally in a tired echo of the first violin.
The passage is heavy with a sense of impending anguish
and sorrow, beset by the interminable beating rhythm

Ex. 123.

of the inner parts; yet this drifting obscurity is dispersed as though by the sunlight breaking through, as
the rising harp-like *pizzicato* returns once more. ' The
significance of this delicate *motif* is now clearly revealed,' so T. Helm imagines, ' and we see Beethoven
as the psalmist, harp in hand, uttering a prayer for
divine succour in distress, and singing a song of adora-
tion to the All-Highest.'
Beneath a long-sustained chord on the first violin
there grows out of the harp *motif* a long soaring *pizzicato* moving continually upwards, first in crotchets,
then in crotchet triplets, in quavers, and finally in
quaver triplets, at which point the *pizzicato* gives place
to an *arco* passage of broad design, and a pedal point leads

crescendo to a statement of the original chord figure
which introduces the final section of the movement.
In accordance with the rules of sonata form, this third
section follows the plan of the first, though with several
striking changes. Before the entry of the harp *motif*,
for instance, the link-bars are extended, and the *motif*
itself stretches over twice as many bars, introducing
interesting modulations. The second subject and the
development that follows, originally in B flat, are here
in E flat, according to rule. Following a series of
strange and lovely *pianissimo* progressions from E flat
through C minor to G minor, then again to C minor,
the final section leads to a *Coda* that reaches symphonic
heights :

Ex. 124.

The ' psalmist's rapturous song ', as Helm describes
it, reaches its culminating point in this magnificent
section. The three lower instruments pick out the harp
motif in an increasingly emphatic *pizzicato*, contending
on a broken chord of the diminished seventh against
a semiquaver figure in ascending and descending
arpeggi on the first violin—one of the most brilliant
passages for the violin in existence (Ex. 125).
The tension is relaxed for a second, when the chord

is again established in the lower parts, still against the *arpeggi* of the first violin, and the harp *motif* merges into the original form of the principal subject. There it gives birth to a new melody (on the second violin):

Ex. 125.

When at last the dominant seventh of E flat is reached the strains of a great organ seem to break upon the ear. At this point the climax of the *Coda* is attained, yet there is no flagging of interest in the succeeding bars to the conclusion. . . . After firmly establishing the tonality of E flat, Beethoven brings back the *pizzicato* harp *motif*, heard on the second violin and the 'cello simultaneously in contrary movement, beneath a long-held chord on the first violin and viola. In these concluding bars every note seems to release an infinity of emotion, every bar seems charged with the vital force which has triumphed over the despair of the introductory *Adagio*, and dispelled its haunting melancholy.

II. *Adagio ma non troppo.* In his work entitled *Beethoven, Liszt, Wagner*, published in Vienna in 1874, L. Nohl, with signal injustice, accuses Beethoven of being often 'sentimental'. 'In most of his works', he says, 'he never gets away from the stale flavour of sentimentality that mars the music of to-day.' But it is no longer possible to misconstrue the work of the artist who once finely wrote that 'music must spring like a flame from the heart of a man'. If one were looking for traces of sentimentality in Beethoven's music one could perhaps find it in the slow movement of Op. 74, but of a quality so noble and sincere as to transcend criticism, and to lift it out of all possibility of comparison with the false emotion and sentimental hypocrisy found so often in the work of Beethoven's successors, and even in Mendelssohn. The *Adagio* of the quartet in E flat is one of the unbroken melodies that characterize the slow movements of the last period. From the point of view of strict analysis this falls into its three parts, constructed on a principal theme, a second theme, and including a middle section; nevertheless these melodies are woven together into so unified and homogeneous a whole that the removal of even one bar would mar the significance of the whole movement.

The first twenty-four bars, quoted here entire, afford an example of this continuous development:

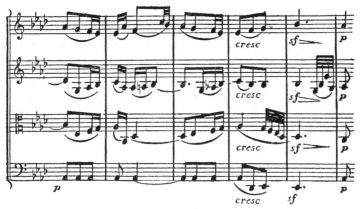

Ex. 126.

The melancholy of this opening passage is borne out in every progression, every slurred note and suspension ; it is felt in the shrill intensity of bars 13 and 14, in the drooping stretch of melody in bars 15–17 before it takes breath in the eighteenth bar. Marx said of this opening section that 'every note is a tear'. As the first phrase reaches its conclusion the second theme rises without any bridge passage, moving, not to the dominant key, but down to the tonic minor :

Ex. 127.

At this point the agony of grief reaches its apex ; through thirty-six bars it twists and turns in strange modulations, sinking into silence, spurred on by sudden impulses, finally submerged ; with the return of the principal theme Beethoven realizes in the music the gradual lifting of this bitter despair as it loses itself in the apathy of the first melody. The continuous melodic period (Ex. 126) now recurs with new vigour, accompanied by rapid triplet figures in the inner parts.

The conclusion of the period on the chord of A flat is not followed this time by a return of the second theme in A flat minor, but by a middle section in D flat minor :

Ex. 128.

This broad melody develops over sixteen bars and
ends in the key of A flat,[1] followed by a statement of
the first theme, a sad *pianissimo*, in the tonality of A flat
minor. After four more bars it breaks into the dominant of F minor with a repetition of the moving phrase
of bars 13 and 14 of Ex. 126, now in a rousing *fortissimo* unison in all four parts (Ex. 129), a phrase of
considerable importance in the interpretation of the
movement. This four-note unison is, as it were, the
turning-point where the spirit of the musician gathers a
sudden strength to cast away despair and find consolation.
The short *fortissimo* outburst relaxes into a chromatic

---

[1] This section of the development is not unlike that in the *Adagio*
of the VIIth quartet. Compare the corresponding entry of the theme
in the *Adagio* of the VIIth quartet, and from bar 73 onwards.

triplet movement, at first of a sombre cast, in which as
the voices slip into place the first violin begins the
soothing strain of the principal theme. This third entry
of the theme is even more full of movement and life than
the second; the melody is at first in its original simple
form, later in a demisemiquaver variation; the second
violin accompanies in *staccato* demisemiquavers, the

Ex. 129.

viola in *pizzicato* semiquavers, and the 'cello in short
notes on the second semiquaver of each beat. As the
first violin takes up the demisemiquaver variation, the
second violin abandons its *staccato* accompaniment for
a continuous counterpoint, followed by an appealing
little phrase drawn from the first theme (bar 18 of
Ex. 126), given alternatively by the first violin and by
the inner parts:

Ex. 130.

Beneath the melody flutters a little demisemiquaver
figure, recalling the harp *motif* of the first movement.

Like the memory of a forgotten sorrow, the second theme in A flat reappears, wistful, as though apprehensive of a return of the hours of bitterness, and in reassuring response the 'cello, for the first time, murmurs in its lowest register a fragment of the principal subject, which is taken up by the other voices in broken phrases, finally leaping note by note from one part to another through the entire range of the instruments until it disappears. (The F flat twice repeated on the viola, imparting a weird tinge of harmony to the score, gives the distant effect of a clarinet.) A last shadow of the theme slips from the 'cello, and spaced chords of A flat die away to a *morendo* conclusion.

III. *Presto*. After Beethoven's expression in the *Adagio*, with an eloquence that he had never before attained, of the bitterness and despair that beset his whole life, we find him, by strange contrast, giving rein in the succeeding movement to a creative impulse that radiates force and vitality.

The abrupt turn of phrase of the *Presto* theme recalls the *Allegro* of the C minor symphony. Rising at first through intervals the same as in the chord *motif* of the first movement, it sinks to the dominant in a fluttering rhythm borrowed from the accompaniment:

Ex. 131.

This first phrase of eight bars is repeated, and leads
without a break to the second ; the *motif* is hammered
out eight times in unison by all the four instruments,
with a fire and intensity that only Beethoven could
achieve. Suddenly the first violin breaks away from
this clamour, and leaps triumphantly upon the tonality
of D flat, as it were taking it by assault. A modulation
to F minor is followed by another descent bursting
with showers of sparks upon the original theme ; it
passes to C minor and to G minor, the dominant of
C minor, and to the dramatic opening of a new section :

Ex. 132.

The second violin keeps up incessantly the rhythm
of the original theme, while a disjointed *motif* appears
on the first violin, and the 'cello leaps from low G,
through alternate intervals of a tenth to B, and an

eleventh to C, dropping each time back to the dominant, and relieving the monotony of the accompaniment.
After a fleeting modulation to G minor, C is taken as
the dominant of F, and the tonality of F minor is established ; C is hammered out in the bass in the original
rhythm, while the dramatic passage reappears in altered
form : the violins at the octave give out the disjointed
motif, and the rising intervals of a tenth and an eleventh
are now played by the viola, on a dominant bass. A
modulation to C minor recalls the fundamental tonality
of E flat ; the theme descends in a *diminuendo*, arrested
for a second on the dominant of C minor, as though
shaken with emotion and on the brink of despair. . . .
But this second section is to be repeated, and the defiant
spirit of the Master springs to new being in the beating
of the theme in four-voice unison ; before the imagination reappear in succession the pictures of irresolution,
triumph, resignation, and finally the trembling agony
of the concluding bars. . . .

It is terminated abruptly by a *forte* chord of C major,
leading straight away to the energetic opening theme
of the *Trio*, given by the 'cello (*più presto quasi prestissimo*) : [1]

Ex. 133.

Several bars later a *Canto fermo*-like melody appears
on the viola, a melody ' without precedent in Beethoven's work ', as Marx describes it. Further still, the
first violin takes the theme in a high register, and the
second violin, the viola, and ultimately the 'cello pursue

[1] *Si ha s'immaginar la battuta di* 6/8 is written here in the score.
(Two of these 3/4 bars should be taken as one and compressed into
the *tempo* space of 6/8.)

a steady counterpoint beneath it. The unhurrying *Canto fermo* melody is heard, first in the lower, and then in the upper parts, moving up and down the scale in contrary motion to the energetic crotchet theme: the whole passage breathes unshakable conviction, a spiritual force that recalls the work of J.-S. Bach; rarely is the inspiration of the two masters so closely akin as here. Marx offers the comment: ' In the *Presto* of the Op. 74 Beethoven's abundant energy and power seem literally to break their bounds, so that he can barely bring himself to hold them in.' After the *Presto* proper, in two twice-repeated sections, there follows the long *Più presto*, worked out on a unique plan. The *Presto* returns with a repetition of the first section only; then the *Più presto* again and, finally, for the last time, the *Presto*,[1] extended in conclusion by a forty-five bar *Coda*. Marx finds in this *Presto* movement an interpretation of a decisive moment in Beethoven's life, and explains the unusual succession of repetitions, in the following way:

There can be no doubt that in this persistently recurring expression of confident hope Beethoven deliberately indicated his mastery over uncertainty and despair; and no fresh theme could have created the sense of power conveyed by the repetition, time after time, of one *motif*. To this end Beethoven was forced to repeat the *Trio* section (*Più presto*) several times, and the re-entry of the principal section (*Presto*) followed each time as a natural consequence.

The *Coda* begins at the point where the hesitating *tremolo* figure, hitherto heard as an accompaniment in the conclusion of the *Presto*, appears in the bass (Ex. 134). The 'cello murmurs the figure *ppp*, and through a veiled obscurity the key of A flat breaks like a sudden glimmer of light; above the beating of the 'cello the

---

[1] In performance the *Trio* is usually only played once, and the principal section only once repeated; nevertheless from a psychological standpoint more importance attaches to these repetitions, specially marked by Beethoven, than in the E minor quartet, Op. 59.

rhythm of the original theme is heard, slowly dispersing the gloom in sunlight. . . .

It is in the same way that the third movement of the C minor symphony seems to sink, towards the end, into a mysterious and impenetrable shadow, suddenly flooded with the splendour of the finale. . . . In Op. 74, however, the finale is of a less brilliant type.

IV. *Allegretto con variazioni*. Marked ' *attacca il se-guente* ' in the score, the theme of the last movement follows after the *Presto* without a break, a smooth, flowing melody, instead of the expected outburst of

Ex. 134.

brilliance. Beethoven develops six variations on the theme (ten, if the different sections of the sixth are to be considered separately).

The melody is in two detached phrases : in the first, the rhythmic figure ♩. ♪♪ is used seven times, in the second, ten times. Each phrase is repeated once, and the variations follow. In this movement Beethoven is still influenced by the twofold inspiration that dominates the whole work, the expression at one time of confident vigour, at another of despondency ; but while the alternating moods effect in each variation a sharp contrast to the one before, there is no longer any sense of clashing forces. The *Presto* sufficed to reveal the hard-won triumph of the artist over the man, and it is in perfect peace of spirit, in the calm after the storm, that

Beethoven turns to the composition of this incomparable movement, written, like the finale of the first Op. 59 quartet, in pure ecstasy of musical creation.

(*a*) The first variation has an air of almost boisterous confidence, the caprice of a spirit tried by adversity. Beethoven here breaks no new ground, confining himself entirely within the classical form. The parts move in imitative counterpoint, and it cannot be denied that the part-writing, alternating between similar and contrary movement, is sometimes angular and even crude.

(*b*) The second variation possesses a quality of soft tenderness, more appealing than the rude strength of the first. The viola part gives it its character, a flowing triplet melody that encircles the entire variation like a wreath.

(*c*) The third effects an immediate and vivid contrast. Florid figuration of the theme appears in hammering semiquavers on the 'cello and second violin, separated by the interval of a tenth; breathless with the effort to keep pace, the first violin and the viola mark the off-beats in short quavers until the semiquaver figure finally extends to all the parts.

(*d*) The fourth variation is most closely allied to the original theme both in feeling and treatment. Leisurely and untroubled, the first violin sings the melody in

Ex. 135.

sustained crotchets above the soft murmur of a quaver figure in the lower voices. Harmonically, this variation affords a glimpse of Beethoven's last period, especially in these advanced progressions (Ex. 135).

(e) The fifth variation is akin to the third, though here expressed with still more abundant energy. A leaping *arpeggio* design on the first violin recalls a passage in J.-S. Bach's Violin Concerto in A, from the first *Allegro* (Ex. 136). Below, the other voices provide a flexible accompanying figure whose rhythmic insistence in itself makes it a further variation of the upper part.

(f) The sixth variation, or rather, the first section of the sixth variation—since the continuity is from this point unbroken to the end—contains the germ of many different later developments, heralding the IXth symphony, and the music of Schubert and Schumann.

Ex. 136.

With its strange harmonic colouring its tendency is to leave the quartet idiom for that of the orchestra ; the 'cello triplets might well be written for drums, the interwoven harmonies of the upper instruments for wood-wind and horns.

At the opening of the second section there is an unusual transition from E flat to D flat, and to E flat again :

Ex. 137.

After the repetition of these first two sections the movement flows on without further interruption. The viola, followed by the violins, and at last the 'cello, seizes upon a fragment of the figure in bars 3–6 of Ex. 137, and gives it a new vigour as a theme in 4/8 *tempo* accompanied by a cross-rhythm in triplets, which ultimately gains the advantage, and sweeps the variation to a rapid conclusion. Out of the violin phrase :

Ex. 138.

grows first the following figure :

Ex. 139.

then :

Ex. 140.

and finally the figure of the concluding *Allegro, accele-rando e crescendo poco a poco* :

Ex. 141.

In this unison passage one recognizes the semiquaver figure of the third variation, and here its passionate significance is fully revealed. Four *piano* chords, after a fiery *fortissimo*, conclude the quartet.

III. *Op.* 95. '*Von Perlen baut sich eine Brücke . . .*' (Schiller.)

Quartet No. XI, Op. 95 (*in F minor*).

Allegro con brio   ($\downarrow$ = 92).
Allegretto ma non troppo   ($\downarrow$ = 66).
{ *Allegro assai vivace*   ($\downarrow\cdot$ = 96).
{ *Più allegro*   ($\downarrow\cdot$ = 80).
{ *Larghetto*   ($\downarrow$ = 56).
{ *Allegro agitato*   ($\downarrow\cdot$ = 92).
{ *Allegro*   ($\circ$ = 92).

Beethoven wrote the Op. 95 quartet in the year after the Op. 74, and the manuscript bears the date, October 1810 ; but it was not published till December 1816, and the *opus* number dates from that period. The year of 1810 brought Beethoven one of the keenest sorrows of his life, in the breaking of his engagement to Thérèse von Brunswick, for reasons that have never been explained, and which will probably always be shrouded in mystery. 'Love has deserted him. In 1810 he finds himself once more alone—but with a new glory . . .',[1] writes Romain Rolland. When Bettina Brentano went to see him in May, the agony of suffering he had gone through had made him a changed man, but without the bitterness of disillusionment. He had gained increased knowledge of his own power, and his own suffering evoked a divine pity for all men.

This sense of goodwill to the whole human race flows out of his music : ' a truth deeper than all wisdom and philosophy'.—' Like the glow of rich red wine, music irradiates inspiration,' he exults, ' and I, Bacchus incarnate, will give humanity this wine to drink and drown its sorrow. . . . No evil fate can touch my music; he who divines its secret is freed from the unhappiness that haunts the whole world of men.'[2]

Bettina Brentano was fascinated by this spiritual power. She writes to Goethe :

When I am near him the world slips away—I forget even you. I may be young to give an opinion, but I feel I cannot be wrong in saying that Beethoven is far in advance of modern thought. . . . One evening he took me to hear an orchestral rehearsal. I was alone in a box at the end of an immense empty hall in darkness; here and there shafts of sunlight broke through, with a thousand particles of dust dancing like tiny fairy creatures in a shining world. . . . Here I saw this wizard wield his baton. O Goethe! no prince or emperor was ever so conscious of the reality of his omnipotence, and the sense that he is the source of all power and strength. If I could grasp its significance as I can feel it, then no door of the mind would be closed to me. . . . One felt that a day must come, when, in a new and perfect existence, he would reappear as the Lord of the world!

His power is the strength of maturity; careless of everything, he abandons himself to his own fierce riot of emotion, without a thought for the world's little opinion, or the forms and conventions of others. What forces has he to guard against, to

---

[1] R. Rolland, *Beethoven*, Paris, E. Pelletan, 1909, p. 49.
[2] Bettina Brentano's letter to Goethe, 28th May 1810.

contend with, now that love and ambition are for ever buried? All that is left to him is the splendour and joy of his genius, and the craving to exercise his creative power and to spend it recklessly.

The VIIth and VIIIth symphonies are soon to follow (Op. 92 and 93), 'veritable orgies of fantastic creation, works in which Beethoven's nature is perhaps best revealed, wild and unrestrained (*aufgeknöpft*), with bursts of gaiety and passion, sudden contrasts, dazzling flashes of brilliance, and tremendous climaxes.' [1]

The quartet in F minor, Op. 95, the *quartett serioso*, affords a magnificent prelude to these works. Of the sixteen it is the most compressed in form and most full of Beethoven's characteristic effects of expressive contrast; passion and sorrow, despair and exultation follow each other with a quick succession that ' recalls in a sense the *Prometheus* of Goethe', as Chantavoine says, and is finally dispelled by a shout of joy.

A book of sketches dated 1810, belonging to the Royal Library in Berlin, contains work relating to all the movements of this quartet. Like those for the Op. 74, the studies for the first movement are very advanced; probably Beethoven began the preliminary outlines in a note-book now lost, and took it up here where he left off. It is even possible that this book only shows superficial alterations made to a work already finished somewhere else in its main lines. The next example is a study for the idea in bars 34 and onwards of the first movement (Ex. 142).

The semiquaver figure in the fourth bar of the example is the same in the manuscript as in the early editions, but the manuscript has also a variant reading in Beethoven's hand, where the semiquavers are replaced by triplets. The alteration was made later on the engraved plate of a later edition, and written in by Beethoven on the manuscript. The latest editions give the variant reading.

[1] Romain Rolland, *Beethoven*, p. 53.

At the eighth bar of this same sketch Beethoven notes down a hesitation about the sequence of keys, uncertain whether to move to D flat, C sharp, or D major.

The themes of the third and fourth movements are written straight in, almost without any corrections, and their development is fairly extended.

Among these studies are scattered various notes, themes for *Egmont*, the draft of a letter to Breit-

Ex. 142.

kopf and Härtel, ideas for a *fandango*, and songs of Goethe,[1] &c.

Between January and September 1810 Beethoven composed the following works : The music for *Egmont*, Op. 84 (without the overture); quartet in F minor, Op. 95 ; Songs of Goethe, Op. 83, Nos. 1 and 2 ; trio in B flat, Op. 97 (dedicated to the Archduke Rudolph) ; Songs of Goethe, Op. 83, No. 3.

The manuscript of Op. 95 is preserved in the Library at Vienna, and bears the following title :

Quartett serioso—1810 im Monat Oktober—Dem

---

[1] Among others the song *Trocknet nicht* (Cease not, tears of eternal love), that Beethoven sang to Bettina Brentano, the moment after he had written it, ' in a voice whose harsh intensity filled the listener with melancholy ' (quoted from a letter).

Herrn von Zmeskall gewidmet von seinem Freunde L. v. Bthvn, und geschrieben im Monat Oktober. (' *Quartett serioso*—October 1810—dedicated to Herr von Zmeskall by his friend Ludwig Beethoven, and written in the month of October.')

The quartet was published in parts by S.-A. Steiner & Co., in December 1816, under the title : *Eilftes Quartett für Zwey Violinen, Bratsche und Violoncelle. Seinem Freunde dem Herrn Hofsekretär Nik. Zmeskall von Domanovetz gewidmet von Ludwig van Beethoven. 95tes Werk. Eigenthum der Verleger. Wien, im Verlag von S.-A. Steiner und Comp.,* etc., etc. (' Eleventh quartet for two violins, viola, and 'cello, dedicated by Ludwig van Beethoven to his friend Nicolas Zmeskall von Domanovetz,[1] Court Secretary. Op. 95. Copyright of the publishers, S.-A. Steiner & Co., Vienna.')

[1] Nicolas Zmeskall von Domanovetz, Hungarian Court Secretary, was a fine musician, a 'cellist and composer, and, as one of Beethoven's closest friends, bore for him a boundless love and admiration. He was one of the intimate members of Prince Rasoumowsky's musical circle, and proved a providential aid to Beethoven on many occasions, and in the details of his daily life, going so far as to provide him with pens, pencils, and paper. Beethoven used to call him by the most familiar of nicknames, and was continually asking all sorts of little favours from him, in whimsical notes, like the following dated 1811 :

More than Excellency ! Please make me a present of some more quills ; I will send you a whole packet as soon as possible, so that you shan't be short yourself. You really should be decorated with the Grand Order of the Violoncello, in reward for your services !

Your affectionate friend,
BEETHOVEN.

(Chantavoine, p. 85.)

To Zmeskall, 16 December 1816.

Here is my dedication to you, dear Zmeskall, that I hope will be a cherished token of our long intimacy. Please accept it as a proof of my continuing love, and not as the end of a long strand of friendship, for I number you among my oldest friends in Vienna.

Goodbye, and keep away from rotten fortresses. An attack does more harm to them than to those in better repair.

Always your friend,
BEETHOVEN.

(Chantavoine, p. 148.)

L. Nohl considers the quartet in F minor the most intimately individual of all, and places it in the front rank of Beethoven's work; but, without any misconception of the work, one cannot honestly say that it deserves so high a place, for the Op. 95 has neither the symphonic grandeur of Op. 59, nor the depths of feeling of Op. 74, only to speak of those of the same period. It is characterized by an attempt to express a condensed idea in the simplest, though also the most expressive, 'thematic' form, and by restraint of method; technically the work is a pure piece of 'quartet' writing, and never oversteps the limits of the genre.

From this point of view there are in Op. 95 traces of a return to the style of some of the Op. 18 quartets, but this by no means implies that Beethoven had any idea of returning to his early manner. The form alone of the quartet in F minor refutes such a suggestion. Von Lenz remarks : ' The quartet in F minor bears at least one unmistakable mark of Beethoven's second period, in that the *Allegro* is written as a continuous whole, without repetitions,' and the model of sonata form is so little observed in this first movement, that if one were analysing it from that aspect one would find that the development section contains only twenty-two bars,[1] against fifty-nine in the exposition and fifty-nine in the recapitulation, as Jean Chantavoine comments. The less complex character of this work reveals only the intention of the composer to write a quartet on less symphonic lines than the foregoing, one unencumbered with obscure meaning—a quartet *serioso*, as he named it himself, where the purely musical aspect was to predominate. ' We find here the dramatist's economy of words,' says Helm, ' and the quartet in F minor is often reminiscent of the spirit, though obviously not of the form, of Gluck.'

I. *Allegro con brio*. This movement opens abruptly

[1] This development, moreover, is not constructed upon both principal subjects, but on the first subject only, divided into two parts.

with an agitated unison on the four instruments,[1] a
phrase forming the first half of the principal subject
of the quartet.

Ex. 143.

In the second half, three bars long, the voices rebound
against each other in a heavily accented rhythm. Upon
this twofold theme a vigorous development is to be
built up.

A sudden silence falls upon this abrupt statement of
the subject; then, in one of the unprepared modulations characteristic of the movement, the 'cello gives
the unison figure in the key of G flat beneath a held
chord on the other instruments; from G flat the
tonality returns to F, and the bridge passage begins
with a plaintive phrase on the first violin above long
ascending *arpeggi* on the 'cello. Through the recurring
beat of the unison figure low on the viola the phrase
slowly unfolds, rising at one point by the interval of
a ninth, but it is interrupted by a gradual *crescendo* of the
figure on the viola, leading to another unison statement
that bursts *forte* from all four voices. This time it is
followed by a second bridge passage, where the semi-

---

[1] In a comparison of this passage with the unison that opens the
first movement of the quartet in F, Op. 18, No. 1, and forms the main
theme, the advance in Beethoven's expressive power is clearly shown.

quavers of the unison persist, modulating to the tonality of D flat, in which the second subject, an urgent, agitated melody, is now heard.[1] A triplet figure on the viola gradually overwhelms the other voices and finally even the sustained crotchet melody on the first violin; beneath this prevailing rhythm the semiquaver unison *motif* is boldly asserted as though to dominate the other parts. The chromatic transition from A flat to A natural brings the tonality of A major; two rushing scales unite and break away, and the key of D flat, soft and appealing, returns through the following bar:

Ex. 144.

In this key Beethoven sets the unusually long cadence passage. The semiquaver unison *motif*, in its original form on the second violin and viola, in a modified form on the 'cello, accompanies a smoothly flowing melody on the first violin (Ex. 145), recalling the phrase in the first bridge passage.

An unprepared transition from D flat to D corresponds to the earlier transition from A flat to A, and establishes the tonality of D major; in a *fortissimo* scale the four voices unite in a unison, and, as if nothing had intervened, the key of D flat reappears in the appealing

[1] In the key of D flat, not in A flat, as strict sonata form would demand.

melody on the first violin. The cadence passage merges into the dominant, A flat, and spaced crotchets suggest a tentative hesitancy, immediately answered *fortissimo* by the 'cello, in the stormy *motif* with which the *Allegro* opens. With striking effect, the unprepared chord of F major is sustained by the three instruments above the unison *motif* in the bass, also in the major for the first time. (F is taken as the dominant of B flat minor.)

Ex. 145.

The development follows, a marvel of concise construction. Three times the original *motif* bursts from the 'cello (in the keys of F major, E flat, and B flat), and each time the viola responds in imitation followed by a semiquaver unison of the inner parts, while the first violin works out a crotchet design of diatonic broken chords. At this point the leaping rhythm of the second half of the principal subject returns, and a struggle ensues between it and the unison *motif*. In his treatment of these combined themes, so widely different in rhythm, which together form the principal subject, Beethoven reveals once more his perfect control of rhythmic design (Ex. 146).

After the vigorous twice-repeated outburst of this first bar, with the voices entering in quick succession,

a strange brooding stillness falls in the following bar
on a reiterated *pianissimo* A flat, bringing a chill foreboding of storm. The distant mutter of thunder rolls
from the bass; on the first violin flashes a vivid streak
of lightning, a shrill vibrating C, like the reiterated
A flat of several bars before; this time it is accom-

Ex. 146.

panied by the unison semiquaver *motif*, heavy and
muffled, on the two lower voices, and by a wailing
melody on the second violin. . . . The sombre mood of
the *Allegro* culminates at this point. Without any warning, the opening bars of the movement return, and with
the *forte* unison of the principal subject—a brilliant
effect enhanced by its suddenness—the concluding
section begins.

The leaping phrase that forms the second half of the principal theme is now completely set aside, and the energetic unison *motif* alone remains, dominating the rest of the piece. The second subject reappears again in D flat, and modulates to F major, the prevailing tonality of this third section. Abrupt and unprepared transitions to distantly related keys occur here, as in the exposition (F major here moves precipitately to G minor). Then the key of C appears as the dominant of F, as, just now, at the end of the cadence passage, A flat was taken as the dominant of D flat. Spaced crotchets suggest a tentative hesitancy. . . . Again it is the 'cello that responds with its burst of defiance; the *motif* is now in the key of D flat, no longer in F; and here a *Coda* begins in which one glimpses the bounding energy of the *Coriolanus* overture. Up to this point Beethoven has made full use of the unison *motif*, especially in developing its semiquaver rhythm; now the quaver rhythm is to take its turn. It rises and falls for nine bars, at one time in similar, at another in contrary motion, on the first violin and 'cello with a stubborn persistence, while the inner parts accentuate the weak beats and finally bring back, *fortissimo*, the semiquaver figure; enclosed by the outer parts, the semiquavers persevere to the end, as it were to meet their doom in the concluding chords. Gradually the tone falls away; together the three upper voices give the defiant unison *motif* above a broad phrase on the 'cello, descending to a *diminuendo* in which the movement sinks to a close.

II. *Allegretto ma non troppo*. After the passion of the *Allegro*, the *Allegretto* breathes an atmosphere of calm, 'apathetic and broken with sighs'. This slow movement in D major, described by Beethoven as *Allegretto ma non troppo*, in 2/4 time, provides ample evidence that in the whole range of Beethoven's work there is no gap or break in the continuity of style. It forms a link that bridges the gulf between the second and the last period, or between the two great periods into which the Master's work is perhaps better divided.[1]

From the first period it gathers the broad lines of its general formal construction, and in particular of its principal movement; the second is anticipated in certain modulations and melodic changes expressive of subtle and delicate spiritual influences, and in the entire middle *fugato* section. For this fugue is far from being strictly worked out, and has all the freedom of the fugues of Beethoven's later works, in which form is subordinated to the perfect expression of feeling.

Ex. 147.

[1] 'The division of Beethoven's work into two periods is clearly a logical arrangement; the first period, where his imagination is controlled by traditional and classical forms, and the second, where his imaginative force first extends, then breaks conventional form, and finally re-creates it, to express more perfectly the full breadth of inspiration.' (Liszt, *Franz Liszt's Briefe herausgegeben von La Mara*, Leipzig, Breitkopf, vol. i, p. 124.) See the Introduction.

The first four bars of the *Allegretto* open up to us the depths of the musician's soul; *mezza voce*, single notes on the 'cello sink awestruck, with silent footfall, as though entering a shrine . . .; serenely the melody is lifted above the murmur of the second violin and viola, coming to an end through an expressive development after nineteen bars. (See Ex. 147.)

This entire passage is tinged with a delicate harmonic colour, hovering perpetually between the tonalities of D major and G minor; no sooner is one of the keys established than a sudden modulation brings back the other, with an effect of constantly changing nuance.

The twelve following bars sustain the atmosphere of unclouded calm; a quaver figure taken from the concluding bars of the first melody appears with spasmodic interruptions, leading at last to an unadorned statement on the viola of a fugue theme of fantastic shape (' laborious ', according to Marx) and chromatic construction, that seems to contain a vague uneasiness; the theme comes to an indecisive finish after five bars, and after successive entries on the second violin, 'cello, and first violin, the fugue is established; there ensues a development involving plaintive phrases that echo the *Allegro* in A minor of the quartet in C (Op. 59, No. 3). The movement slackens, and as the melancholy phase exhausts itself, the mood of calm contemplation returns with the single notes of the 'cello that open the movement, receding noiselessly into the distance. Entering *pianissimo* (the original entry was *mezza voce*) they extend over twelve bars through three modulating sequences, sustained by long chords on the other instruments, and finally extinguished on the dominant chord of D. Uneasiness prevails again in the repeated *fugato* section, a troubled oppression accentuated by each successive entry of the subject. It is rather more elaborately presented than before, with contrapuntal figuration recalling the *Fugue* of the Eroica; its movement now has a certain impassioned vigour, a momentary sense of indignation almost, soon spent in an outburst as brief as it is violent.

The contemplative mood regains and establishes the ascendancy as the notes of the opening phrase drop slowly from the 'cello, *sotto voce*, in their original form, and the principal theme rises above a murmur below. This point marks the opening of the recapitulation section. The principal theme appears this time slightly modified; set an octave higher, it assumes a more ornate form, with an air of greater assurance. It develops as before to the sombre *fugato* theme which enters abruptly on the viola, followed by the other voices in uneasy indecision.

But this disquietude is evanescent; the *fugato* figure is lost in a modulation to F major, and disappears to allow the principal melody, intimate and tender, to pursue its way alone, until it, too, rises to a moment of exaltation and dies away; silent and awestruck, as though leaving a shrine, the single notes fall one by one from the 'cello and sink into oblivion on the tonic. This concluding passage carries the same serene inspiration that stamps the works of the last period.

III. *Allegro assai vivace, ma serioso.* A chord of the diminished seventh follows immediately after the last dying notes of the *Allegretto*, like that which concludes the slow movement of the F minor sonata, Op. 57 (*Appassionnata*). The chord is sustained in a long pause and seems to be indefinitely suspended before resolution, when suddenly the *Allegro vivace* bursts upon us, full of Beethoven's fierce energy, reawakened after the twilight of the slow movement with redoubled force. This *Allegro* takes the place of the *Scherzo*, ' being in *scherzo* time, even though without its rhythm, pace, and form '. Marx thinks rather fantastically that Beethoven might have called it a *menuet*, though it has a deeper expressive quality than the old *menuet*: Gluck alone, before Beethoven, could have written a work of this type.

Yet Beethoven here seems to be not so much looking

back to the spirit of Gluck as anticipating the spirit of the future; this individual rhythm, striking and clear-cut, is unmistakably modern; it lives again in the music of Weber, Schumann—especially in the symphony in C, for instance—and Wagner.

This rhythmic vigour makes itself apparent from the first two isolated bars of the opening, separated by rests, where the latent force of the movement seems to pause to gather strength. The theme develops with abrupt stops and sudden climaxes, invested with a heroic grandeur by the effect of an unprepared transition to D flat major, a return to F minor, and the rhythmic verve of the concluding bars. A diminished seventh chord struck *sforzando* on the up beat of the last bar, immediately after the tonic, reintroduces the opening bars and the repeat.

At the *seconda volta* a G flat accentuates the up beat, forming the point of departure of an *Alternativo* or *Trio* [1] of a character radically opposed to the principal section. As though from another world, the slow march of a solemn melody falls upon the ear, chanted by unseen voices to an accompaniment of harps.

Ex. 148.

[1] In his course of lectures at the *Schola* (1900), M. Vincent d'Indy observes that this G flat, for F sharp, is explained by the necessity for linking the tonality of this section to that of the one before (in D).

Beethoven has chosen here the form of accompanied chorale used in Op. 74, but in the expression of very different feeling. In Op. 74 the chorale of the C major *Prestissimo* irradiates glowing conviction, in the spirit of Handel or J.-S. Bach; here all is dark, with mysterious shadows. Chanted later by the 'cello, the theme passes with constantly changing harmonic inflections through D major and then B minor, sinking *diminuendo* to *pianissimo* depths, until it almost seems to merge into the quaver figure on the first violin. Infinitely remote, *pianissimo*, the stressed up beat makes itself heard, heralding the return of the principal section four bars later. This section works out as before, but without repetitions, until the last bar, which is repeated three times with the *sforzando* chords on the up beat changed each time, and reintroduces the *Alternativo* in the key, not of G flat, but of D major. Once more the hymn-like chorale extends, moving through momentarily disturbing modulations to G major, C minor, and F minor. At the conclusion of the chorale the return of the *Allegro* is anticipated, not by the *pianissimo* stressed up beat, but by the blending of the rhythm of the first part with a fragment of the chorale, leading to the third and last repetition of the principal section:

Ex. 149.

The introductory bars in C minor of the original
statement and of the first repeat are omitted, and with
quickened pace (*più allegro*) it plunges into the key of F
minor, and concludes the movement with a flourish
of characteristic vigour.

IV. *Larghetto—Allegretto agitato*. A short Introduction of several bars' length, purely modern in feeling—
foreshadowing Schumann's symphony in C, and perhaps
even *Tristan*—leads to the finale in 6/8 time (*Allegretto
agitato* in A minor). The first opening bars reveal the
passionate emotional content of the movement:

Ex. 150.

Towards the end, a sense of impending uneasiness is felt,
and with it, at a dramatic moment, the *Allegretto* opens.

The theme is composed of two separate *motifs* (I and II) and a concluding phrase. The first *motif* is based directly on the last notes of the introduction, and has an air of whimsical caprice, but *motif* II gives expression to a dreary desolation (in the first studies for it Beethoven marked it *languente*), and the concluding phrase to a still more poignant grief. The whole theme forms a plastic melody that lends itself perfectly to development. At the end of the first statement of the subject a beating semiquaver phrase on the first violin, urged to a climax by the other instruments, rushes wildly up to a sudden D flat, struck *fortissimo* by all four voices. In the following bar a strange effect is achieved by the minor chord of G–B flat in a long *pianissimo* sustained by the two violins. According to Helm's description : ' A thousand heroic scenes flash before the imagination, evoked by the passion and martial vigour of this passage. We see the figure of a soldier leaping wildly from the ranks to raise his standard on the enemy's walls, and shot dead in the moment of triumph.' It is, in fact, a sort of heroic chant, qualified by the contrasting plaintive character of *motif* II.

The struggle continues as the main theme of the movement reappears an octave lower, on the first violin and the viola in unison, upon a simple 'cello accompaniment and a characteristic semiquaver figure on the second violin. This time the concluding *motif* of the theme extends into a broad phrase leading to a stormy episode : in the inner parts a semiquaver figure rolls, and in the outer parts—the first violin and 'cello— short crotchets, single notes, and isolated chords crack like pistol-shots. . . . The clamour dies down a little as the second violin gives out a second principal theme in C minor (Ex. 151).

Accentuated by vigorous *sforzandi*, this figure thunders like a 'storm' *motif* through lightning flashes on the first violin. After several imitations on the viola and 'cello, calm once more supervenes, while an unusually

truncated development section begins. *Motif* II of the
principal theme is energetically treated in close imitation
between the instruments (cf. the first section of the
Adagio in D major of the Op. 10 piano sonata). The
other *motif* (I), in D flat, dances gaily through four

Ex. 151.

Ex. 152.

bars, but the mood of melancholy returns with *motif* II,
and is concentrated in the conclusion ; the final section
of the *Allegretto* is now reached, also much curtailed.

Again the stormy episode follows with the subsequent imitative figures and the second principal theme,
this time in F minor. Again the principal subject re-

turns, on the first violin only, floating upon long waves
of *arpeggi* on the lower voices. Finally the conclusion
motif reappears, with several bars of dialogue between
the first violin and 'cello, leading to the *Coda*. This
opens with a strongly rhythmic passage (Ex. 152), where
the first *motif* (I), modified two bars later, sounds an impressive trumpet-call with funereal grandeur.

The short phrase following, where the conclusion
motif creeps up on the viola beneath the interwoven
counterpoint of the other voices, must be remarked as
a model of polyphonic writing :

Ex. 153.

As the music fades to the end, this *motif* still persists,
silenced at last in a tentative *poco ritardando* ; the key-
note F is held on the first violin, viola, and 'cello. The
end seems imminent in the tonality of F minor, when
an A natural—dropped from the blue—appears *ppp* on
the second violin, and brings the tonality of F major.
At once is liberated a rapid passage in four-time *alla
breve*, as the instruments rush to the rout of this unforeseen return of the major mode, in an *Allegro molto* in F.
Too short to be regarded as another movement—it is
only forty-three bars long—it forms an epilogue to the
fourth movement. It bears the same relation to the
fourth movement as the triumphant final section, also
in F, of the contemporary Egmont overture bears to
the earlier part of that work. The energy of this short
Allegro molto is not so triumphant as that of the overture ;
here it is marked by a certain air of irresponsibility.

The passage is constructed upon a rapid violin figure, against which the other instruments weave a delicately spun counterpoint. The theme passes to the viola, to the 'cello, with an accompanying counterpoint on the violins, then to the two violins, and finally to a four-voice unison ; and in default of a heroic climax, all the parts join in an exuberant burst of gaiety.

Note 2, p. 51.

Ulibishev, who as a rule has little to say for Beethoven, has curiously enough devoted several pages to quite extravagant praise of Op. 29. Certainly, he may have done it in order to be able to disparage the works that follow, without being accused of deliberate prejudice ! (*Beethoven, ses critiques et ses glossateurs*, p. 146) : ' Having once heard this work,' he says, ' who could ever forget the opening of the first *Allegro*, with that theme that seems to be stricken with a shuddering awe, like the troubled spirit of a prophet in the anguish of revelation ? ' At the same time he observes very truly that this theme, in spite of its profound significance, is a characteristic *motif* for strings, as distinct from the genre of opera or symphony.

'The *Allegro*', he goes on, ' expresses no active purpose, no definite thought, but rather the formlessness of a half-developed idea, uncertain alike of motive force and of ultimate purpose. Such is the character of the first theme. In the triplet figure that follows, one seems to see an opposing force becoming active, and involving the long drawn out struggle that ensues. A third influence, expressed in a soft persuasive melody, seems to act as arbiter between the irresolute will of the first theme and the opposing force of the triplet figure, an influence so pacific that by dint of argument and skill it effects a reconciliation ; the triumph of the will over the antagonistic force is expressed in a rapidly descending figure on the first violin, and a triple volley of trills. . . . The musical picture portrayed on the five instruments and by these three subjects has neither passionate nor dramatic power, it could be expressed neither through the medium of the voice nor through the orchestra and piano. . . . Psychologically and musically conceived within the limits of the genre (discussed earlier in relation to the quartets of Mozart) this *Allegro*, and, indeed, the entire quintet, seems to me from the point of view of intellectual criticism to be Beethoven's most perfectly constructed work.

' The same unimpassioned meditative air characterizes the 3/4 *Adagio*, in F major. A resolute calm follows the spiritual strife of the preceding movement, but it is disturbed by momentary misgiving. High up on the E string the first violin gives out little troubled broken figures, answered by the bass, and interrupted by syncopated figures on the second violin. But this argumentative vein never rises to any real importance ; the main theme dominates and controls, at one time noble and impressive, at another persuasive, at another self-assertive. Towards the middle of the piece the obedience hitherto exacted becomes as it were a solemn homage, an effect created by the harp-like character of *pizzicato* broken chords. So, surely, must the harpists of old have reverently greeted some mystic apparition, revealed in divine condescension. At the third bar it becomes evident that the composer is using an unusually idiomatic construction. Having hitherto never heard the theme complete, in spite of frequent entries, we now hear it in its entirety for the first, and as the ear instinctively guesses, for the last time. After this, there is left only the gradual fading away of the *Adagio* to a close ; we hear echoes of the theme on the first violin with an accompaniment in the lower parts, the whole dying away to silence in a final distant farewell. How Mozart would have loved this *Adagio* !

' Then at once comes the *Scherzo* to stimulate and arrest the attention. . . . Following two movements of profound meaning, the vigour and gaiety of a 3/4 or 3/8 movement is always effective, if only as affording a contrast. So it is with this *Scherzo* in C, although the first section has no particular interest beyond a difficult technical passage taken at breakneck speed. The *Trio* in F is more interesting ; in it one can already trace peculiarities of style that characterize his second manner, though kept strictly within bounds. It opens with a melodious phrase given out at first on the viola ; passing from one to another, it finally breaks abruptly into the key of A♭. Then it is as if, for some unknown reason, the composer bursts into a fit of annoyance, and seizes upon the last turn of the phrase, the short falling *arpeggio* and twists and turns it time after time in a unison of twenty-seven bars, almost as if he were grasping some one by the hair, and crying " Oh ! you don't want to, don't you ? I'll make you, then." In the half-comic effect created by this means, he shows that nothing in the world is half so effective as dumb-show threats, for the little swinging *motif* hurriedly starts climbing up like a squirrel, and when breathless and at the last gasp, the *Scherzo* slips in and takes up the tale again.

' We now come to the celebrated 6/8 *Presto* in C major, never surpassed even by Beethoven himself for its weird originality, one of the early works which already bears marks of the third and most advanced manner. By this I mean the interpolation of several lines absolutely foreign to the main tenor of the piece, written in a strange tonality and with similar differences of rhythm and construction. It is consequently a point that needs to be explained in detail in order to be understood. . . .

' To avoid appearing dogmatic in analysing this movement I endeavoured, by a study of the foregoing movements, to arrive at the most

logical of the many interpretations that this amazing finale might suggest, and to find the most obvious metaphor in which to cast the main
theme of the *Presto* itself. One at least is self-evident. From the very
start one seems drawn into a veritable whirlwind. In the upper part,
flash after flash of lightning vies with the crash of thunderbolts hurled
by the bass in answer, as if the gods were making merry in the clouds ;
these dazzling flashes herald a gay procession of sylphs gliding along in
fairy boats on a river of mist, seen in fantastic shapes and mad frolics,
a babble of gaiety cut short by the return of the rippling triplets that
brought them (the second theme), which in their turn give place to the
thunder of the first theme, as it crashes with redoubled force into the
second section of the finale. What could be the significance of these
musical pictures flickering through the mist of metaphor before one's
dazzled imagination ? They are too full of meaning for a dream.
Recalling the anguish of prophetic revelation that the *Allegro* seemed
so perfectly to portray, one imagines that anguish to have given birth
to a vision of the spirit, not yet made completely manifest. For this first
part of the *Presto* only, as it were, prepares the *mise en scène* ; in the
second section the mist of clouds and the blinding brightness will be
lifted, and we shall see clearly. And to compass this miracle Beethoven
has recourse to a third means, more expressive than the two used
before. A new theme crosses the 6/8 with a beat of 2/4, with imitations
in canon in every part, of a nobility and force that dominate the
brilliance of the principal theme, and subdue the syncopated counter-
subject, rising higher and higher until the syncopated figure gives way
before it. A final statement high up on the E string seems to deliver
an ultimatum ; we hear it for the last time. The climax is reached, and
with the 3/4 *Andante* in A major the mist clears from our eyes, and we
see the vision of divine grace brightening upon us suddenly eclipsed.
The revelation of happiness, most elusive of all, vanishes as we stretch
out our hand to grasp it, promising immortal love, the solace for tears
that the soul has shed in bitterness—a bitterness felt and expressed in
another work, closely akin to the quintet, the piano sonata Op. 27,
No. 2.

' After eighteen bars of the *Andante* the *Presto* takes it up again, and
with slight variations repeats the earlier section without the 2/4 theme.
One glimpses again the vision of beatific happiness in the *Andante*, seen
from a different aspect, and expressed in the tonic key of C, as if to set
the divine seal upon the promise held out to us before. And immediately
the flood of the *Tempo Primo* is loosed from its bounds, and one hears
in its flying rush to the conclusion a mighty cry of triumph. And not
without reason, for never was the triumph of an idea more perfectly
realized.'

Ulibishev's note is certainly ingenious, though extravagant and
fantastic. It is surely difficult to find grounds for the assumption that

the finale is psychologically the climax of the whole piece, to find there, in the midst of a tumult of divine revelation, the consummation of the abstract thought up to which all the preceding movements have hitherto been leading. Certainly it is borne out by evidence to be found in no other work of Beethoven's of this period, and it implies a sudden transition into the middle of the period that was then only on the point of beginning, and in which his genius was to find fuller expression, if one is already to assume his perfect comprehension of ideas that did not reach their full growth until much later. Schumann, in his *Écrits pour la Musique,* also speaks of the quintet, but makes much less of it. This is his interpretation of the anomaly of the new theme in the finale for which no purpose can be assigned. After having pointed out the passage of forty-six bars, where a harmonic chaos with a particularly poignant effect is produced by the continual contrast of two different rhythms, he comes to the *Andante,* which he finds light-hearted in character, and says, ' Does it not seem as if Beethoven himself steps in here with pretended horror, crying, " Great Heavens ! What have I done ? Why should I try and upset the old ways ? I will stop, and don't go on shaking your pigtails (Zöpfe) at me ".'

CHAPTER III

THE LAST QUARTETS

(Op. 127; Op. 130 (133); Op. 131; Op. 132; Op. 135.)

THE composition of the five quartets, Op. 127, 130, 131, 132, 135, and the fugue of Op. 133, occupied the last three years of Beethoven's life. Setting aside, for what he hoped would be only a short time, all the other ideas in his mind—overtures, oratorios, and symphonies, &c.—the Master devoted himself entirely to the quartets, beginning work on them in the summer of 1824, and finishing them in November 1826, hardly four months before his death. They grew to maturity in the midst of all the sufferings of mind and body that made these last three years one long agony: ill, poverty-stricken, and alone, he found in these intensely moving *Adagios* and pain-racked *Allegros* an outlet for his anguish of hope and distress, often, as Schindler tells us, weeping as he wrote. . . . The five works are intimately linked with the daily existence of one of the greatest and most desolate figures in history, during the saddest period of his life; they are in every respect 'the last revelations of his spirit', inspiring the listener to an admiration mingled with infinite pity and awe. . . .

Fourteen years had elapsed since the series of quartets of Op. 59 (Nos. 1–3), 74, and 95, years in which Beethoven at once touched the pinnacle of his glory and plumbed the depths of desolation.

Success came first. Master of his mature genius, at the height of his most brilliant phase, he composed the magnificent trio in B flat, Op. 97, dedicated to the Archduke Rudolph, and the VIIth and VIIIth symphonies, where the full force of his 'concentrated, unified power'[1] was made manifest as never before. He was freed from material cares by the generosity of influential patrons, and surrounded by an atmosphere of warmth and affection in a circle of devoted friends, in the affection, too, of Amélie de Sebald. The year 1814 marked the zenith of his fame, and at the Congress of Vienna he reaped the glory of an international reputation. Royalty paid court to him, and he haughtily received the homage of princes as a right, as he boasts to Bettina von Arnim.[2] A cantata composed for the occasion, *Der glorreiche Augenblick* (The Glorious Moment), was played before an audience of emperors and kings.

This same year Lichnowski died, and the loss of his most zealous patron marks the beginning of a succession of troubles and disasters in store for him. One by one, his other patrons disappeared, as Rasoumowsky left Vienna in 1815, and Lobkowitz died in 1816; his friends left Vienna or deserted him; he was cut off from the world by absolute deafness, and after 1816 writing was the only means of communication with his fellow-men. His conversation books, now his only resource, begin with this cry of desolation: ' I am friendless and alone in the world! . . .' In 1815 his brother Caspar-Anton-Carl died, leaving him the care of his son, but unfortunately making his widow joint trustee. Beethoven was passionately fond of the child,[3] and in his anxiety for his welfare tried to keep him from the bad influence of his mother,[4] engaging in an interminable lawsuit in which the necessity for

---

[1] Marx, *Ludwig van Beethoven*, vol. i, p. 281.

[2] Romain Rolland, op. cit., p. 52.

[3] ' A new affection has come into his life,' writes Mlle. Giannastasio del Rio, the daughter of the head master of the school where Beethoven sent his nephew.

[4] ' I have been made guardian to my brother's son. It is hardly possible for you to have had so much trouble as I have had through this death, but at least I have the satisfaction of saving an innocent child from the hands of an unworthy mother.' (Letter to Ries, February 28, 1816.)

taking action against his own relations broke his heart; the affair did not come to an end till 1820.[1] Through unwise advice he also took action against Mälzel, the inventor of the metronome, and against Lichnowski's heirs, &c., long and costly proceedings that drained his remaining resources. ' I am almost destitute,' he writes to Ries in 1818, and Spohr relates that when he went to see him, about this time, he could not go out because his shoes were worn through. Worse still, he was often in bad health. He had bronchitis badly in the winter of 1816–17; it left him with a chronic catarrh, and he was in terror of consumption, the disease of which his father and brother had already died.

This period of distressed circumstances is marked by a consequent falling off of creative work. . . . Between 1815 and 1818 he composed only the piano sonatas of Op. 101 and Op. 106, and a few unimportant pieces. In Vienna they were already saying that his capacity was exhausted, and that he would never produce anything again : ' *Er hat sich ausgeschrieben, er vermag nichts mehr* ' (' He can do nothing more . . .'). The *Allgemeine Musikalische Zeitung* writes : ' Beethoven seems now to be beyond writing great works.' One knows that there was nothing in all this ; the Master regained strength and composed two fresh masterpieces one after the other : the Mass in D (1818–22), and the IXth symphony (1822–3). At this moment he had a world-wide reputation, and even in far-off Russia the publication of a new work by him was an event. There was no greater artist living, and at the same time no living creature more desolate ; until the day of his death his creative genius was haunted by

---

[1] ' O God, my sole strength and refuge ! Thou canst read the inmost thoughts of my soul, and Thou knowest my utter desolation, that I must cause suffering to those who would take from me my darling Carl ! Hear my prayer, Great Being that I cannot name, bring succour to the most wretched of Thy creatures.' (Conversation books, 1818.)

illness and misery. In 1821 he fell ill with jaundice,
' a wretched disease,' he complains, and in 1823 his
sight failed altogether for several weeks.

During this year, the most terrible time of his whole
life, not a month passed without some domestic crisis. He
owed money to his publishers, and his brother John not
only refused to stand security for him, but tried to make
money out of his financial distress : ' My fine brother
John, already a rich man, has also tried to profit by my
misfortunes ; without asking my leave he has offered
this overture (Op. 124) to a London publisher. He
bought it from me as a speculation. O Frater ! '
Desperate to get out of debt at all costs, he appealed,
but in vain, to his friends. He writes to Ries on
15th April 1823, ' I am in such terrible straits that
I am forced to write down immediately what will bring
me in money for my immediate needs. What a sad state
of affairs this letter will reveal to you ! As a result of endless worry I am far from well, and my eyes are very bad.'

And several months later, on 16th July : ' Truly my
position is hard to bear. I am writing a new string
quartet.[1] Do you think that I could offer it to the
highest bidder among these musical—or unmusical—
Jews in London?—*En vrai juif!* '

He also wrote to Cherubini in 1823, on 15th March,
a letter to which he got no reply : ' My situation is so
critical that I can no longer keep my eyes fixed on the
stars ; I have to concentrate upon the barest necessities
of life.'[2]

He was bitterly ashamed of having to make these
demands upon his friends, and pleads in excuse : ' I
would willingly write for all the greatest artists in
Europe, for nothing—if I were only not poverty-
stricken Beethoven ! ' But his appeals met with no
response, and he was obliged at last to sell his shares

[1] The XIIth. See later.
[2] Translated into French from German by J. Chantavoine, p. 208.
The lines quoted are in the text.

in the Austrian Bank, that he had bought after the Congress of Vienna to keep for a legacy to his nephew.

He was living all the time at the wretched lodging, small and dirty, where Rossini had visited him the year before.[1] Weber's son, staying in Vienna for the performances of *Euryanthe*, went to see him, and described the place afterwards as 'a bare and poorly furnished room in terrible disorder : money, music, clothes, all scattered on the floor ; a pile of linen on the bed, dust thick on the piano, cups and cracked plates strewn over the table '.

After the IXth symphony and the brilliant success of the Kärnthnerthor Concert, some peace of mind and spirit returned, but it proved only a short respite from misfortune. He always had the best of intentions, but his irritable nature, aggravated by his infirmity, estranged from him his best friends. He was reduced to the companionship of Charles Holtz, the second violin of the Schuppanzigh Quartet, 'a young man with the face of a scamp, shallow and sly, half artist, half counter-jumper '.[2] In spite of the difference of age and tastes between them, Holtz became his inseparable companion and worked him up into a terrible state of over-excitement. He dragged him off to restaurants, and urged him to drink to excess, encouraging his drunkenness and involving him in vulgar jesting that disgraced his true character.[3]

[1] In a letter to Schindler of 2nd July 1823, Beethoven bursts into a complaint about his lodging : ' I should not have believed that a chimney so shockingly inefficient and so dangerous to health could have been allowed to stay by the government inspectors ' (Chantavoine, p. 218). It was the Abbé Carpani who introduced Rossini to Beethoven. 'The composer of the *Mass in D*, deaf and almost blind, could only answer Rossini's questions by signs ; and Rossini went away from this melancholy interview almost broken-hearted.' See, on this point, Fr. Kerst, *Die Erinnerungen an Beethoven*, i, p. 289.

[2] T. de Wyzewa, *Beethoven et Schubert*, p. 154 (in the section *Beethoven et Wagner*).

[3] Later, Holtz managed to extract from Beethoven the exclusive right of biography. Beethoven afterwards bitterly repented of this

During this time Beethoven was in the depths of disappointment and despair on account of the reckless behaviour of his beloved nephew Carl. One should read his letters from 1824–5 to understand fully the agony of mind this worthless young man caused him. Nothing could be more disillusioned or more eloquent.

. . . I have been deeply grieved by your faithless behaviour, and it is difficult to forget that you have betrayed my love for you. Even though I may be willing to endure it all without complaining, you will never keep any one else's affection if you treat every one like this. Before God, I wish I were a hundred miles away from you and your wretched family! As God is my witness, I shall never believe in your good faith again. (From Baden, May 31st, 1825.)

God has never yet forsaken me, and even now I shall find some one to close my eyes. I understand that you have no intention of staying with me any longer. Naturally, I can well believe that my household is too *particular* for you! Last Sunday you again borrowed money from the housekeeper, that coarse old slut! And yet it was forbidden! But it is the same with everything else; I wear my old clothes for two years, but that is not good enough for Mr. Carl. What else is my money for, you say. (September 1825.)

And as though sorry to scold, he immediately adds a postscript:

Never mind, one's Viennese customs stick, and I used to take such pleasure in helping my parents; what a difference in your attitude to me! Goodbye, young scamp! Your loving father.[1]

promise, given on August 30th, 1826, and tried to cancel the agreement, but in vain. Holtz after all did not put the promise to account, and sold his right, on November 4th, 1843, to Dr. Gassner, the Court Musician at Carlsruhe, to whom it was also of no advantage, for death overtook both of them before they had published anything (Holtz died on November 9th, 1858). See Mme Audley, *Beethoven*, p. 214. Nevertheless, Holtz's memoirs have been collected by Mme Fanny Liegbauer, and more recently by Ludwig Nohl, in his book, *Beethoven, Liszt et Wagner*. Schindler was the first to write a complete biography of the artist.

[1] Nohl, *Briefe von Beethoven*, pp. 305, 314; Chantavoine, pp. 243, 258.

In the summer of 1826, sick of continual reproaches, Carl van Beethoven tried to commit suicide. For Beethoven this was a devastating disaster. Schindler saw him at the time, and relates that he seemed suddenly ' stricken with age, an old man of seventy, nerveless and stunned. . . . He would die if Carl was dead . . .'

We cannot but be moved by the appealing letter that the unhappy man wrote to his nephew on the news of his attempted suicide :

My dear son,

I beg you to come back to me, and there shall be no word of reproach. For God's sake do not rush to cast yourself off. You shall be received as you always were, with tenderness and affection. We can talk over the future together, and consider plans, and I promise you that no reproach shall pass my lips; in any case, what purpose would it serve? You have only love and interest in your welfare to expect from me. Come back quickly to your loving father, Beethoven. And come at once—as soon as you receive this letter.

On the envelope is written (in French) :

Si vous ne viendrez pas vous me tuerez sûrement. Lisez la lettre et restez à la maison chez vous, venez de m'embrasser votre père vous vraiment adonné, soyez assuré que tout cela restera entre nous.

Return home to-day, for the love of God, who knows what dangers may be awaiting you. Quickly! [1]

The rest of the story is still sadder. Attempted suicide was a grave offence in Austrian law, and Carl only escaped imprisonment through the influence of his uncle, and was forced to leave Vienna. Beethoven decided to go with him, and accompanied Carl to Gneixendorff where his brother John lived, a self-made man, grasping and selfish. The musician was making a difficult recovery from some serious internal inflammation, and needed the greatest care ; at Gneixendorff he was left deprived of physical comforts, in an attic

[1] Nohl, *Briefe von Beethoven*, p. 317 ; Chantavoine, p. 260.

room without a fire, during the rainy season of the year. He soon discovered, moreover, that a guilty intimacy existed between his sister-in-law and his nephew, and felt he could stay no longer under that dishonourable roof. He left at once for Vienna. The weather was damp and cold, but John would not give him his closed carriage for the journey, and it was in an open cart that this great desolate figure went away, never to return.... That was on the third of December. A few months later he was dead. Two days before the death of the Master, Schindler wrote to Moscheles in London, March 24, 1827, a letter in which he gives a moving account of the illness destined to be his last:

The moment of death has not yet arrived, but by the time this reaches you, Moscheles, Beethoven will have passed away. He is rapidly losing strength, and one is forced to pray that the end will not be long when he will be delivered from pain, since there is no hope. For a week he has seemed more dead than alive, scarcely able to ask for what he wants. . . . He lies in a kind of stupor, with his head sunk on his breast, and his eyes fixed and unseeing. He cannot recognize even his most intimate friends, and asks the names of those who are with him now. Very many people have come to see him for the last time, and none have broker. through the mist of failing memory, except those who were cruel enough to torment a dying man with questions. . . . His funds were so depleted at the end [1] that he had to stint himself of food. . . . We have bought him a big arm-chair which cost us fifty florins; he rests in it for an hour every day while his bed is being made.

When you were here at the end of 1826, I spoke to you about Beethoven's financial straits; I did not imagine then that I should see so soon his last moments. It was on December 3rd that he was attacked by the illness that will take him from us now; he was leaving the country to return to Vienna with his

---

[1] In February 1827 his resources were exhausted in providing fresh equipment for Carl, whom the Baron von Stutterheim had just taken into his regiment as a cadet. In spite of the opposition of his friends, who considered it beneath his dignity, Beethoven had at this point made an application for help to the Philharmonic Society in London.

graceless nephew, and the bad weather compelled them to spend a night at a wretched inn. There he caught cold so badly that inflammation of the lungs set in almost at once, and he arrived here in a terrible state.[1] The inflammation had barely subsided when dropsy set in, so acute and progressive that on December 18th an operation was necessary; a second operation was performed on January 8th, 1827, a third on the 20th, and a fourth on February 27th. Imagine the suffering this must have meant to Beethoven's impatient nature, in the grip of so painful a disease! The ingratitude and misconduct of his nearest relation accentuated his mental sufferings, and the doctors assign the cause of the illness to the agony of mind that this noble soul must have endured on his nephew's account, and to the enforced stay in the country during a damp time of year, which was only undertaken on his nephew's behalf.

. . . But I am not with Beethoven, and his last hour is very near at hand: before the arrival of this letter, his magnificent spirit will have left us. He is now in full possession of his faculties. I have just cut off the enclosed lock of hair for you. I must close now, and hasten back to him.

Your sincere friend,
A. Schindler.

That same morning Beethoven received the last sacraments; the agony of the end, increased by his marvellous vitality, began at a quarter to one; in the evening he lost consciousness and fell into a delirium; in the evening of the 25th, it became apparent that death was not far away, and he died on March 26th, 1827, at half-past five in the afternoon, while a hailstorm raged outside.

Enfeebled, racked with suffering, starving, betrayed by his nearest of kin and abandoned by his friends, broken with misfortune, how Beethoven ever achieved the last five masterpieces is the miracle of his great genius; still more amazing is it that his last work of

---

[1] On arrival in Vienna, Beethoven sent his nephew for a doctor. Carl stopped on the way for a drink and a game of billiards, and forgot all about his errand. Remembering after an hour or two, he sent the waiter instead of going himself. It happened to be Dr. Wawruch who was then called in.

all, the glowing finale of Op. 130, breaking from a
wounded heart during the days of misery and shame
at Gneixendorff, throbs with the unspoilt gaiety of
youth ; it is the supreme token, perhaps too the most
heart-breaking, of his mystical courage, at once intimate
and sublime, his ' universal goodwill ', revealing not
the superman but the saint. In the evening of his life,
so radiant with this spirit, Beethoven once more expresses his lofty conception of the meaning of his work,
as he said to Bettina von Arnim : ' I am Bacchus
incarnate, to give humanity wine to drown its sorrow,'
believing that the artist must fulfil his mission in bringing joy to the world. The hundred voices of his last
symphony overflow with this joy, but still he is not
satisfied. After this transcendent climax he has still to
find a subtler, more intimate expression for his divine
joy, sorrow-born ; he casts a veil of beauty over his
griefs, and through his suffering confers a benediction
upon all men. ' He who divines the secret of my music
is delivered from the misery that haunts the world.'

As R. Wagner acutely observes, once more he wishes
to express his conviction of the fundamental beneficence
of human nature, in spite of all the apparent contradictions that life had offered him. The last quartets are
a living witness of this faith. ' All the unkindness, the
lack of sympathy, and selfishness discovered anew, he
saw in the light of blasphemy against the fundamental
beneficence of man.' All these apparent contradictions
of this law were only a nightmare unreality, hiding the
truth ; rising from the heart of his suffering breaks
once more the cry of divine optimism that is many
a time expressed in the conversation books during his
worst struggles : ' Yet man is, in spite of all, a bene-
ficent being ! ' . . .

Wagner again observes :

Fallen from the Heaven of his harmonious inner life to the
hell of his jangling, discordant material existence, he hastily
turns from material reality, and slips into the harmonious cosmos

of his soul. . . . An inviolable serenity becomes for him the very essence of music, and graces all he sees or imagines. Even the melancholy that lies at the heart of all sound is transformed into laughter: the world recaptures the innocence of childhood. . . .[1]

* *
*

It is to an artist named Zeuner that the world owes the fact of the composition of the last Beethoven quartets. Now quite unknown, his name should be saved from oblivion on account of the signal service rendered to music at this time. This Zeuner was a violist, and in this capacity one of the pillars of the St. Petersburg Quartet, in which Nicholas Borisowitch Galitzin, a wealthy amateur, was 'cellist. In 1822 Galitzin returned from Vienna, where Weber had just put on a performance of *Der Freischütz*, full of the idea of having a score of the work, which was then causing widespread interest, made for his own use. When he spoke of the matter to Zeuner, the latter gave it as his opinion that the money spent on a score of *Der Freischütz* would be put to better use if Beethoven were commissioned to write three new quartets—by which the whole musical world would profit. Prince Galitzin thereupon wrote the following letter to the musician:

As a deep admirer of your genius, I am taking the liberty of writing to ask you if you would agree to write one, two, or three new quartets, for which I should be delighted to pay you whatever you think adequate. I should be very much obliged if you would give me the name of a banker to whose care I can have directed the amount of whatever fee you name. The instrument I study is the 'cello. I shall await your reply with the greatest impatience. Will you be so good as to direct your letter to the following address: Prince Nicholas Galitzin, c/o MM. Stieglitz and Co., Bankers, St. Petersburg. Please accept the assurance of my deep admiration and attention.[2]

---

[1] *Beethoven*, by R. Wagner (translated into French by Lasvignes); published by the *Revue blanche*, Paris, 1902, *passim*.

[2] According to the biographers, this letter is dated 1822. But Prince Galitzin himself, in an article dated from Kourtsk, August 27th, 1845

Beethoven was at this period in appalling financial difficulties, as the foregoing account relates. He was looking everywhere for commissions, especially in London, through the agency of Neate, and was in fact offering to compose a quartet. He wrote to Ries : ' If God will only grant me health, I shall be able to comply with all the requests made me from every country in Europe, and even from North America ; and I might yet come to prosperity ! ' So that Nicolas Galitzin's letter was a providential arrival. He replied at once. ' Only a month later I received his answer,' relates Galitzin, ' and as a proof of his pleasure in discovering that " I was anxious to know more of his work ", he declared himself willing to accede to my request ; he could not yet put a definite date to the fulfilment of the commission, seeing that his inspiration would not come to order and he was unable to work at a fixed rate day by day ; and since he was in the unfortunate position of having to earn his living by his music, he suggested that fifty ducats should be paid him for each quartet.

' No letter was more impatiently awaited than this reply. Following these first overtures, a regular correspondence was established between us, written in German,[1] which has made me the possessor of a large collection of autograph letters from the great man.' [2]

Beethoven, nevertheless, did not set to work at once. Other ideas were filling his mind, and he had said to Rochlitz in 1822, when the latter had suggested his writing music for Goethe's *Faust* : ' I can undertake nothing else until I have brought to light three big works already conceived in my brain, an oratorio and

(September 8th), which was published in *La Presse* on October 13th; 1845, dates it 1823.

[1] Prince Galitzin wrote in complete agreement to the suggestion of the composer, on May 5th; 1823 : ' I only ask for myself the dedication, and a manuscript copy when you have finished with it ' (Wilder).

[2] See the article in *La Presse*, October 13th; 1845.

two new symphonies quite different from any I have hitherto composed.' One of these symphonies was the immortal Ninth, which he began in June of 1823 and finished in February of 1824. Other works were roughly sketched out while he was busy with this : an *Overture on the name of Bach*, of which studies for the working out are to be found in the note-books of 1823–5, and which was never finished ; an Introduction (*grave introduzione*) to the cantata *The Glorious Moment*, recalling the splendid days of the Congress of Vienna ;[1] the six *Bagatelles* for the piano, Op. 126, finished in 1824. . . . His brain was overflowing with ideas, and writing from Baden on September 17th, 1824 to Schott the publisher, he says : ' Apollo and the Muses cannot yet leave me free to die in peace, for I am still much in their debt ! Before I pass over to the Elysian Fields I must finish what the Spirit moves me to write. I seem to have scarcely composed a note yet. . . .'

Nevertheless death prevented him from accomplishing all the projects coming to birth in his vast imagination, and after the IXth symphony he wrote only the five quartets ; but these contain the essence of that boundless inspiration that might have flowed through a hundred masterpieces. He began the XIIth quartet in E flat (Op. 127) in 1824, and its first studies are scattered among the last sketches for the IXth symphony.

These early notes are innumerable, and ideas for all four movements of the work are jumbled together in disorder. Some are extended studies—like that for the lovely *Adagio* ; the long curving melody of this perfect movement, which seems to express in its balance of design and emotional serenity pure joy of artistic

---

[1] He began to outline it in 1823. On June 12th, 1825 he wrote to Haslinger, his publisher, saying : ' I am keeping the score of *The Glorious Moment* a day or two longer ; I want to add an overture.' (Nottebohm, *Zweite Beethoveniana*, p. 577.)

creation, was slowly evolved by laborious thought, in spite of its air of absolute spontaneity and freshness ; it was only after repeated attempts that the final shape unfolded, and its eighteen bars were wrought one by one in almost isolated fragments. Beethoven soon decided on the outline of the first phrase of the theme, except for the bar or two of introduction, but he takes it up again and 'ruminates' over the musical idea, according to Nottebohm's phrase, with endless experiments in tonality and rhythm, trying the effect of contrary movement and an unbroken accompaniment of thirds. This preliminary work occupies forty-three pages.

The sketches for the other movements are short and written in feverish haste, often barely legible. From the first they approach very closely to their final form. One of Beethoven's friends, constantly in his company at this time, remarked : ' Beethoven is inspired by the ecstasy of his joy, and by the joy of his ecstasy.' Among these notes for the quartet he suddenly breaks in with a five-page study in a totally different tonality, *tempo*, and manner, written in one stroke at great speed, often illegible, and scored for string quartet. This fragment, in C major, bears the epigraph, ' *La Gaieté, allegro grazioso* ', and the music expresses a passionate joy. Beethoven never used it in any form. ' This piece has no relation whatever to the quartet in E flat,' remarks Nottebohm, ' but it bears on its history.'

Opus 127 was finished in October 1824,[1] and was sent to St. Petersburg in the spring of 1825. As von Lenz comments, ' It must have been a wonderful moment when it was performed for the first time '.

The second quartet commissioned by Galitzin, Op.

---

[1] Beethoven wrote from Baden to Schott the publisher on September 17th, 1824 : ' You shall have the quartet without fail by the middle of October. I am in very bad health, and you must have patience with me ; I am staying here on account of my health, or rather, on account of my low state, but already it is improving.' (Chantavoine, p. 239.)

132, in A minor, was already begun. The original
studies sketched down on paper are even of the same
date as those for the beginning of Op. 127. They are
to be found in a note-book for 1824. None of the
ideas reach their final form in these memoranda, and
all are many times modified and recorrected. But these
experiments were by no means wasted labour, for in
the theme of the *Grand Fugue*, Op. 133, Beethoven
uses a form that he remembered from these sketches
for the introduction to the first movement. Illness was
a constant interruption to the composer, but out of it
came for us the *Canzona di ringraziamento*, which
Beethoven wrote in the spring of 1825, and incorporated into the quartet. There remained only the
finale. But his illness had delayed him, and he was
probably afraid lest he should not get the work finished
in time for his noble patron in Russia; consequently
he abandoned the scheme for the finale that he had
started on, and took up an earlier study from the
note-books of 1822–3, intended originally as a *finale
instromentale* to the IXth symphony. From this he
evolved the *Allegro appassionato*, that ' *valse tragique* ',
as it has been called, full of passionate and throbbing
intensity. Op. 132 was finished in May 1825.[1]

The quartet in A minor, though thirteenth in chronological order, is numbered fifteenth in the list of the
Master's works, and therefore follows Op. 130 and
131, which actually were both written after it. It was
published after Beethoven's death, and the two *opus*
numbers before it had already been assigned by assidu-
ous publishers to the B flat and C sharp minor

---

[1] On March 19th, 1825, Beethoven wrote to Neate (in French):
' In regard to the quartets, I have finished the first and am now at
work on the second, which will be finished shortly with the third.'
The first in question is Op. 127, the second Op. 132, and the third
Op. 130. The two works that come between Op. 127 and 130 are:
Op. 128, *The Kiss* (A major), for solo voice, to the words of Weisse,
I was all alone with Chloe, composed in 1822, published in 1825;
Op. 129, *Rondo capricioso* (G major), posthumous work.

quartets; it became for posterity the XVth quartet, and that order will be followed here.

The quartet in B flat, Op. 130 (the XIIIth) is of the same year of composition, 1825. It was begun in March, finished in September,[1] and scored between September and November. Three books from a set of six containing sketches from 1825–6, formerly in Schindler's possession, and now in the Royal Library in Berlin, include studies for the four last movements of the quartet.[2] Beethoven was working on all these different movements at the same time. The *Danza tedesca* was originally intended as part of the preceding quartet in A minor; and the theme of the dance is to

[1] On August 29th, 1824 Beethoven wrote to his nephew Carl: 'The third quartet (Op. 131) has six movements, and will in all probability be finished in ten or twelve days at most. . . . I am giving the last quartet (Op. 130) to Artaria, and the earlier one (Op. 132) to Peters.' This last sentence refers to negotiations started by Beethoven with the firm of Schlesinger, in a letter written at Baden on July 15th, of which Nottebohm reproduced the original text with marginal notes; in this letter Beethoven offered the two quartets to Schlesinger, Op. 132 and 130, the first finished, the second in course of composition.

By the date of the letter to Carl, Schlesinger still had not replied, which explains why Beethoven was considering sending his quartets to Artaria and to Peters. To the latter, with whom he had had difficulties on another occasion, he wrote the following letter : ' The quartet (Op. 132) that I am now offering you will prove to you that I do not bear you a grudge for your previous conduct, but, on the contrary, am giving you the best I could give my best friend. I can assure you on my honour as an artist that it is one of the best works I have ever produced. If I am not telling you the strict truth, may I be held the worst of men.'

One wonders if Peters held out against Beethoven, or whether, in the meantime, Schlesinger accepted the suggestions of the musician. At all events, at the end of August—according to Schindler during the last two days of the month—Schlesinger became possessor of the quartet in A minor for the agreed sum of eighty ducats.

[2] The second book, which contains the last three movements of the quartet, is dated early in September, and the third, containing the last two, is dated on the last page, December 1825. But it also contains the early sketches for Op. 131, and its opening pages must certainly have been filled up in September.

be found in a little note-book devoted to the quartet in A minor, unmistakable, and already quite developed; it is in the key of A major.[1] When using it for the quartet in B flat Beethoven transposed it into the key of G major, and called the study for it *Allemande*. The melody of the *Cavatina*, so moving in its apparent simplicity, was, like many others of the same type, evolved out of thematic scraps after countless attempts. The following is the beginning of one of the longest of the studies for it :

Ex. 154.

Beethoven himself accounted this little movement the best in the quartet ; he had written it in the summer of 1825, and confessed that the composition of it had moved him to tears.[2] ' Never have I written a melody that has affected me so much,' he added, ' nor with so poignant an emotion.'

The finale of the quartet in B flat was originally the *Grand Fugue*, Op. 133. The idea of the fugue subject is to be found sketched out in one of the themes for the introduction to the quartet, Op. 132, as mentioned before. Beethoven has extended this simple four-note phrase into two magnificent pages of working out, another example of his genius for development. . . . As one might imagine, this colossal fugue was a màtter of great labour : Beethoven worked at it for a long time before the counter-subject satisfied him, experimenting with several and hesitating as to the final choice. But though the final form of the counter-subject caused so

[1] See the transcription of this sketch in Nottebohm's *Beethoveniana, Aufsätze und Mittheilungen*, Leipzig, 1872, p. 53.

[2] Wilder, p. 480.

much trouble, many ideas for later development and part-writing were born of this exhaustive preliminary research.

At the first performance of the quartet in B flat, on March 21st, 1826, this tremendous finale, 745 bars in length, had little success, and the publisher, Artaria, advised the composer to write another. During the following summer, when he was busy with the composition of the quartet in F, Beethoven sketched out ideas for the new finale; these were quite different from the later studies, and quite different from the plan he ultimately adopted, being more restrained and less ebullient in feeling. It was during the days of suffering and sadness at Gneixendorff that Beethoven conceived the movement in its final form, radiant with gaiety and wit. It was finished in November, and sent on November 26th to Artaria, who paid him the sum of fifteen ducats for it. In all probability it was the last work that the Master actually completed, as he died four months later.[1]

The three quartets commissioned by Nicholas Galitzin were now completed; and the two later ones were dispatched soon after the first. It only remained for the prince to fulfil his obligation with the artist, as only the first quartet, Op. 127, had been paid for. Once in possession of the other two, however, this generous Maecenas completely forgot his debt, and on receipt of urgent letters of request from Beethoven, he excused his negligence in the following letter:

My dear and honoured M. Beethoven, you must be thinking me both careless and negligent to have kept you waiting for so

---

[1] Nohl contends that the last inspiration of Beethoven was the *Adagio* of the quartet in F major, Op. 135: *lento assai, cantante e tranquillo*. But it must be pointed out that the manuscript of the F major quartet was sent to Vienna at the end of October, while the finale of Op. 130 was not sent till November 26th. Besides, we are here only concerned with finished works; we shall see later that Beethoven's last inspiration was neither the *Adagio* of Op. 135 nor the finale of Op. 130.

long for a reply, especially after the receipt of the two fresh masterpieces of your incomparable genius; but I have been awkwardly placed, and am now in distant Russia, leaving in a day or two for the war in Persia. Before my departure I will send without fail the sum of 125 ducats to MM. Stieglitz and Co.[1]

In spite of this promise and the prince's formal arrangement, Beethoven died without having touched the money due to him.

In 1832 Seyfried wrote in his *Beethoven's Studien* that it was still owing, and Schindler declared in his turn, in the first edition of his book, that the prince's debt to Beethoven's heirs was even yet unsettled. Under the weight of these charges, Galitzin wrote a recriminative letter to the editor of the *Neue Zeitschrift für Musik*, in which he asserted that Beethoven had already received the money that was now being claimed in his name. This letter, printed on August 6th, 1832, only fanned the flame of resentment, and a second letter, sent to the *Gazette musicale de Paris*, had no better result. In the third edition of his book Schindler took up the defence against these charges, in loud support of Beethoven.[2] He brought forward incontrovertible evidence that in claiming the money, the musician was claiming no more than his due, and that the prince would have spared him the agony of his last illness if he had paid him the money at the time. This wretched altercation ultimately came to an end. After lengthy correspondence between the prince and Beethoven's heir, and by the intervention of the Count von Nesselrode, then ambassador in Vienna, the Prince paid first fifty ducats, and later seventy-five more, to Beethoven's nephew Carl, thus relieving himself of his obligation, but too late to avoid accusations on all sides.[3]

These petty vexations did not hinder Beethoven from composition. Once given an impulse, his inexhaustible inspiration flowed in a widening flood that nothing could stem. ' During the composition of the quartets

[1] Fifty ducats for each quartet, plus twenty-five ducats for the dedication of the *Grand Overture* in C major, Op. 124.

[2] He devoted nine long pages to a discussion of the dispute.

[3] Mme Audley, *Louis van Beethoven*, p. 208. Naturally the prince did not breathe a word of this miserable affair in his article to *La Presse*, quoted above.

for Prince Galitzin,' remarks Holtz, then the great man's constant companion, ' Beethoven seemed so overwhelmed with continually springing ideas that the completion of the quartets in C sharp minor and in F major was almost an effort of restraint.' 'My boy,' he would say, coming up to his friend with a smile, ' another inspiration has just occurred to me, and I must make a note of it.' And for the rest of the walk the note-book would be filled up with sketches and rough notes.[1]

An examination of the six note-books mentioned above reveals the fact that Beethoven went on without interruption from the composition of the quartet in B flat to the quartet in C sharp minor, and that he worked on all the movements at the same time, in the method adopted with the last four movements of the preceding work. The early sketches for the quartet are in the third book, dated December 1825, and the later ones in the sixth, dated May 1826. A letter from Beethoven to Schott the publisher, of May 20th, 1826, gives the date of the completion of the work. ' At that date (April 6th, 1826) the quartet was still not quite completed, but it is now finished.' Nevertheless, Op. 131 was still not ready for the press in July; on September 29th Beethoven wrote to Schott, ' It is to be hoped that you will very soon have the quartet in C sharp minor.' And he did send it soon after : ' I hope you have already received the new quartet,' he wrote on October 13th from Gneixendorff (Chantavoine, p. 280).

The XIVth quartet in C sharp minor, Op. 131, was a source of long-continued labour to Beethoven. It was not only that the fashioning of the themes was, as usual, a matter for patient experiment; on the contrary, these reached their final shape fairly soon. The subject for the fugue was soon evolved, and the answers were found at the fifth above and the fourth below; the theme for the *Andante* (No. 4) only underwent

[1] Wilder, p. 478.

slight alteration of notes and modification of key;[1] it is the same with that of the *Adagio* (No. 6),[2] and most of the others. Only the theme of the finale is at first entirely different from the form it ultimately takes. But even here the final theme quickly displaces this abortive attempt. . . . Beethoven's method of work is this time on new lines, and it is the same in the quartet that follows; the themes are quickly found, and the broad lines of the quartet decided upon, and then Beethoven embarks on an endless polishing of detail; he takes a passage and repeats it in various ways; he tries different combinations of voices, and every possible variety of part-writing; and it is not till he has exhausted every possibility that he makes the final decision between them. All these numerous studies accumulate on odd leaves that together form a book three times as large as the manuscript score.[3]

The XVIth quartet, in F major, Op. 135,[4] also gave rise to similar studies, but considerably fewer. Of all the quartets it is the one that took Beethoven least time to compose. It was begun in the summer of 1826, after Op. 131, and was completely finished at the end of September. At least, so Holtz asserts. At any rate it is certain that twelve days after his arrival at the 'house of Cain', as Beethoven always stigmatized his brother's home, the Master told his publisher that the manuscript would be sent directly, that is to say, in the very

[1] See the series of modifications in Nottebohm's study, quoted above, note 1, p. 213 (twelve sketches for the first violin part of the last four bars of the *Andante*).

[2] A study of the sketches for this *Adagio* shows Fétis to be mistaken in saying (*Revue musicale*, 1830, 2nd series, vol. i, p. 351) that Beethoven had used here an old French melody. If it had been the case, Beethoven would not have omitted to mention the source of the theme, in the same way that he did with the Russian folk-*motifs* of Op. 59, and would not have modified the form of the melody.

[3] Nottebohm, *Beethoveniana*, p. 54.

[4] Op. 134 is an arrangement for four hands of the *Grand Fugue*, Op. 133, by Anton Halm, revised by Beethoven. According to the title, it is 'arranged by Beethoven' (Artaria). See Schindler, p. 254.

early days of October, and Johann van Beethoven took it to Vienna [1] himself on October 30th. Beethoven did not write a dedication until much later ; on March 18th, 1827, a week before he died, he offered it to Johann Wolfmayer, one of his finest friends and first admirers in Vienna.[2] He had originally dedicated the quartet in C sharp minor, Op. 131, to Wolfmayer, but in October 1826, when the work was being dispatched to Schott for publication, General Baron Stutterheim had just taken Beethoven's graceless nephew Carl into his regiment, and the Master wished to show his gratitude to the baron by inscribing his name in front of his new work. In the dedication of Op. 135 he made amends to Johann Wolfmayer. Op. 131 appeared in print in April 1827, after the death of the composer.

On October 7th, 1826, Beethoven wrote to his old friend Wegeler : ' I still hope to give several more great works to the world, and then, like a tired child, to end my earthly existence among friendly souls ' (Chantavoine, p. 279). Five months later his sufferings and his life were at an end, without his having realized half the projects pent up within his imagination.[3]

[1] Wilder, p. 481. A note in Beethoven's hand on the first violin part of Op. 135 gives : Gneixendorff, October 30th, 1826.

[2] On March 24th, three days before his death, Beethoven asked Schindler to write to Schott, and to send him the agreement by which he gave him the copyright of the quartet in F major. The signature to this letter is the last he ever wrote.

[3] Among the works Beethoven had in mind, symphonies, oratorios, . . . &c., of which scattered sketches are to be found in the later books, there is one in a fairly advanced stage of development. It is a quintet commissioned by the publisher Diabelli in the summer of 1826, and Beethoven was working on it at the same time as the quartet in F, and the finale of Op. 130. It is uncertain exactly what instruments this quintet was intended for ; in the list drawn up after Beethoven's death, for his heirs, we read : *Violinquintett* ; but, in a letter on the subject to Diabelli, the Master speaks of his idea of a Quintet for Flute (*Quintett für Flöte*). But again, none of the sketches seem to imply the use of this instrument.

One movement in the work, *Andante maestoso*, in C major, was almost complete at the time of his death, and Diabelli printed an

A fundamental difference of outlook separates the last quartets from those that preceded them, including the one in F minor, Op. 95, even though it approaches the spirit of the later works in a certain subjective intensity of emotion. Impassioned they may be, these earlier quartets, but they are primarily objective, and the later works are stamped with a profound and undeniable subjectivity; the mind that formed them is now wholly independent of external things for its inspiration, detached from the outside world, and careless of traditional form; the last quartets are essentially the direct expression of Beethoven's most intimate spirit, the channel of inspiration flowing from another sphere. These melodies came to birth in the soul of the musician, and no external influence can touch them. As though unable to tear himself away from the task of interpreting his own inner consciousness, Beethoven extends it endlessly, delighting in his inexhaustible creative gift.[1] For this reason he is especially drawn to the form known as the *Grand Variation*.[2] From him it gains a new lyrical vitality and force, expressing all the possible shades of emotional variety and contrast. He draws the inmost subtleties of feeling from a theme already profoundly conceived and profoundly moving, and develops its expressive capacity with limitless musical resource. Once embarked upon these confidences,

arrangement. The rest remained in outline, and the pocket-book which contains them belonged to Schindler, and is now in the Royal Library in Berlin. The last thirteen pages are blank; after the last note, Schindler wrote in his own hand on the page : ' These sketches were written in my presence, and were the last Beethoven ever set down, about ten days before he died.'

[1] ' The Master's genius seems to break its chains, and, escaping from the restraint of the bar, it is even freed from the restraint of rhythm, for nothing can now confine nor set a limit to its powers. . . . In an ecstasy of freedom and creation he soars for a second into infinite time and space.' (C. Bellaigue, *Études musicales : les Sonates pour piano de Beethoven*, p. 181.)

[2] Cf. Vincent d'Indy, *Cours de composition musicale*, pp. 476 onwards, with examples taken from the XIIth and XIVth quartets.

Beethoven's ardour is unquenchable, and he does not stop till the last secret of his soul has been laid bare. The most beautiful example of this colossal variation form is to be found in the C sharp minor quartet, Op. 131.[1]

It is not only that each movement of these quartets assumes gigantic proportions, by reason of this uninterrupted flood of musical ideas, but each main theme is itself on a larger scale, occupying a greater number of bars than before. The theme of the *Adagio* of the quartet in E flat, Op. 127, stretches over eighteen bars of 12/8 time. And these eighteen bars, enclosing one of those indescribable passages that only Beethoven could write (like the *Adagio* of the IXth symphony, the *Benedictus* of the Mass in D, the *Adagio* of the great sonata in B flat Op. 106), lead on to variations where the original theme shines through a brightness of rarefied purity.

If these last quartets are marked almost invariably by thematic length and extension of development, there are none the less to be found in them passages where the inspiration changes rapidly from moment to moment in the most unexpected way (*Andante* in D, of the B flat quartet, Op. 130), or in which short snatches of *motif*, sometimes figures of two notes, give rise to an amusingly elaborate piece of construction (finale of the quartet in F, Op. 135).

Lack of comprehension of Beethoven's motive force in the composition of these quartets is the chief reason why they are so often thought obscure. The attitude of mind in which most people listen to chamber music must undergo a radical change before the listener can understand them. As a rule, the concert-goer is accustomed to notice, especially at the first hearing of a piece, mainly that aspect of it which appeals to the ear—*Aria* and *cantilena* passages, for example, and technical details of theme and melody. The rest he considers an

[1] Von Lenz says of these variations that 'they are not so much variations as different expressions of a sublime inspiration' (op. cit., p. 255).

elaborate development of the thematic material, which
it is unnecessary to follow with the same close attention
as the theme itself, and where the ear may rest for
a space in order to pick up the return of the subject
with revived interest.

Such an attitude is impossible with the last quartets,
where this type of development is non-existent. Like
Wagner's unbroken melodic line, Beethoven's thought
is linked, bar by bar, from start to finish, into a continuous organic whole, in which all must be grasped or
nothing; in the loss of but one bar the thread is broken,
and one wanders in a maze. Owing to their broad
extended construction, the themes alone of the quartets
are difficult for an unaccustomed ear to grasp, but how
much more so their complicated development and continuous working out. One cannot afford to miss a single
note. Another reason for their apparent obscurity is
the complex part-writing, particularly advanced and
free. Von Lenz remarks : ' The five last quartets are
less quartets than discourses between four string
instruments.' Beethoven uses the instruments as four
separate voices, each interpreting an idea with the
utmost freedom and individuality, yet uniting in a perfect and significant whole. Certainly, from this freedom of
part-writing there result occasional angularities of style
and harshness of effect, of which the *Grand Fugue*,
Op. 133, offers many examples. This fugue is one of
the two works by Beethoven—the other being the
fugue from the piano sonata, Op. 106—which should
be excluded from performance. Op. 133, described by
a note on the manuscript as ' *tantôt libre, tantôt recherchée* ', is one of the greatest works of genius in existence
to read, but reading gives more pleasure than hearing.
Studying the score, one is struck by the novelty of
counterpoint, the vigour of each part, the logical development of transformations and modifications of the
subject chosen, but on hearing it one also realizes that
this time the Master has missed altogether the intimate

and contemplative appeal to the ear, found to perfection
in his last works (to recall again the *Adagio* of the
IXth symphony, and the *Benedictus* of the Mass in
D). Abandoning himself with an almost demoniacal
pleasure to his mighty genius, Beethoven heaps one
discordant effect upon another, and the general impression of tiresome waste of sound cannot be dispelled
by the marvel of its technical construction, nor by the
perfection of detail (the impressive introduction, the
Andante in G flat—a dazzling peak—and the magnificent conclusion). It is impossible to share W. von
Lenz's view that this fugue is the climax of Beethoven's
art; one can only consider it the outcome of pheno-
menal vigour and fantastic power. It is a work that
Beethoven rightly set apart from his last quartets.[1] In
them, by contrast, the sensitive ear, familiarized with
the work by previous hearing, finds complete satisfaction; nevertheless the study of these quartets could
not fail to surprise any one who had forgotten the lapse
of time between these and the preceding group; the
quartet in F minor, Op. 95, was written in 1811, and
the quartet in B flat, Op. 127, in 1823; and one knows
what Beethoven had written in the interval, all he had
lived through and expressed in his music. In studying
this music written during those intervening years, one
discovers here and there, in some orchestral, choral, or
piano work, tendencies that hint at the later manner,
advanced details that bridge the gulf, as von Lenz
observes, between the early period and the five epic
poems of the future. The Op. 95 quartet, and in it
particularly the *Andante*, possesses already the peculiar
intimacy of feeling that inspires all the later quartets,
and, in consequence, it possesses their long-drawn-out
development and extended melodies. Religious feeling
—the inspiration of the Mass—is echoed in the *Adagios*
of the later works (especially in the quartet in A minor,

[1] Nevertheless, on account of its original position, it is studied after
Op. 130.

Op. 132); and the conception of universal goodwill
and happiness, long felt, and expressed to perfection in
the IXth symphony, flows through them in an abound-
ing tenderness and serenity.

The last piano sonatas—the second movement of
Op. 111, for example—already contain a hint of this
emotion, the impelling force of the last quartets, so
purely subjective that it often tends to become veiled
and enigmatic; through the two staves of the piano
score, as afterwards through the four staves of the
quartet, he tells the secret of his soul, heedless of conventional form or public approval, for himself alone, and
in pure self-expression. Once one has plumbed these
spiritual depths, and grasped this individual conception,
once one has been inspired by the *Adagio* of the B flat
sonata to feel with the artist the infinite tragedy of
universal unhappiness, one has divined the secret of
the last quartets, and they lie open to complete comprehension both of meaning and detail. Yet these works
present wide differences of purpose and style. According to von Lenz, ' they represent the emancipation of
the quartet form from the fetters of past tradition '.
A gigantic imagination gave them birth, and joy of
creation inspires them; here is lavished a wealth of
bold counterpoint, massive design (as in some movements of the B flat quartet, Op. 130), poignant harmonies and heart-breaking melodies, bursts of wit and
laughter. Some of the quartets are from first to last
the concise and logical development of one idea (Op.
132, in A minor; Op. 131, in C sharp minor); in
others his imagination runs riot, and successive movements create sparkling contrasts. But through it all
surges the essential personality of the artist, giving
impulse to passages of constant recitative, as in the later
sonatas, and to the frequent expression marks in the
text, indicating to the listener the drift of imaginative
meaning.

Other characteristics of these later works remain to

be pointed out. First and foremost they are peculiarly
true to the quartet genre, from the listener's standpoint;
whereas in the earlier quartets, and especially in Op. 59,
the form tends to slip from the confines of its genre,
and to approach the idiom of the orchestra or at least
to suggest it, here it has become impossible to conceive
of any other interpretation of the work apart from the
medium of the quartet. No other instrumental ensemble could convey the imaginative idea to the listener
with equal clarity and depth. When one thinks, for
instance, of the opening bars of the A minor quartet,
Op. 132, expressed through the supple medium of
the four instruments, one can imagine nothing that
more perfectly assimilates the creeping mystery of
this theme, as it slips like a phantom spirit across the
page.

Though perfectly expressive of musical ideas, the
character of these last quartets has also an entirely
individual and remote quality, spacious but unsub-
stantial, of itself, and alone of its kind in the realm of
music. Its effect on the sensitive ear is so intense as to
be often agonizing. Marx says that ' it tortures the
nerves '. So perfect a unity between idea and expression, whether spontaneous or the outcome of slow
growth, reveals the fact that in his last works, in spite
of the harshness that is sometimes said to mar them
(a result of his loss of hearing, and not of a weakening
inspiration), the deaf Beethoven heard his music more
clearly than in the far-off days of strength and vigour.
They are marked by yet another characteristic, a point
touched upon earlier in this chapter : the almost total
absence of the brilliant lyrical quality that lightens the
quartets of the second period. Beethoven here pene-
trates to the very spirit of the quartet genre, lingering
over effects by which he can express the subtleties of
his emotion, but no longer does he bestow upon it the
ecstatic flights of purely lyrical character—' symphonic ', according to Helm—which formerly swept

the stream of sound before it. Yet several movements of the later quartets are notable exceptions;
as, for instance, the finale of Op. 131, in C sharp
minor.

We must not draw the conclusion from this that his
inner flame of inspiration was dying out; it had never
burnt more clearly than in the brilliance of these last
works. The *scherzi* of the E flat and A minor quartets,
Op. 127 and 132, are perhaps comparable with the
earlier *Allegretto scherzando* of the Op. 95 quartet in F,
but in all the quartet music ever written, there is
nothing that can equal the inspiration of the *scherzi* of
Op. 130, 131, and 135.

*
* *

It may be imagined that these works were little
understood at their first performance. Prince Galitzin
writes :

I must admit that these eagerly-awaited quartets were a
source of deep disappointment in musical circles in St. Petersburg. They had been expecting music in the form and manner
of Beethoven's first quartets ; these were anything but that.
Moreover, the demands upon technique were now further increased, so that perfect ensemble became a matter of long and
hard study.

The poetic idea was hidden beneath phrases of seeming
angularity, and only revealed, even to the discerning, after long
imaginative researches into the mind of the composer, through
the medium of perfect technical performance. Nevertheless I
was not discouraged, and at all the concerts at my house nothing
but Beethoven was played, in all his various styles. I was the
object of ironical reproaches for this mania for Beethoven, but
I was undeterred by disparaging criticism from my effort to
make known among artists and amateurs the last works of a
genius several decades ahead of his generation. My perseverance
was rewarded at last, because ten years later Beethoven's music,
so far from being called extraordinary and harsh, was being
played all over the capital in drawing-rooms and concert halls ;
the world of fashion was in ecstasies over works that even distinguished artists had hitherto failed to appreciate. Now, it is an

ill-educated person who does not sing the praises of Beethoven;
he has become the fashion, and the last concerts in Bonn are an
overwhelming confirmation of my predictions in the old days
when his genius was completely misunderstood.

Upon receiving the first quartet, Op. 127, I lost no time
in sending the original manuscript to M. Baillot, in Paris, in
recognition of the great pleasure I had experienced at his quartet
concerts in 1821 and 1822. I believed that this famous artist
would prove one of the first to appreciate this new work of the
great composer. When he sent me back the manuscript, the
celebrated violinist expressed the following opinion : ' Beethoven translates one to a new world, where one wanders in wild
desolation, on the edge of chasms, in the darkness of night. One
awakes in an earthly paradise of ravishing beauty, and all the
splendour of life shines in the sunlight.' No metaphor could
better describe the last works of Beethoven ; the arid stretches
of dimly understood obscurity only throw into greater relief the
sunlit passages, where divine harmonies seem to break out of
chaos, reflecting the soul of the artist in all its variety of emotion.
One cannot form any conception of the suffering he must have
endured, misunderstood by his friends, isolated from the world,
and deprived of his chief faculty for enjoyment and usefulness.
To create the most glorious works of art, without ever being
able to hear them performed, is surely a more agonizing torment
than all the pains of Tantalus and Ixion.

According to Schindler, contemporary criticism of
the quartets was very guarded, although there were
even then critics who, after long and patient study of
the works, declared that these involved developments,
worked out to their furthest possible point, were certainly only the logical conclusion of linked ideas.
Schindler goes on to say :

One of the most enlightened critics of Beethoven was Count
Brunswick of Pesth ; and he could deservedly call himself Beethoven's pupil. For two winters we studied these quartets together
with two other distinguished performers, and finally we arrived at
a point where we grasped their harmonic and technical beauty
to the full, but were still groping for the clue to the continuity
of idea and development. Count Brunswick sometimes thought
he had discovered the elusive secret, but lost it again in the mist

of speculation, declaring that he must be dull-witted,—*schwach-kopf*. After years of study, he told me that certain passages were still as obscure to him as they had been when we separated in 1829.

The first performance of Op. 127 took place on March 6th, 1825, played by the Schuppanzigh Quartet. It failed completely in effect, and the audience, who had come expecting a beautiful work, went away in disappointment and mystification. The following criticism appeared in the *Leipziger Allgemeine Musikalische Zeitung* : ' The work was understood by very few, and made a bewildering impression ' (the critic adds that he himself was no exception). The failure was considered due to Schuppanzigh, whose playing was not subtle enough to give full justice to the poetic refinements of this very difficult work. There was a lively dispute on the subject between Beethoven and Schuppanzigh. After such a fiasco Beethoven was anxious to re-establish the fame of his work, and wrote to Joseph Boehm, a professor at the Conservatoire, who was also a talented virtuoso ; after having surmounted the technical difficulties, he obtained better performance ; nevertheless certain passages were still quite incomprehensible, though the composer was told, too hastily, that it was an unqualified success, and as perfectly understood as his early quartets. Before this first performance Beethoven wrote a personal letter of encouragement to the four artists.

The second quartet in A minor, Op. 132, was played for the first time in November 1825. It was far more immediately effective than the first, owing to sustained study on the part of Schuppanzigh and the rest of his quartet. The only obscurity lay in the variations of the *Canzona*, &c., which Beethoven had written on recovery from his illness. As early as August in 1825, Beethoven had tried over this new work at the request of Maurice Schlesinger, at a private music club where Charles Holtz was first violin. The composer was present with the artists, and Schlesinger had the copyright of this quartet for France and Germany. He took the manuscript with him to Paris.

Generally speaking, most critics of performances of the quartets, in the years following the publication of the works, emphasize the curious blending of ' genius and extravagance ' that they seem to present. Certainly there was recognized here extraordinary beauty, but marred by blemishes and by passages of inexplicable obscurity. One gains the impression of admiration mixed with an uneasy, even awestruck, astonishment. At the same time, criticism is less clearly defined and precise than it was of the Op. 59 group, for instance. Obviously, contemporary opinion was entirely bewildered by these works, which are still fascinating mysteries to us after a century of advance in musical thought.

The following extracts show the direction in which criticism tended.

The Bohrer Quartet performed the quartets of Op. 127, 130, 131, and 132 in the music rooms of A. Pape, a pianoforte manufacturer, during the years of 1830 and 1831. The *Revue musicale* published the following account of the concert on March 6th, 1831, when Op. 132 (XVth) was played:

Part of the evening was devoted to one of the last quartets (in A minor) of this extraordinary artist. Here, I must confess, it seemed to me that genius was overwhelmed by fantastic extravagance. Without doubt the work could only have been written by Beethoven, and one recognizes his style from time to time, but these moments are few and far between. The first movement, the least involved of them all, is nevertheless full of a harmonic vagueness which offends a sensitive ear. The *menuet* and *trio* recall the Master's finest period, and have the greatest novelty of effect. The *Adagio* is a thanksgiving offered to the Almighty on convalescence after a long illness; one can only express doubt as to whether the Master was yet quite restored to health. . . . As to the last movement, comment is impossible; one must respect even the aberrations of so great a musician.

In the *Revue musicale* of July 27th, 1834, Fétis again speaks of the 'caprice which mars the admirable qualities of Beethoven's last works. In the two last quartets by this celebrated musician . . . there is much to occasion surprise; it is difficult to imagine how so powerful an inspiration could be linked with so much sheer extravagance. . . .'

H. Blanchard writes on February 18th, 1844, in his *Silves musicales* in the *Revue et Gazette musicales de Paris*:

With the unwavering faith of a devout believer bowing down before his prophet, M. Maurin presented his audience with a performance of the XIIth quartet, Op. 132 (*sic*) . . . the work belongs to Beethoven's last period, when deafness had overtaken him, and his broken faith in humanity had driven him to take refuge in a half-defined religious mysticism. He had reached a stage of premature senility, brought on by illness and discouragement rather than by his actual age. His last works bear a sort of analogy with the *Rêveries* of J.-J. Rousseau. The grammatical and musical forms are respectively observed, but the inspiration flickers. It must be obvious to those who read the works of the philosopher of Geneva carefully and without prejudice, that when he wrote the *Rêveries* he had lost something of his old intellectual keenness. Might it not have been the same with Beethoven, writing these later works deprived of his hearing, the most precious faculty he possessed? His manuscript is covered with marginal notes expressing religious aspiration, entreaties, and introspective doubts—*Muss es sein? Es muss sein! Es muss sein!*

It cannot, however, be denied that there are still, in these last compositions, qualities which have always marked his quartet writing—splendour of inspiration, broad curves of melody, and daring harmonies; but he seems no longer careful of the formal excellence to be found in his earlier work, his idea wanders in a waste of formless development. Those who worship him blindly see in this the ecstasy of a misunderstood genius; his true admirers pity him, and realize that it is now the dying fire of genius still bursting fitfully into flame. . . . Frankly, we can declare that the *Adagio* of the twelfth Beethoven quartet, except for the opening passage of grave religious fervour, is intolerably long, and without sequence of idea, in spite of the long inscription which explains the emotions of the writer, and might well be considered the forerunner of the ' programmes ' of the great Romantic composers.

A professor of the Conservatoire who was present at the concert and who had patiently listened to this quartet, and in particular to the *Adagio*, with mingled respect and curiosity, remarked afterwards to me : ' If this work had been played for the first time before competent judges as the work of a young composer at the beginning of his career, the verdict would very likely be that there were plenty of ideas in it, but little conciseness of form, and that when the young man had shaken off his youthful exuberance he would probably produce a work of art.' I will not reveal the name of the author of this far-sighted dictum, as it is possible that he would not care to stand by this private expression of his convictions. . . . To say that Beethoven became at the end of his life a sublime madman, like Tasso, is to commit a sacrilege in the eyes of his most ardent admirers, but I am not ashamed to uphold the statement.

From the pen of the same critic we read, in the number for 15th April 1849, in reference to the XIIIth quartet :

That work is the *Agésilas, hélas!* of its composer ; one imagines that the musicians for whom it is a foregone conclusion to admire anything that Beethoven wrote, and who are forced to admire these last works of the great composer's decadent old age—one imagines that these musicians, possessing only a smattering of the knowledge of beautiful sound, will be hastened on their way to join the uncultured adherents of musical romanticism, which the great writer has thus opened out to them.

To the complete quartet form—consisting of a first movement, a *menuet* or *scherzo*, an *adagio*, and a *finale*—in which it is difficult enough, as it is, to obtain perfection of balance, Beethoven has added two extra movements, in his XIIIth quartet in B flat major. The first movement is remarkable for the elaboration of strange harmonies, the long delay in the resolution of discords, and a consistent avoidance of the perfect cadence in concluding melodic phrases. It seems to point to an exhausted imaginative power, which is using every possible technical conceit and device of composition in default of fresh inspiration.

The fifth and sixth movements especially (the *Cavatina* and the *Finale*) are full of these interrupted resolutions, although still lightened by flashes of brilliant melodic writing. In the striking phrase of one of our best composers, whose instrumental quartets and quintets every one admires, Beethoven's worn-out imagination in the finale of the XIIIth quartet makes one think of a tired swallow imprisoned in a fast-shut room, beating its wings wearily against the closed window.

Quartet No. XII, Op. 127 (in E flat).

I. *Maestoso* (Introduction) and *Allegro*.

Maestoso (in E flat, 2/4), vigorous chords are struck, inspired with a throbbing energy that springs for six bars from the sinewy *sforzandi* of the bass:

Ex. 155.

suddenly, out of a preliminary trill, grows a tender curving melody in 3/4, *Allegro*:

Ex. 156.

It forms a striking contrast, to be reasserted in the pages that follow in intermittent repetitions, and gives the movement an air characteristic of Beethoven, dominated by the tender outlines of the principal theme. Murmured, *teneramente*, caressing, upon the first violin, it is thrown into relief by the web of counterpoint woven beneath it, the typical linking of bar with bar, and the steadily moving bass.

At the ninth bar of the *Allegro*, the viola takes the theme, immediately followed by the second violin, and together with the first violin they extend the two phrases of the theme, the one *motif* in crotchets, the other in quavers, in beautifully blended movement of parts. The second theme follows, given with long sweeps of the bow by the first violin, bringing back the energy of the introduction, sustained by a *forte* accompaniment on the inner parts :

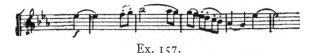

Ex. 157.

As it comes to an end, the four instruments take it up in imitation ; then, modulating to G minor, a plaintive melody appears on the first violin, against a sort of contrary movement on the second violin and viola. The advanced chromatic harmonies of the fifth and sixth bars of the phrase, which is based on the first theme, are worthy of remark :

Ex. 158.

The melody broadens and rises to a climax on the first

violin, above imitative phrases on the other instruments,
and then becomes attenuated, merging into the crotchet
motif of the first theme (Ex. 156), and finally leads back
by a series of modulations in trills—a device Beethoven
often used in his later works—through G major to an
unexpected return of the *Maestoso* figure of the Introduction. Firmly establishing the key of G major, in
vigorous spread chords on all four strings of the violins,
it gives place as before to the *Allegro* theme (Ex. 156)
in the same key as the *Maestoso*, growing out of a preliminary trill in G major. The development this
time, however, is different. The exposition is followed
by a broad *Canto fermo* melody spreading on the first
violin above a rising sequence of the crotchet *motif*
from the earlier theme (Ex. 156) on the intermediary
voices :

Ex. 159.

The new theme passes to the viola and then to the
'cello, returns on a high E flat to the first violin, struck
forte three times, and then loses itself in a short modulation to C. The crotchet *motif* from the first theme
recurs on the second violin, with the *Canto fermo* melody
imposed upon it by the first violin, and a rapid *crescendo*

brings in a dramatic figure distantly related to the
quaver *motif* of the first theme:

Ex. 160.

This vivid episode works quickly through the tonality
of B flat and the diminished seventh of C minor, but
instead of the extended development that one expects,
it falls away suddenly before the re-entry of the *Maestoso*
of the Introduction, *con tutta forza*. This time it is heard
with all the force of which the quartet is capable
(*fortissimo*, while the second entry is *forte*, and the original
opening only *sforzando*) in C major, and the *Allegro* theme
follows in the same key, imbued with a corresponding
increase of vigour. A twenty-bar episode ensues, in which
the crotchet *motif* of the theme is given in rhythmic
unison on the lower voices, in movement sometimes
contrary and sometimes similar; against it is set, sweet
and insistent, the following characteristic figure:

Ex. 161.

rising on the first violin a tone at a time. This close
conflict between the parts is brought to an end, as
though exhausted, by a return of the initial theme in

E flat an octave higher. From this point the development is mainly similar to that sketched out at each previous return of the *Allegro*, but very free and original in its working out and moulding of the musical meaning of the work, a sequence of ideas perfectly clear after reading the score, or hearing a performance. The form of composition is more condensed, and from the psychological aspect the work seems to broaden, and progress towards a goal that constantly recedes as it is approached. The two principal *motifs* (Ex. 156 and 157) lend this section of the *Allegro* a keen vitality, shadowed over by a distant reminiscence of the plaintive melody of Ex. 158. Not till after sixty-nine bars is the conclusion reached, marked by the rhythmic crotchets which heralded the first return of the *Maestoso*, this time in the tonic key (E flat). But the sonorous vigour of the Introduction is expected in vain. Instead, a mood of resignation to an implacable fate supervenes, felt in the sombre gloom of a bass C flat. This melancholy is lightened by an interior peace, and after a bar of suspense, a confident hope in the future is expressed by a return of the original theme on the first violin, at first in A flat, and then in the tonic key. The *Canto fermo* theme, which was in its earlier appearances abruptly cut short, is here made the subject of a long statement, alternating in importance with the original theme, in its complete form. The web of sound tightens, and the voices, *mezza voce*, gain strength ; it seems as if the great melodist can barely tear himself away from the quaver *motif* which recurs incessantly on the second violin and the viola, as though to fix its image indelibly upon the hearts of its hearers, while the first violin soars away into the heights, only leaving them to sing the first *Allegro* theme (Ex. 156) for the last time, an octave above. The music fades into a *pianissimo* as the 'cello and first violin murmur the seven last notes of the theme, in a conclusion charged with the tender feeling of the opening.

This entire first movement of the quartet is a delicate and subtle portrayal of the artist's soul, and a perfect example of true Wagnerian unbroken melody, adorned with *motifs* of varied construction. Here we are far from true sonata form, and yet the new style shows itself to be as coherent and unified as the old; its unity is here assisted by the *Maestoso* opening, outlining the massive proportions of this monumental structure.[1] In this work, the first in the manner of his later quartets, Beethoven reveals himself—not only his power of psychological expression, but his genius—as a creator of musical form.

II. *Adagio ma non troppo e molto cantabile* (A flat, 12/8). The predominating effect of the first movement of the XIIth quartet is one of mystical contemplation. In the slow movement Beethoven's inspiration frees itself from the last restraining influence; the *Adagio* is one of the broadly conceived movements rising out of a depth of concentrated feeling that only his last works reveal, and which is found first of all in the IXth symphony and the great B flat Sonata, Op. 106.

The apparently complex construction of the work, in which every note is of vital importance, is never merely the result of technical art, but springs from the artist's brain as a natural flowering of his complex emotions and aspirations.

From a mysterious distance the dominant E flat is heard on the 'cello, followed by D flat on the viola, and B flat on the second violin; the three notes, broadly sustained (the E flat for more than two and a half bars), firmly establish the ruling tonality of A flat; the tonic chord is then asserted as a basis for the ethereal melody that rises from it on the first violin. The lower voices are limited for the first few bars of the theme to a sustained harmonic accompaniment, soon to gain melodic interest of their own, as they move in contrary motion with the

[1] Von Lenz gives a rather inadequate criticism of this construction (op. cit., p. 277).

principal part. As the theme fades away on the first
violin it passes to the 'cello and is extended during
eight bars, while the first violin answers in imitation;
the second violin moves with the 'cello, and the viola
fills up the harmony. Then the theme moves back to
the first violin, and continues almost uninterrupted until
the four voices unite in a conclusion of extraordinary
harmonic effect (the 'cello part in the last bar but one,
D flat, F flat, D), where a harsh and piercing melancholy prevails:

Ex. 162.

Apart from the three bars of introduction, this opening section of the *Adagio* is, from beginning to end,
eighteen bars of uninterrupted melody, like a slow continuous melopœia. This melopœia is to be the theme
of five variations, which one can describe, with Marx,
as 'an increasingly sublime transfiguration of the
melody'. From the point of view of style, it can be
compared with the variations of the *Adagio* of the
IXth symphony, and perhaps with the piano sonatas
in E and C minor, Op. 109 and 111 respectively. But
in detail of formal construction they are quite different;
the variations here are purely contrapuntal, and wholly
in the genre of the quartet.

In the first variation (eighteen bars in length, like
the opening statement of the theme), already the latent
vitality of the melody is expressed in the substitution
of two semiquavers for a quaver, wherever it occurs in
the course of the theme, and in every part, giving an

effect of added animation, a restlessness, and intensity of thought.

The second variation, twenty bars long, is of opposite character (*Andante con moto*, 4/4):

Ex. 163.

The theme appears at first on the second violin, continued in contrary movement on the first; it acquires at once a rhythmic decision, as the lower voices establish a monotonous *staccato* that resounds like the distant beating of a drum. (Notice the fifths on the 'cello.) The inspiration becomes almost martial and heroic, but still as though enshrouded in a half-light. Shades of heroes seem to cross the path of the imagination, ethereal and shadowy. As the development extends, this impression deepens; melodic imitations on the violins are heard against the redoubled *staccato* of the bass, and from the principal theme new melodic and rhythmic life seems to spring and flourish. The half-light persists, with barely perceptible changing nuance. One bar only (the twelfth from the beginning) contains a *forte*, and that is a *sforzato* on a D flat held by the first violin, accentuated by a vigorous syncopated figure in unison on the lower voices. The modulation to the minor at the end of this bar casts a passing shadow of melancholy over the theme, now adorned with imitations, trills and turns, on the two violins alternately, against the monotonous beating of the bass. This restless variation, a dream-like fantasy of the imagination, is linked to the next by a modulation in a unison of the four instruments (C sharp–E). Immediately, a striking contrast is produced between the new variation (*Adagio molto espressivo*, 4/4) in E major and the one preceding.

Adagio molto espressivo.

Ex. 164.

The eighteen bars of this variation breathe a deep religious feeling. Like a prayer, the notes of the sustained melody on the first violin fall slowly upon the ear, repeated by the bass, in a stretch of melody of a type often found in the chamber music of Schumann. As it comes to an end, rhythmic triplets, struck *pianissimo* on E natural, bring in the fourth variation of eighteen bars in 12/8 time, and the tonic key of A flat major through a modulation to E flat. This section combines the fullness of inspiration of the first variation with the subdued melancholy of the second. The triplet rhythm persists on the lower voices, and the first violin broadens into a melodic flight in which the theme appears in an altered and ornamented form, incorporating a modification already heard in the course of the variation in E major.

The 'cello follows with a statement of the theme almost in its original form, written on the tenor clef (C on the fourth line). The development is built up on a method in which all the instruments share in the theme and in the accompaniment; the theme passes between the first violin and the 'cello, and they share, too, a triplet figure of accompaniment, with strongly marked rhythm and vigour, a sort of progressive movement urged on by short trills, a device Beethoven so often used in his later works. The inner parts beat out the same harmonies in the rolling drum accompaniment of the second variation, and then join the 'cello at the thirteenth bar in a statement of the melody, to which is given a new impassioned energy. Alone, the first violin provides the accompaniment of endless trills and grace-notes, with an almost fantastic effect.[1]

Between this variation and the last is a thirteen-bar episode on a thematic basis borrowed from the cadence passage of the principal melody (Ex. 162), stated by the first violin and the viola, at first solo, *sotto voce*, then strengthened by isolated *pizzicati* on the second violin and the 'cello. Through modulations first to E major and then to A flat, snatches of melody are tossed about, as it were, now in succession, now in extraordinary contrary movements, to which the first violin puts a stop by a figure of trills derived from that of the preceding variation, which lead on to the fifth and last variation of nine bars.

It is this last variation which makes the movement akin to the *Adagio* of the IXth symphony. Here, as there, the first violin gives a metamorphosed statement of the principal theme in a fluent semiquaver passage, taken up afterwards by the other three instruments; above the wave of melody, for four bars, held notes on E flat and A flat leap up on the first violin through several octaves, till a *crescendo* is reached, when they drop from the heights to join the other instruments in a transformed version of the concluding cadence passage (Ex. 162), remarkable for the flexible movement of the parts. The actual conclusion is still to come; as though reluctant to bring this inexhaustible stream of sound to an end, the artist introduces a *Coda* reminiscent of the fourth variation. The beat is marked by 'cello *pizzicati*, the inner parts have the triplet figure, and the first violin a melodic design floating amid trills, and modulating to D flat major; the whole passage of five bars is *mezza voce*, swelling to a fugitive *crescendo* in the last bar but one on the first violin. A strange

[1] See the verses of Musset on the serenade of Don Juan (*Namouna*).

enharmonic G sharp, the length of a dotted minim, seems to suggest a return to the key of E major, and thus to a fresh field of exploration, but the principal tonality is re-established, and a last figure on the first violin, joined by the 'cello, murmurs a farewell as the dream slips away; the parts unite on the last bar in *crescendo* quavers, *ritardando*, leading to a final sustained *pianissimo* A flat. So fades from view this vision of a supernatural existence, where, with Schumann, one ' seems to have lingered, not fifteen short minutes, but an eternity. . . .' [1]

III. *Scherzo* (*Scherzando vivace* in E flat, 3/4). With those of the IXth symphony and of the VIIth quartet (Op. 59, No. 1), this *scherzo* is the most advanced work Beethoven ever wrote. But while the *Allegretto scherzando* of the Op. 59 derives its highly developed construction from variety and musical treatment of *motifs*, the *scherzo* of the quartet in E flat is evolved from the germ of an idea gradually developed to complex maturity.

After a breathless summons by vigorous *pizzicato* chords on all four instruments (one of Beethoven's most characteristic traits, instanced again in the Eroica) the 'cello introduces a fragmentary theme, *pianissimo* and whimsical, followed four bars later by a reply in contrary motion on the viola, while the violins have seven bars of silence (Ex. 165).

[1] The following details borrowed from von Lenz are interesting additions to the history of this *Adagio*. At the fifteenth bar of the episode in E major, the slur from the A to F sharp in the 'cello part was omitted from the manuscript. Beethoven wrote specially to Prince Galitzin to ask for the correction to be made.

At the sixteenth bar of the viola part of the *Andante con moto*, the original performers wished to substitute a C for the second B flat. Zeuner opposed the suggestion, and Beethoven wrote to thank him, adding that the proposed alteration would give the chord of C minor, unsatisfying to the ear.

These stories, among many others, prove how unceasingly careful of detail Beethoven always was, even long after the completion of his works.

Whether taken as a whole or in its four component *motifs*, A, B, C, D, this theme contains the elements of a development that seems to stretch as far as the eye can reach, extending over a hundred bars; the unfettered imagination of the artist roams at will through endless thematic and rhythmic changes, where each

Ex. 165.

new idea is the germ of the next, and the impact of one against the other leads to countless fresh developments, unprepared, but always in logical and vigorous sequence.

The *scherzo* is of the old classical form, in that it

consists of a principal section and an *alternativo* or *Trio*,
both of which in their turn contain two subdivisions or
development sections. The subdivisions of the principal section are both repeated according to rule ; in
the *Trio*, only the first is repeated. After the *Trio* the
principal section reappears without repetition, and leads
to the conclusion with a backward glance, as it were,
towards one of the *motifs* of the *alternativo*. In the main,
it is the construction of the *scherzi* of the VIIIth and
IXth symphonies, but here infinitely enlarged both in
form and detail.

After the two bars of *pizzicato* introduction, the first
section occupies thirty-four bars. New voices join the
low-toned whispering between the bass instruments,
and in the bar immediately following the last of Ex.
165, the second violin takes up *motif* D, followed by
the first violin entering four bars later with the same
motif, which forms the subject of an ensuing dialogue
among all four parts. At the fifteenth bar, an abridged
motif A appears in an original form, given by the 'cello
(E, Ex. 166 *a*):

Ex. 166 *a*.

worthy of notice because it gives rise to a new design
of *motifs*, working out, with *motif* F, to a robust conclusion, after a change of rhythm (Ex. 166 *b*), where
this first section ends on the dominant B flat, as the

first violin· hammers out *motif* F above a falling scale
on the lower voices (Ex. 166 *c*):

Ex. 166 *b* and *c*.

Before the conclusion, the music was already growing
in animation and complexity, due particularly to the
ritmo di tre battute (Ex. 166 *b*; Beethoven's own indication), which presents itself without warning at the
twenty-fifth bar, and of which the *motif* G serves to
hasten the conclusion; later in the movement this *motif*
reappears as the subject of fresh and original treatment.

The second section opens with a unison statement
of the *motif* A-F, *fortissimo*, on all the instruments,
leading to a modulation to C minor; then several bars
of a monodic type, suave and graceful, where the first
violin has *motif* C, accompanied by a valse rhythm on

the 'cello, and the figure F on the inner parts in turn.
Polyphonic writing returns again, as the voices clash
in a feverish chromatic modulation to a point where
the first violin declaims a new figure in G flat major,
in contrary movement with the lower voices, but in
rhythmic unison :

Ex. 167.

For four bars the clash of parts continues *fortissimo* in
the key of G flat (tonic, subdominant, and dominant);
then (following Ex. 167) in a sudden *pianissimo* they
together modulate through F sharp minor, D major, and
finally C minor, falling once more in an energetic unison
upon *motif* A. Breaking off unexpectedly on E flat, the
tumult of sound is arrested for a second ; on the lower
voices alone, in unison, a theme appears *piano* (*Allegro*,

2/4), in a short period of five bars, thematically derived, apparently, from the *motif* G of the *ritmo di tre battute*:

Ex. 168.

One cannot fail to notice here the resemblance between the last two bars of Ex. 168 and a certain passage from the *Mastersingers* (in the third act, during the dialogue between Sachs and Beckmesser. Beckmesser: 'The writing is fresh!' Sachs: 'And the ink still wet!') which thus furnishes further proof of the imaginative kinship between Wagner and the later Beethoven, and shows the aptness of Wagner's remark that the greatest musical effect could only be attained by the use of Beethoven's method of dramatic expression.

The mysterious interlude, significant as introducing Beethoven's innovation of duple rhythm in the *Scherzo* form, comes to an abrupt stop on the diminished seventh, on C, bringing back *pianissimo* the 3/4 *tempo*. The *motif* C drops from high up on the first violin, answered in whimsical response by *motif* A on the second violin. The theme of the interlude returns, shortened to three bars and modulating to F minor. Then follows forty-two bars of the triple rhythm in a diverse development of *motifs* already stated, until the double bar; the section is not usually repeated in performance, owing to the length of the movement. An extraordinary episode of twenty-one bars precedes the *Trio*; the tonic key is asserted in an E flat pedal on the 'cello, eight bars long. The tone drops to a murmur, the *motifs* fade away in barely perceptible beats in the rhythm of the *ritmo di*

tre battute, pianissimo, forming the tonic triad on the lower
voices, E flat, G, B flat. With a transition on the viola
from G to G flat, the *alternativo* in E flat minor, 3/4,
bursts out *presto, crescendo.* This *Trio* is composed of
two sections, lasting with the repeat (formed this time
of the first section) for a hundred and forty-six bars.
It offers a striking contrast to the thick polyphony of
the principal section, being monodic almost from start
to finish. The melody is a long slurred passage on the
first violin, with an underlying accompaniment of regular crotchets in the middle parts, and of groups of three
crotchets on the 'cello, separated by corresponding
groups of three-crotchet rests. In the second section
the four instruments join forces, to take up an advancing
figure which follows in the key of D flat major:

Ex. 169.

from which the melody on the first violin springs up with revived strength. In it is to be found a familiar melodic trait of Beethoven's early manner (notably in the first movement of the C minor sonata, Op. 30, No. 2, for violin and piano, though here with less vigour).

So the *Trio* ripples on, in a stream of sound essentially melodic in type, in turn ethereal and misty, decisive and heroic.

The principal section reappears, slipping back as smoothly as it receded. The development is exactly the same as the original exposition, including the twice-recurring episode in 2/4 time. During its course, even the *Trio* section reappears exactly as before, but after the twelve opening bars the composer brings it to an abrupt stop as though suddenly realizing his mistake. An expressive pause follows, and the *ritmo di tre battute* returns, *pianissimo*; its last beats mingle with a final whimsical statement of *motif* C on the first violin, and in an unexpected *crescendo* the *Scherzo* concludes *fortissimo*, breaking with *motif* E on all the instruments upon the chord of the tonic.

IV. *Finale* (E flat major in 4/4). Characteristically, the *tempo* is left to the discretion of the players, and is not indicated at all. In this finale the passionate and bitter emotions of the first movement, the unearthly twilights of the *Adagio*, and the fantastic movement of the *Scherzo* are set aside; here all is gaiety and charm recalling the genial wit of Haydn, in which the imaginative intensity of the preceding movements is relaxed. The *motifs* are simple and almost popular in form, their development of a unique originality.

In the first twelve bars the whole content of the movement is revealed (Ex. 170). The first four bars of unison (presenting something of a resemblance, though purely superficial, to the opening of Mozart's quartet in E flat) appear at first as a simple introduction, but later it is seen that they contain germs of thematic

material. On this account, the first bar is marked
motif A, and the three others *motif* B.

At the fifth bar, above held semibreves on the middle
voices (B flat on the second violin, and E flat on the
viola), and a thrice-repeated minim figure on the 'cello,
the first violin gives out the simple melody that

Ex. 170.

dominates the movement. Played *piano*, but on the
fourth string, it gives an effect of distant bells. At
the third bar of the figure derived from *motif* A, and the
seventh from the beginning, is a curious chromatic
change from A flat to A natural ; the rest of the theme
grows out of *motif* B, and is followed by a repetition of
the entire melody, with the exception of the four introductory bars, concluding in the tonic key.

This exposition is mainly remarkable for the alternate repeated groups of three and five bars, respectively based on *motifs* A and B, creating an irregular, halting effect, and giving the passage a gay and popular air. The whole movement is developed from these two basic *motifs*, and preserves this character throughout; it is easily analysable, with the exception of certain passages which demand special study.

First, at the fifty-fifth bar, occurs a passage rippling with gaiety, after Haydn's manner, but revealing Beethoven's own essential humour in the vigorous rhythmic descent of the bass from E flat to F. Reinforcing the rhythm with grace-notes, the first violin follows in pursuit :

Ex. 171.

Linked to this passage from bar sixty-seven onwards are *motifs* A and B, in reverse order to their original appearance, and with a curiously stressed rhythm ; the *sforzando* on the weak beats in the inner parts gives an effect of latent energy (Ex. 172). This irresponsible jesting works up to a *fortissimo* conclusion, where all the voices unite on *motif* A (Ex. 173).

The three bars of Ex. 173 are striking in harmonic audacity, in the double effect of clashing discords, shrill and harsh, against perfect fifths, resounding like

a wild shout of joy. After a bar of transition, these
daring harmonies recur with interesting changes ; the
second violin alone hammers out *motif* A, and the B flat
octave of the first violin gives place to a martial figure.
The bass fifths, C-G, accented *fortissimo*, form a hard

Ex. 172.

Ex. 173.

and unyielding foundation, as though hewn out of solid
rock. The whole passage, from Ex. 171 to Ex. 173,
affords a typical example of Beethoven's strain of heroic
gaiety, to which the light-hearted wit and humour of
Haydn forms a perfect contrast.

Through a passage of sixteen bars derived from the
transition bar of Ex. 173, and actually from *motif* B,

the section terminates; the energy of the preceding
bars is gradually dispelled in a tender dialogue in thirds
on the two violins, *pianissimo*, punctuated by thirds on
the basses at the fourth below, in intermittent figures:

Ex. 174.

This dialogue brings back the exposition, but by no
means an exact repetition of the section. The *motif* B
is extended for eight bars on the first violin, in a
mysterious *piano* passage, linked immediately to the
heroic phrase of Ex. 171, heard at first *pianissimo* in
C major, then *forte* in C minor, with a *fortissimo*
modulation to G major. At this point Beethoven
suddenly interrupts the continuity of the development.
In the next four bars is the germ of a new development, in a fresh combination of themes.

Ex. 175.

THE LAST QUARTETS 253

The *motif* A (fifth bar of Ex. 170) is placed on the
first violin, *pianissimo*; and on the second violin, also
pianissimo, the heroic *motif* of Ex. 171, while the viola
works out a plaintive figure in minims, derived from
motif B; the 'cello is silent for two bars. In the next
two bars, the viola figure passes to the second violin,
motif A to the viola, and the heroic theme to the 'cello.
Then ensues a harmonic passage based on the combined themes, which constitutes one of the striking
beauties of the XIIth quartet. Straight away, in a
modulation to F minor, the *motifs* are repeated unaltered, but in varying positions of pitch. Then, in the
key of C major, taken as the dominant of F minor,
the *motifs* shed their original form; the heroic figure
of Ex. 171 becomes an insistently repeated note on the
first violin, and then on the second (in thirds, C-E);
motif A on the viola, then on the first violin, becomes
a simple design of accompaniment, and the combined
polyphony rests on a B flat pedal in the bass. The
ensemble gives a hollow and monotonous effect like
the drone of bagpipes, and the uncertainty of tonality
between C major and F minor (established by the bass
B flat) conveys a sense of uneasy gloom, wherein is
felt the weird, fantastic side of Beethoven's personality. This is one of those passages where the artist
seems to stretch his mental hearing to its fullest extent
towards some unearthly revelation; no one has ever
seemed to delight so keenly in the mysterious effect of
groping harmonies.

Out of the disquietude of these combined *motifs*, the
theme A rises on the violins in smooth and fluent
imitations, like a Bach prelude. The 'cello gives *motif* B
in minims, modulating to A flat major; the *motif*
passes to the inner voices, while the first violin sustains
a long trill, heralding the return of *motif* B in its original
form.

The course of the development brings back the
thematic combinations heard before, but with an added

independence of part-writing, which slightly mars the
logical clarity of construction. It must be pointed out
in this passage how Beethoven has turned to account
a little figure hitherto unnoticed (twenty-eighth bar of
the final section):

Ex. 176.

evolving from it a melodic period of great beauty:

Ex. 177.

But instead of fading into a dream-like sleep, this
tender lullaby is rudely broken by a return of the
original exposition. The recapitulation follows the
rules of the ordinary third section in sonata form,
though modified in detail, and enriched in technical
construction (for example, notice the use of quaver
movement against the crotchet movement). Again the
second principal section is heard—this time in E flat,
though it was originally in B flat—with the combined
thematic passages of Ex. 172 and 173, the latter this
time on the dominant chord of B flat major. The dialogue of Ex. 174 seems about to introduce a conclusion
in E flat, but an unprepared modulation to C major

brings the *Coda* (*Allegro comodo* in 6/8). From a purely psychological point of view this *Coda* epitomizes the emotional content of the entire work, but it is also, musically, a marvellous structure of sound. The prevailing 4/4 rhythm is completely routed by the 6/8, but Beethoven, doubtless intentionally, does not allow the change to strike a jarring note as an obvious technical device. The even crotchets of the first violin in the last bars of the *alla breve* tempo merge into a trill; the modulation is effected by the transition from A flat to A natural on the first violin. At the third bar, the intermittent bass figures noticed in Ex. 174, having already made an appearance in the last bars of the *alla breve*, reappear, but *pianissimo* the second time, beneath a *pianissimo* triplet design on the violins that imperceptibly re-establishes the rhythmic beat. Introduced in this way without any thematic change, the *Coda* links on to the main body of the finale in the most fluent possible manner, although in a totally different rhythm. At the fourth bar, the *motif* A enters on the first violin, above the triplet design on the second violin, in its new and strange rhythmic guise, broken on the weak beat. The entire *Coda* is based on the combination of this theme with the triplet design, in a shining web of modulations working slowly to the principal tonality of E flat. The effect of the triplet figure and the even motion of the parts is that of a rippling stream of sound. At the same time, a robust vitality is given to the conclusion by the substitution of A natural in the melody for A flat, especially in bars 23 and 27 of the *Coda*.

It almost seems as if the Master could not tear himself from this theme, the instrument of so many confidences; after all four voices have declaimed it in a mighty chorus, a sudden *pianissimo* falls, and the triplet design dies into a chromatic murmur, like a distant fairy rustling. For the last time the theme is heard, finishing on a note of interrogation (A-B flat), answered by the two vigorous chords of the tonic, which conclude the movement, and with it bring the quartet to an end, with its wealth of inspiration and spiritual power, its overflowing vitality and brilliance of technique.

Quartet No. XIII, Op. 130 (in B flat).

According to Schindler, after the XIIth quartet, Op. 127, Beethoven wrote next the XVth, Op. 132, in A minor, and after that the XIIIth quartet, Op. 130. The latter, in that case, ought to receive the *opus* number 131. But habit has established the custom of numbering the B flat quartet as Op. 130, No. XIII, and this is a good reason for following that order.[1] If the XVth quartet, Op. 132, bears signs of having been composed during the period of serious illness that Beethoven suffered in the spring of 1823, the XIIIth, written in 1825, radiates the vigour of perfect health. Its youthful vitality, instinct with the enthusiasm of recovered strength, leaves little room for melodies of a melancholy cast, but overflows in bursts of infectious gaiety and humour. If one accepts the term 'humour' in its broadest meaning, as the expression of imaginative freedom and the triumph of the mind over the sorrows and sordidness of the world, the Op. 130 quartet can be said to be the most 'humorous' of them all.

In terms of technique, this quality is realized by sudden modifications of inspiration, the creation and blending of apparently conflicting ideas. Broadly speaking, a logical and continuous psychological analysis, like that of the first two movements of the XIIth quartet (and of the Op. 131 and 132 quartets), must not be looked for in Op. 130. In the old revived joy of creation the Master is swept away by the force of his inspiration, in a flood of fresh melodies and big designs, and technical effects hitherto unknown in music. This fund of spontaneous invention makes the work, in addition to being the gayest of the quartets,

[1] See above, pp. 211 onwards.

also the most rhapsodical (W. von Lenz describes it as
' intoxicated with fantasy ').

The XIIIth quartet is in six movements : an *Allegro*
in B flat major, in very freely treated sonata form, like
the first movement of the other quartet in the key of
B flat, Op. 18, No. 6 ; a *Presto* in B flat minor, *alla
breve*, taken at a wild pace ; an *Andante scherzoso* in
D flat major, 4/4 time, in an entirely free form ; an
Allegro assai written in the popular style,· *alla tedesca*
(G major in 3/8) ; a *Cavatina* in a soft and poetic vein,
Adagio molto espressivo in E flat major, 3/4 ; finally, an
Allegro in B flat major, 2/4, at first serene in character,
afterwards exuberant.

At any rate, this is the form in which the quartet
has finally reached us, though originally the *Grand
Fugue*—' *tantôt libre et tantôt recherchée* '—formed the
finale in place of the present movement ; but in
addition to its length (stretching over thirty-five pages
of the score), this was completely misunderstood by
the musical public, as indeed it still is, and when the
publisher urged the Master to write a new finale,
Beethoven agreed, writing the new movement at a time,
November 1826, when he was ill again and almost
dying. It was to contain the very consummation of
Beethoven's genius, for the Master's inspiration rises
triumphant above the plane of bodily anguish ; knowing nothing of sorrow and suffering, this new finale
breathes an unclouded serenity and joy from the first
to the last bar.

Technically, the first movement of the XIIIth
quartet is, like that of Op. 127, remarkable for the
unbroken continuity between the slow introduction and
the *Allegro* that follows ; the link here is even closer,
for the introductory *motif* is given a thematic importance in a combination of themes in the middle of the
development section of the *Allegro* ; with amazing
assurance, Beethoven realizes here an effect suggested,
but not developed, in the first movement of the Sonata

Pathétique (development section in E minor). But as
far as the imaginative significance of the themes goes,
their inter-relation in the Sonata is quite different from
their relation in the XIIIth quartet; the introduction
expresses a passionate vigour, the principal theme a
passive tenderness; in the XIIIth quartet the significance is almost reversed.

I. *Adagio ma non troppo*, 3/4; *Allegro*, 4/4. Like
the XIIth quartet, the first movement of the XIIIth
is preceded by a slow introduction, linked on to the
Allegro. Here, as there, the bond between them is
extraordinarily close, with an added strength in the
Op. 130 quartet, because the *motif* of the introduction
is later to assume a thematic importance denied to the
introduction of the Op. 127. This significance becomes
apparent in the middle of the development section of
the *Allegro*, where the idiom that was no more than
a hint in the first movement of the Sonata Pathétique
(development section in E minor) finds full expression.
In addition to this, the emotional inspiration of the two
themes of the introduction and the *Allegro* is in reverse
order from that of the same themes in the Op. 127
quartet; here, it is the introduction that expresses a
mood of passive tenderness, the *Allegro* impassioned
vigour.

The introduction is at first closely woven and condensed in form; but at the eighth bar a more definite
figure appears on the 'cello :

Ex. 178.

which is later to give impetus to a lively development
in the *Allegro*.

The animated twofold theme, A-B, of the *Allegro*
proper, is first of all heard on the violins, almost unaccompanied :

Ex. 179.

At the fifth bar all the parts take up the theme in semi-quavers ; the exposition is, however, interrupted at this point by a return of the introduction ; the figure of the opening phrase of the movement is given by the 'cello, with imitation on the other voices, for four bars in contemplative vein, suspended on an expressive pause in the fifth bar. . . . Suddenly, the two themes of the *Allegro* burst headlong forth from all the instruments at once, *motif* A on the second violin and viola, *motif* B on the first violin and 'cello. At the thirteenth bar, the part-writing is complicated by the entry of the theme from the introduction (Ex. 178), bringing in this new rhythm an element of grace and strength to the development. The semiquaver theme broadens into quavers (bars 21 to 24) in a *staccato* unison, accentuating the strong beats *sforzando* ; in bar 23 the first violin breaks the unison by a bold, free figure in contrary movement. Then follows, for twenty-two bars :

Ex. 180.

a passage characteristic of the last period, in its heroic rhythm, the bold outlines of its design (notice the leap on the first violin from F in *altissimo* to diapason A), and the freedom of its polyphony. (See the first two bars of the example.) In the next two bars a chromatic progression, *diminuendo*, seems to fill the air with mysterious suspense.

The progression comes to an end on D flat, the dominant of G flat major; in the key of G flat the 'cello gives out on the fourth string a questioning semiquaver *motif*, *sotto voce*, derived from theme A, answered by the upper parts (the melody on the first violin, the harmony sustained on the other voices):

Ex. 181 *a*.

This smooth dialogue is repeated, and then gives place, seven bars after the last of the preceding example, to another little *motif* murmured by all the voices [1] (Ex. 181 *b*), followed at once by a passage of mocking laughter, as it seems, in all the parts; after which the theme A of the *Allegro* reappears in G flat major. The next fourteen bars are without any special significance; theme A, slurred and no longer *non legato*, seems almost ready to disappear within itself; nevertheless it works gradually up to a *crescendo*, where it is heard *fortissimo*,

---

[1] R. Wagner remembers this phrase in one of the mysterious, tender passages in the Siegfried Idyll.

first on the viola and then on the 'cello, against a background of held semibreves and minims, taken by the
first violin up to A flat two octaves above diapason A,
in a culminating effort that thus forms the climax of

Ex. 181 *b.*

the movement. The excitement dies almost at once in
a unison quaver figure, an eloquent curve of melody
fading to a *piano* (suggestive of certain phrases of
R. Schumann) and finishing on the leading note of
B flat major :

Ex. 182.

This first section is repeated, but at the *seconda volta*
the melodic phrase (Ex. 182) undergoes an extra-

ordinary change (Ex. 183). The thrice-repeated G flat, *pianissimo*, before the pause on F, gives a warning effect, probably quite accidental, like a premonition of an identical phrase in the bars that follow. The ensuing development (Ex. 184) is a masterpiece of bold construction and flawless design. Still in the key of G flat major, for two bars the 'cello sings the opening *motif* of the introduction with all the expressive power of which it is capable (*Adagio ma non troppo*, 3/4). A sudden burst of the *Allegro* tempo follows for one bar of 4/4 time where the violins are heard alone, *pianissimo*, in the two-fold theme of Ex. 179, modulating to D major by means of the enharmonic change of G flat to F sharp. The *Adagio* reappears in this key for three bars ; in the first, the *motif* B finishes a fourth higher on F sharp, and its effect of imperative summons is heightened by the change of *tempo*. The sustained F sharp sounds like a trumpet-call, in response to which the 'cello gives the last half of the introduction theme. It is in the second and third bars of this episode that we hear on the viola the three reiterated notes, of which the *seconda volta* of the previous section gave warning.

The combination of the themes of the introduction and of the *Allegro* respectively is repeated in D major (one bar of *Allegro* and three bars of *Adagio*). The *Adagio* is this time only represented by the phrase in Ex. 185. It will thus be observed that the nine *Adagio* bars here exactly contain the six bars of the introduction divided into three phrases.

In the same way as the theme of the introduction Ex. 178 was the germ of a dramatic development in the *Allegro*, so the diminished second figure (Ex. 185) is to become the basis of a further development.

The *Allegro* is re-established from this point, and proceeds without a break for some time. The passage in Ex. 186 is typical of the flexible and at the same time sequent counterpoint that follows. The viola and the 'cello take as *motifs* the diminished second figure in

Ex. 183.

Ex. 184.

contrary motion (thus forming a double *motif*) ; the first violin sounds the trumpet-call of theme B, A-D ; the second violin at the third bar plays a fragment of theme

Ex. 185.

A, *non legato*, to which is linked the diminished second design in a modified form, with the interval increased to a third, while the viola version of the figure has an interval of a sixth :

Ex. 186.

Above this poised rhythm, at the third and fourth bars, the 'cello in a high register sings a melody derived from the first violin phrase in bars 3 and 4 of Ex. 181 *a*. In these five bars, five different *motifs* are combined with consummate skill and remarkable rhythmic balance, —the clear call of the first violin, the even poise of the lower instruments, the fragment of *staccato* semi-quavers on the second violin, imposed upon the sustained *cantabile* of the bass. The light and shade of tonality stretches over the harmonic colour of this elfin fantasy, bright with a luminous clarity. Polyphonic writing for quartet has never reached a higher pitch.

The next twenty-four bars of development are

worked out on the plan of Ex. 186, but with great
variety of detail. The rhythm flows on in smooth
measured beat, enlivened from time to time by successive entries of the semiquaver figure (it appears once
in imitation in the inner parts). The tonality of D major
is followed by G major, with a change of signature, and
C minor. The untroubled serenity of the passage is
deepened when the first violin takes the 'cello theme,
while the latter sounds the trumpet-call figure. After
another interchange of themes between the two instruments, the all-pervading sense of mystery increases to
a culminating point; the musician seems to come to a
sudden decision to drive away the shadows in which
the *motifs* are enshrouded, and theme A returns in *forte*
semiquavers on the lower voices, while the first violin
sounds its original *fanfare motif* in the re-established
key of B flat major; the entry of this *motif* marks the
opening of the third section of the movement.

This is no less freely constructed than the others;
several passages are remarkable, and may be noticed in
detail, without entering into a study of its free imaginative development bar by bar.

Six bars after the return to B flat a new figure slips
out of the rapid semiquaver theme:

Ex. 187.

its rhythm is noticeably square and hard, with a harmonic harshness later to recur in the *Coda* with a special
significance.

As before, the questioning *motif* of Ex. 181 re-appears, after a modulation to D flat major, on the viola, with a grave and distant solemnity at first, then the subject of canonic imitations on the viola and 'cello in a mood of tender contemplation. A return to the key of B flat brings back a development almost identical with that of the first section of the *Allegro*, interrupted by a four-bar repetition of the *Adagio* with greater harmonic richness than before. A striking *Coda* follows, opening with a brilliant play of alternate bars of the *Allegro* and of the *Adagio*, with the last note in one *tempo* the first of the other. The *Allegro* gains the advantage, and introduces a development of the figure in Ex. 187, but this time the harsh *staccato* gives place to a soft and tender *legato* :

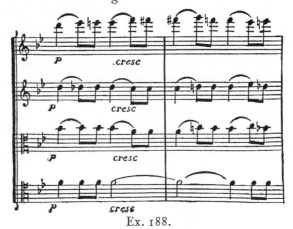

Ex. 188.

This sings a farewell in which every note is charged with meaning. As in others of the later quartets, one feels the artist's gathering reluctance to leave the fantasy of his creation as he approaches the end. . . .

But the shiver of melancholy is evanescent, and merges into the vigour of the original opening of the *Allegro*, repeated once more. The two themes A and B are heard again, but moulded to a different shape from the original, in a more closely condensed combination.

In a far-away *pianissimo* of four bars the two themes swell and finally subside beneath the short energetic conclusion on the tonic chord.

II. *Presto*, 4/4. Although this movement is not so named, it is in reality a *scherzo* of the most robust type. Its brevity, its striking rhythm, and its concise four- and eight-bar form make it one of the most popular movements among the later quartets. The combination of different elements invests it with a fantastic fairy charm, a sort of wild dance of elves; its remote tonality of B flat minor (not before used in the work), and the flying pace of the *tempo*, all in an almost continuous *pianissimo*, conspire to cast over the movement a weird unearthly light; the clash of themes from the start:

Ex. 189.

the little *motif* on the first violin, hurried and insistent, yet in an undertone, the graceful clarity of the second violin, the fluent figure on the viola, the energetic *staccato* of the bass, unite in forming a firmly woven design of perfect quartet type.

The four bars of Ex. 189 are followed by four more in symmetrical balance to the first: the first bar of each phrase is identical (the first and the fifth). This eight-bar sentence comes to an end on the tonic B flat, and is at once repeated. A second sentence of eight bars follows in logical response: the first four bars in D flat major provide a melodic phrase on the first violin of a pastoral character, reminiscent of the finale of the G major Concerto; the next four bars lead up to a second conclusion in B flat, and the period is repeated, concluding the short first section of the *Scherzo*.

The *alternativo* (*l'istesso tempo*, 6/4 in B flat major):

l'Istesso tempo

Ex. 190.

maintains the same symmetrical balance, except that the second period develops to twenty-three bars instead of eight. This section of the movement is marked, first by the persistence of the figure on the first violin, based on the principal theme, which recurs no less than fifty-four times, counting repeats; by the peculiar rhythm of this figure, with its stressed weak beat, and its alternate *fortissimo* and *pianissimo*, giving a striking effect of light and shade; by the regular three-note accompaniment on the lower voices, marking the weak beat with mocking fury; and by the powerful *crescendo*, working up to a tremendous climax on the tonic. . . . A veritable ' ride to the abyss ' !

The transition from the *alternativo* back to the principal section is brought about by means of the episodic passage (Ex. 191). The scales in crotchets which follow, *presto*, after the conclusion of the second repeat, are changed into scales of dotted minims in unison, *ritardando*, occupying four bars instead of one. The first violin waits for a bar and a half (*l'istesso tempo*), on the final C, then falls in a daring chromatic

descent to one *alla breve* bar of the principal theme,
of which the three-note *motif* (F-F-G flat) is identical
with the conclusion of the first four bars of the theme
(Ex. 189), played in a *forte* unison by all the instruments.

This phrase is played twice more, with a bar's expressive pause in between each statement. The second time,
the chromatic descent starts from E flat; the third
time from G flat. Each time the phrase also quickens
its movement; it was at first composed of five crotchets
and two quavers; it is now composed successively of
three crotchets and six quavers, and of one crotchet and

Ex. 191.

ten quavers. This last statement of it brings back the
feverish pace of the mysterious fairy dance. . . .

Few pages in the literature of the quartet are so full
of dramatic intensity as this. The very essence of it
seems to be contained in the two conflicting themes
and the two rhythmic clashes, evoking an imaginative
fancy of an elfin dialogue; the chromatic phrase is
twice answered by the three-note *motif*, and at the third
time a tumult of excitement is let loose. Such a musical
tour de force gives point to Wagner's critical appreciation of the later works of Beethoven : ' One no longer
finds melody of definite shape and form; melody is
all-pervading, contained in every note of accompaniment, in every inflection of rhythm, even in every rest.'

The return of the exposition of the principal section
is essentially the same as before in rhythmic balance,

but with several differences of melodic detail and construction, in particular the graceful imitations on the
lower voices during the first eight bars (on the second
violin in bar 4, on the basses in bar 8), binding the
melodic continuity, and in the second period (corresponding to the repeat in the exposition) the addition
of trills and octave leaps on the first violin, transforming
the design of Ex. 189 into the following:

Ex. 192.

This modification is applied in the same way to the
repeat of the last 'strophe' of the exposition.

The *Scherzo* concludes with a ten-bar *Coda*, built on
the same *motifs*, but in different positions of pitch on the
various instruments. The viola gives a muffled *pianissimo* statement of the first violin theme; the first violin
takes the light *motif* of the second violin, which strikes
clear-cut *pizzicato* chords, stressing the weak beat; the
'cello alone keeps its original *staccato* figure (Ex. 193).
The last two bars of this example are repeated as though
in interrogation; the *pizzicati* of the second violin are
heard an octave higher. The first violin echoes the
question of the viola in a hesitating *ritardando*: an
eloquent pause ensues, and, *a tempo forte*, the movement
ends.[1]

[1] From the point of view of technical construction this conclusion
resembles that of *l'Apprenti Sorcier* of M. Paul Dukas.

Ex. 193.

Andante con moto, ma non troppo

poco scherzando

Ex. 194.

III. *Andante con moto, ma non troppo,* common time, in D flat major. This movement, called by Schumann *intermezzo* (though it is to be played *poco scherzando*), is the most deeply inspired of the XIIIth quartet, by reason of its depth of fantasy, its whimsical blending of conflicting melodies, from the gayest to the gravest, its ethereal yet firmly coherent construction built upon unified themes growing one out of another and making the movement a unique example of thematic variation, its continuous *pianissimo* half-light, in which the *sforzandi* seem barely to be felt, and finally its novelty of technique.

It opens in the key of B flat (Ex. 194). Two bars of sighing melancholy seem to anticipate a long period of gloom, but at the third bar an unexpected melody appears on the viola, gay and vivid, above *staccato* semiquavers on the 'cello. The first violin takes it up in a higher register, and it is for a moment transformed into a new figure, imitated by the second violin and brought to an end in D flat major. All this thematic movement is erected upon a foundation of *staccato* semiquavers in the bass, reinforced in the inner parts by harmonies at once buoyant and complex.

The last three quavers are echoed first by the 'cello and then by the voices above, in a modulation to A flat major. Three bars based on a variant of the original theme follow:

Ex. 195.

They form a sort of introduction arrested on a suspended discord of Ab-C-Eb-Gb.

The 'cello proceeds with a new figure, completed on
the viola, and imitated on the first violin ; it is followed
by a dialogue between the basses, in which the 'cello
has the same *staccato* quaver design that concluded the
first phrase, beneath a florid demisemiquaver *legato* on
the viola ; the whole passage is *pianissimo* throughout :

Ex. 196.

The gay interchange of these *motifs* is only a free
development of the original melody, upon which it
seems as if the Master would graft an element of irresponsible jesting. A break on the chord of C, the
dominant of F, introduces another gay *motif* derived
from the first theme (Ex. 197).

Ex. 197.

It leaps from part to part in a vivid animation that breaks off suddenly upon a sullen note on the first violin, a D flat held for a half-bar in isolated silence. The ear expects a modulation towards A flat major, but with disconcerting suddenness the first violin asserts the principal theme in C major:

Ex. 198.

which gives place to a fluent canon with the second violin and the viola, leading to the tonality of F major. In this key the 'cello has the theme, and a new *motif*, giving a strange colour to the passage, is sounded like a call on the two violins:

Ex. 199.

Two bars follow in A major, in which the voices
emerge from the shadows to build up a massed contrapuntal episode, and to lead up to a lovely tender melody
on the first violin, springing from the metamorphosed
main theme; it rises out of all the gaiety and irresponsibility, as though the Master had hitherto been
reluctant to reveal his true feeling through such a welter
of sentimentality :

Ex. 200.

This *cantabile* melody is accompanied by a beating
of wings that links it in the most enchanting way with
the gay inspiration of the earlier part of the movement.
Interrupted for a moment by a bar of vigorous inter-

lude, it is extended on the first violin in the key of
D flat, and then passes to the inner parts and finally
to the bass, all the time moving with incomparable
grace above a bird-like, fluttering accompaniment; it
then passes to the first violin, raised aloft in jubilant
triumph. These few bars are written with a novelty
of technique without parallel before our time. The
counterpoint splits up and fades away in the two bars
of episode, based on the two opening bars of the introduction, which bring back on the first violin the
principal theme in the principal tonality. From this
point, for the next twenty-five bars, the movement pursues a course symmetrical with the development already
analysed, following the rules of sonata form freely
treated with harmonic and rhythmic modifications, as
though governed by an inspiration at once whimsical
and controlled. One modification among others has the
effect of increasing the playful character of the original
theme by accentuating it in the accompaniment. The
following example should be compared with the last
bar of Ex. 194:

Ex. 201.

The tender *cantabile* melody reappears, but simpli-
fied at its second statement, heard only once on the

first violin and once on the viola, and coming to an end without any development on a long A flat trill on the first violin ; this trill merges into a sudden rapid flight marked *non troppo presto*, which resolutely establishes a melodic and rhythmic phrase arising from Ex. 195. But the light *pizzicati* modulating from the tonic to the dominant key are here replaced by the opening of a *Coda*, and the *pizzicati* form a broken diminished seventh chord in chromatic descent:

Ex. 202.

Then again the melodic design of the principal theme appears on the first violin ; the triplet figures on the inner parts reveal the quickening of pace, as the inspiration becomes breathless and agitated ; the plaintive theme and the restless anxiety disclosed in the second bar of the following example finds relief in the serenity of the next bar, effected by a simple harmonic change ; it recurs, more plaintive still, in the fourth bar, and culminates in the fifth and sixth bars in an access of impassioned tenderness [1] (Ex. 203). All this development can be traced back to the original gay theme, expressed in lively good humour by the viola at the beginning of the movement. It is difficult to conceive

[1] It must be pointed out that the extraordinary character of the phrase repetition in this passage (G–G flat), the germ of a passionate vitality and melodic freedom, is an instance of what the ordinary critic considers an achievement of modern technique. . . . The passage might well have come out of a work by César Franck, whose technical methods it strikingly anticipates. Yet this is no isolated example of it in this quartet.

Ex. 203.

of constructive technique carried to a higher point
of perfection.

The advent of a more forceful *motif*:

Ex. 204.

adds an element of stability to this delicate tracery
of sound. It appeared in a slightly different form
before the entry of the *cantabile* theme. Here one
sees in it a manifestation of the artist's resolute
will, that for a moment dominates his inspiration. The
motif is given by the first violin in semiquavers, a sort
of fluent musical discourse made expressive by means
of varied accent. The third bar of Ex. 204 heralds the
return of the *cantabile* theme, as will be seen six bars

later. The phrase concludes on a *pianissimo* chord, Bb-F-D, and is immediately followed by a *pianissimo motif* on the second violin, unaccompanied:

Ex. 205.

The distant echo of the theme seems to evoke fresh visions in the Master's imagination. There follows a free combination of the opening phrase of the *cantabile* theme with the rhythmic quaver design of Ex. 196 on the viola. The *motif* passes freely from the second violin to the other voices, and then the passage in the third bar of Ex. 204 returns with increased vigour, bringing back the *cantabile* theme. More intimate, more contemplative still, it floats above the fluttering accompaniment where the quaver theme murmurs a last farewell. The tone dies away. A sudden rustling from the lower voices, at first *pianissimo*, grows in a veiled *crescendo* like a swelling breeze; on the first violin a long *pianissimo* demisemiquaver scale soars up to A flat in *altissimo*, where it merges into the quaver figure, falling with fairy-like touch upon the leading note with the chord Ab-Eb-Gb-C. This suspended discord is suddenly resolved after a sustained pause, on to the broken chord of D flat major, struck *fortissimo* (Ex. 206). The whimsical suddenness of this chord is significant of the character of the piece. One can imagine the composer breaking into amused laughter at himself and his own sentimental outpourings—as heartless Bettina

Ex. 206.

Brentano used to laugh at his protestations of love !—
and resigning himself with a shrug to the cynical
comedy of life. Von Lenz could have written a book on
the famous C sharp, the 'startled cry' of the finale of
the VIIIth symphony, or on the *Sourire de la Chimère*
of the return of the principal theme in the Eroica. . . .
The *intermezzo* of the XIIIth quartet no doubt also
contains matter for volumes of psychological study !

IV. *Alla danza tedesca, Allegro assai*, 3/8, in G major.
The fourth movement of the XIIIth quartet is a
triumph of whimsical humour, without the interruption
of the emotional periods of the *Andante* to mar its
gaiety. In a way it is a second *scherzo*, and its structure
is that of Beethoven's earlier *scherzi*, comprising a main
section and a *Trio* with customary repetitions. But its
inspiration is simpler and much less imaginative than
that of the *Presto* ; the *motifs* are in the popular vein
of the German dance form, and recall the unaffected
simplicity of Haydn. The uncomplex key of G major
makes the similarity closer, and the impression is
further increased by a brief study of its technique.

The first four bars contain the essence of the whole
movement :

Alla danza tedesca

Allegro assai

Ex. 207.

Later, the development acquires a richer hue. The phrase on the first violin:

Ex. 208.

forms the basis of a graceful variation, vividly reminiscent of Haydn, in the repetition of the principal section after the *Trio*:

Ex. 209.

The *Trio* uses a charmingly rustic valse theme:

Ex. 210.

which is made the subject of a rippling play of imitative
figures among the instruments, in the course of a
modulation to E minor. The principal section reappears
with artless simplicity, concluding with a delicate echoing repartee which confirms the pastoral character of
this charming movement:

Ex. 211.

V. *Cavatina* (*Adagio molto espressivo*), 3/4, in E flat.
The contrast between light-hearted wit and deep
emotion which characterizes the XIIIth quartet is nowhere more striking than in the juxtaposition of this
famous movement and the dance that precedes it.

According to Beethoven's own statement, this *Adagio*
was composed during a time of deep melancholy, in
the summer of 1825, and he himself accounted it the
masterpiece of his last period and the crowning achievement of all his chamber-music works. ' He composed
the *Cavatina* of the quartet in B flat amid sorrow and
tears; never did his music breathe so heartfelt an
inspiration, and even the memory of this movement
brought tears to his eyes.' So Charles Holtz, a member
of the famous Schuppanzigh Quartet, described it, after
having been Beethoven's constant companion during
the last years of his life.

This short movement is an agonized entreaty, an
intolerable longing for happiness and peace, a longing

broken with sobs that break from the music with deeper intensity of feeling than even the living voice of the musician could express. It possesses a vital expressive force that increases the melodic significance tenfold. Of actual defined melody there is little; the *Cavatina* is a continuous unbroken song, an endless melody in which each phrase is shaded into the next. The effective arrangement of rests makes the piece very closely akin to music of the present day. Few movements defy analysis and comment so completely, but its unity of inspiration and incomparable emotional vitality make it within the grasp of every listener from the first hearing.

The first period of the plaintive theme:

Ex. 212.

becomes still more sorrowful and bitter in the bars that follow, modulating to the minor. Held minims on the stressed weak beat (bars 15–19) strike on the ear like cries of anguish.

The second principal theme is both more resigned and more impassioned, bringing, it seems, a ray of hope. But the most remarkable passage in the whole movement is contained in the eight bars of episode, from C flat major to A flat minor, against the second of which Beethoven has written the expression mark: *Beklemmt* (afflicted):

Ex. 213.

The music here reaches an intensity of feeling that transcends all the agony of grief, all the depths of anguish that human grief could experience.

After this moving passage the original theme brings

something of consolation and repose, dying away (*morendo*) on the distant concluding chords of G :

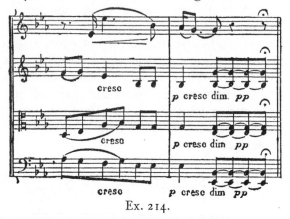

Ex. 214.

VI. *Finale* (*Allegro*), 2/4, in B flat. It has been pointed out before (p. 257) that the original finale of the Op. 130 -quartet was the Grand Fugue, *tantôt libre*, *tantôt recherchée*, published afterwards as Op. 133. It seemed as if Beethoven had spent his emotional resources in the agony of the *Cavatina*, and, as he so often felt, strove to sink himself in a technical *tour de force* in working out this massive contrapuntal design, which surpassed in technique anything he had ever achieved before. From a psychological aspect its meaning is so clear that it cannot be studied apart from the Op. 130, and this fact explains why an analysis of the fugue is appended here to the study of the XIIIth quartet, in its relation to it as the original finale.

Regarding it from a purely commercial standpoint, the publisher pointed out to Beethoven that neither quartettists nor audiences would be likely to do justice to the performance of so long and involved a finale, coming as it did at the end of a series of already very protracted movements. Beethoven realized the force of this objection, and it is worthy of remark that he did, for his fortunes were at the time at a very low ebb. He was staying at his brother John's house at

Gneixendorff, near Krems, the same brother who
darkened the last years of his life by his cruelty and
avarice. Beethoven had only just recovered from a
serious illness, and was already feeling the early symp-
toms of the one to which he was soon to succumb. It
is in these trying and painful circumstances that he
wrote this new gay and exuberant finale, with extraordinary rapidity and with all the fluent ease of the early
period. Constructed on simple lines, and split up into
eight-bar phrases like the earlier movements, it is
rhythmically and thematically cast in a popular style
easily understood by every hearer—a point which
delighted the publisher—like the finale of the XIth
and above all of the VIIth quartet. From beginning
to end it overflows with vivid movement and jaunty
confidence.

The viola opens with two solo bars of a guitar-like
accompaniment, characteristic of this finale; then,
pianissimo, the principal theme appears on the first violin
like a ripple of silent laughter. It is framed into an
eight-bar phrase, at first of a slightly whimsical cast, in
the key of C minor, growing decided after a modulation to B flat :

FINALE

Allegro

Ex. 215.

The whole finale is based on this simple, easily
remembered *motif*, and provides another remarkable
instance of the extended use and development of a
single musical idea, a feature of most of the later works
of Beethoven.

Another similar eight-bar phrase follows, in which

the *staccato* accompaniment passes to the first violin, reinforced by the viola, while the theme is murmured by the second violin an octave lower, and the 'cello works up little imitative figures at a high register.

The sixteen bars do not at once admit of repetition ; they are followed by twelve more bars, repeated, in which the main theme modulates to E flat major and then returns to B flat.

The episode of transition is, with the development, constructed by means of a figure from the third and fourth bars of the theme (fifth and sixth bars of Ex. 215). The *motif* passes successively from the 'cello to the viola and to the first violin. The development itself is very simple, exactly in the Master's early manner, like the IInd symphony, the sonata in D, Op. 10, &c.; here again one is constantly reminded of Haydn, in passages like the contrary movement in bars 5–8, p. 34 (Eulenburg edition), the simple imitations of the last bars of p. 34, and the first two of p. 35. Beethoven's first manner is again recalled in the conclusion of this passage through a descending homophonic phrase, vigorously accented :

Ex. 216.

but certain significant details (for example, from bar 12, p. 35, the 'cello accompaniment on the notes D flat–C) reveal a more advanced technique ; and the broad sweeping phrases which come several bars later from the second violin and the viola are purely modern in conception, and typical only of the composer's last period:

Ex. 217.

The development includes a *da capo* repeat of the entire earlier part of the movement from the third bar.

The second development is much more complex. It opens with a sort of monologue on the first violin above sustained notes of the inner parts, in which the original theme appears in a strangely altered shape:

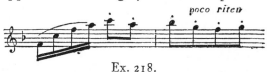

Ex. 218.

The answer appears in the form of a new melody in A flat major of a tranquil design, in vivid contrast with the rhythmic movement of the principal theme. It is heard first on the viola:

Ex. 219.

It stretches over eight bars beneath an accompaniment in which the first violin plays in imitation; the melody is then repeated in unison by the two violins, undergoing a change which gives it added energy and grace.[1]

Ex. 220.

After the repetition of this unison on the lower voices, it gives place to a succession of echoing *motifs* in imitation, based on the same quaver melody; then the original theme reappears in contrapuntal fashion in contrary motion, later with its rhythmic elements split up, as in the following passage :

Ex. 221.

Here the polyphony of the finale reaches its greatest complexity, giving way at the height of its rhythmic and

[1] This characteristic passage seems to anticipate Schumann, who considered the last quartets the summit of all music's achievement, and is himself more influenced by them than one would think, from the point of view of both rhythm and harmony, and even of melody.

tonal force to a big homophonic phrase where the notes
of the quaver melody resound in a *staccato*, *fortissimo* :

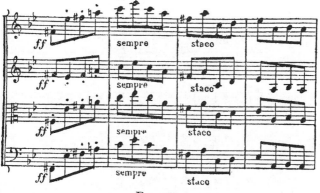

Ex. 222.

These unison quavers first give the notes of the
arpeggio chord of the diminished seventh of G minor,
culminating in a rocking figure alternating between the
major and the minor, and working back to a *pianissimo*
return of the guitar-like accompaniment on the second
violin, on the dominant D ; the original theme appears
on the first violin in G minor and finally in B flat—the
prevailing tonality of the movement. This re-entry is
extraordinarily typical of Beethoven's style.

From this point the first development section returns,
according to the laws of sonata form, but the finale of
the XIIIth quartet also includes, like so many of these
later works, an immense *Coda* in which it seems as if
the artist's inspiration finds fresh vitality and creative
power in every bar, an imaginative strength that increases in proportion as the end draws near.

An intricate play of imitation is worked out between
the quaver melody, the guitar-like accompaniment, and
finally the rhythmic element of the original theme ; as
this last appears it is first seized by the inner voices,
and then by all the instruments in a chromatic contrary
movement, an impassioned *crescendo* leading to a *for-*

tissimo climax in E flat major, where the entire original theme breaks upon us with the luminous brilliance of dawn. The music throbs with light and joy:

Ex. 223.

A short episode brings a *pianissimo* passage where the rhythmic elements of both principal melodies (the second in *staccato* quavers) are skilfully combined; the original theme persists and is heard once more, *fortissimo*, in the last bars of the *Coda*, with unabated force. Bringing yet another contrast of effect, the artist links on to this outburst of vigour a short period that leaves an impression of a subtle and evanescent sweetness:

Ex. 224.

In the above example is shown this unique conclusion, in which the variety of *motifs* and the conflicting voices finally subside; halting on a *pianissimo* pause, F-A-C-F, the end is achieved in a broad tonic chord.[1]

There is no trace here of pain or weakness, yet this amazing conclusion was written in the twilight of his life by the feeble hand of a man diseased in body and broken in spirit.

Grand Fugue, Op. 133 (in B flat).

It remains to examine the Grand Fugue, Op. 133, the original finale of the XIIIth quartet. One cannot do better than follow M. Vincent d'Indy's analysis.[2]

It is a fugue with two subjects and variations. The work is unified by a principal theme, the counter-subject of the first fugue, which is used as the subject of the second. For purposes of analysis the work can be divided into six main sections, each subdivided again.

[1] This *Coda* has an extraordinarily fine effect if played on a string orchestra. One can imagine the effect in calling to mind the *fugato* Overture in C, Op. 124, a piece thematically very like the XIIIth quartet.

[2] Notes taken at the *Schola* by M. Coindreau in 1909.

I. *Introduction.* Exposition, in related keys that lead to the dominant, of the principal subject in its four important aspects:

1. In its aspect as counter-subject of the first fugue.
2. In the rhythm of the second fugue.
3. In the form of the second fugue.
4. Accompanied by the rhythm of the counter-subject of the second fugue.

In this main theme is the germ from which the entire work grows.

II. *First fugue,* with three variations.

1. Statement of the counter-subject alone. Exposition of the fugue according to the usual rules in four entries (S.A.S.A.). The basic theme is characterized by the compass of its melodic intervals. Episode in the same rhythm. Return of the subject in one part leading to the

2. *First variation,* consisting of the subject (S.A.) in the sub-dominant, coupled with a new triplet rhythm. Episode based on the first phrase of the subject. As above, the return of the theme is in one part only, and this time appears as the answer, not as the subject, and leads on through the statement of the answer, transformed, to an exposition of the answer in the relative key. Episode in the rhythm of the subject.

3. *Second variation* in the principal key of B flat. An exposition (S.A.) with a new rhythmic figure of semi-quavers. Episode in the rhythm of the subject accompanied by the semiquaver figure.

4. *Third variation.* Exposition in the original key (S.A.S.A.). The subject is varied by borrowing the triplet rhythm. As in the two first subdivisions the return of the subject appears in one part only, and leads to the

III. *Second fugue,* also with three variations.

1. In the key of D flat, the new counter-subject is first stated alone, as in the first fugue; it is formed from the basic theme in a rhythm announced in the *Introduction.* Exposition (S.A.S.A.) where the new subject is the counter-subject of the preceding fugue. Episode based at first on the answer in canon, then on the develop-

ment of the subject. Development of the counter-subject, which leads to the

2. *First variation*, in B flat, the principal tonality. Exposition (S.A.) of the second fugue, in a rhythm announced in the *Introduction*. Episode based on the subject in this rhythm. Re-exposition as in the first fugue, but here in two sections, based on the subject and leading to the

3. *Second variation* in A flat. Exposition (S.A.) of the subject by augmentation upon the inverted subject, in the rhythm of the first variation.

4. *Third variation. Divertissement* on the subject by diminution, with much modulation.

IV. *Development of the two fugues in three sections.*

1. *Divertissement* on the figure of the principal subject.

2. *Divertissement* on the first subject and the beginning of the second.

3. *Divertissement* on the second subject in similar and contrary motion, with the second counter-subject and the rhythm of the first, leading to the

V. *Re-exposition in the principal tonality.*

1. Re-exposition and repetition of the first variation of the second fugue.

2. Development of the second fugue.

VI. *Conclusion* in B flat, principal key.

1. Reminiscence of the first fugue by its subject.

2. Subject of the second fugue.

3. Recapitulation, based on the first subject in its ordinary form, with the second in augmentation with the triplet rhythm of the first fugue.

4. Concluding bars of massive statement of the basic theme.

Quartet No. XIV, Op. 131 (in C sharp minor).

This quartet is generally recognized to be musically the finest of them all, and undoubtedly reaches the highest point ever attained in quartet literature. Here one finds a rich flowering of all the qualities that mark the later works; originality and freedom of form, which is nevertheless always a strictly logical and supple technique; and intellectual and imaginative conception of idea, of each note, and of each bar of development. As in many of the later works, there is also to be noticed the working out of a continuous psychological idea. A great soul rises above the trials of human suffering, out of the darkness of irreparable grief to spiritual strength and power, vigour, vitality, and triumph over the hosts of evil, over the bitterness of fate, to inner peace and reconciliation.

The splendour of technique that describes this lofty ascent is attained by means of varying *motifs*, and ' quartet' designs and conceptions, with which the mind of Beethoven overflowed at this period of his creative life. It is in this sense that one must read the epigraph set against one copy of the work : *4tes Quartett, von den neuesten*. N.B. *Zusammengestohlen aus verschiedenem diesem und jenem*. (' XIVth Quartet, of the last group. Composed out of scattered fragments and snatches of movements.')

This quartet is constructed in seven movements played without a break.

No. I. *Adagio ma non troppo e molto espressivo*, in C sharp minor (4/4). R. Wagner says of this introduction : ' The very slow introductory *Adagio* reveals the most melancholy sentiment ever expressed in music.' [1] It is a lamentation at once passionate and resigned, labouring under restraint, an endless melodic line from which not one phrase could be taken away without marring the continuity of idea. Technically, this theme is worked out as a close fugue, with episodes of a free character. The melody is at first given by the first violin unaccompanied, in five bars. The second violin, the viola, and the 'cello enter in turn ; each entry is separated from the last by the usual interval of four bars. The counterpoint is complete in four parts after the fourteenth bar.

[1] R. Wagner, *Beethoven*, translated from German into French by A. Lasvignes, published by the *Revue Blanche*, Paris, 1902, p. 68.

The theme can be split up into two elements :

Ex. 225.

The first phrase seems to express a profound sadness, reaching a poignant climax on the *sf* which marks the dotted minim A ; the second phrase is the *motif* of still resignation, felt particularly in the episode in B major (bar 2 onwards) where the theme is in diminution and the slurred quavers played in imitation convey the effect of a chorale, and in the episode in A major (bars 6 and 7 onwards), where the two violins have the theme in its original form in the same chorale-like manner. At this point it recalls certain passages in *Parsifal*, a work that this prelude is often to bring to mind. . . . The division of the main theme into two phrases makes for added interest in the course of the technical analysis, since each *motif* serves as the basis for a development of its own. Even during the prelude this twofold character is several times defined. For instance, see bars 21–25, and the viola part in bars 2–5 of the episode in G flat major.

The *motif* of resignation dominates the ensemble in this introduction on another count, even influencing the other *motif*, in that it sometimes acts as a restraining agent upon its too passionate character, and creates instead an effect of heavy oppression. It is thus that the *sforzato* dotted minim is replaced in bars 23 and 25 by a figure of two crotchets, slurred and *piano* ; and again the same theme is lifted into a higher register by the violin, and there acquires a character of sorrowful calm (from the fourth bar of the episode in A major).

Once, however, the complete double theme breaks forth in the expression of defiant grief. Sombre and fierce instead of despairing, the theme rolls from the 'cello in

augmentation (semibreves and minims take the place
of the minims and crotchets of the opening statement):

Ex. 226.

while on the first violin, the expression of passionate
sorrow swells in a rising *crescendo* to a cry on which
the instrument dwells as if with the deep relief of
deliverance.

Ex. 227 includes the last ten bars of the introduction. In the second bar the poignant cry of grief is
heard in the *sforzato* chord on the bass and the first
violin, B sharp-D.[1]

---

[1] The 'cello only goes down to bass C natural, but, as von Lenz has
remarked, what would this audacity of notation signify to Beethoven,
though it made the pedants wring their hands ? (See similar examples
from von Lenz, op. cit., p. 89.)

That brooding chord seems to absorb the whole soul of the artist. It will also be seen a little later how the two *motifs* of the original theme are combined; the 'grief' *motif* assumes its aspect of inexorable gloom once more. Finally, in the last bars, the succession of solemn

Ex. 227.

chords in elaborate harmony leads to the long-held dominant note above the chord of C♯-G♯-E-C♯-G♯, which falls to the tonic C sharp in a sustained *pianissimo* unison.[1]

No. 2. *Allegro molto vivace*, in D major (6/8). The

[1] The last modulations in the Introduction to Schumann's symphony in D minor recall this passage in a certain degree.

rise of a semitone [1] brings before the imagination a
musical picture of quite different cast, and purely
homophonic; *pianissimo*, its first theme :

Ex. 228.

is delicately wrought on the first violin, dissipating the
sombre despair of the *Adagio*, which fades away, as
R. Wagner describes it, ' into a wistful memory '. In its
turn the viola has the theme, while the accompaniment,
at first only a long harmonic stretch of the tonic chord,
now gains animation in a quaver figure moving from
one instrument to another. The strangely tentative air
that marked the first statement of the theme (*poco
ritardando* at the eighth bar) disappears, to give place
to an increasingly vivid rhythmic insistence, specially
noticeable when the first violin takes the theme again
and strikes an impassioned note. The same quality is
apparent in the second theme, still in D major, which
follows at once with an air of animation and quick
grace—an expressive gesture, typical of the ' last
period '.

The second violin and the viola take in succession
fragments of this melody. The 6/8 rhythm and the
crescendo give a continuous impetus to the passage;
then in a *diminuendo* modulation to B minor the vitality
dies and the gaiety is dispersed; the theme splits up
into fragmentary figures, and sustained dotted crotchets
and dotted minims creep in on the upper voices, as the
'cello breathes little *pianissimo* sighs (Ex. 229). But
the original theme again returns, in E major, and
broadens in a modulation to A major, in which tonality

---

[1] The bond between the first and the second movements, established
by the linking of these two octave leaps from C sharp and D, is significant.
It indicates to the performers that no break must be made at this point.
A pause for applause would entirely spoil the effect.

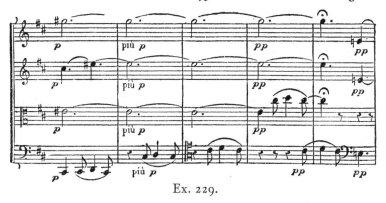

Ex. 229.

it assumes, under the same rhythmic figuration, an accent so entirely different that it almost becomes a third thematic influence in the movement:

Ex. 230.

This new element brings increasing ardour and fire, an effect heightened by unusual harmonic progressions, harsh and penetrating, of a type peculiar to the last quartets, and of which the two last bars of Ex. 230 afford an instance (chords of D-F♯-A-G; E-G-A-F♯; D-F♯-A-E, &c.). These are not deliberate crudities, but the logical sequence of an indomitable polyphonic scheme. . . . A heroic inspiration gives life to this episode, until a modulation on the first violin, like a cloud passing over the sun, gives it a contemplative cast (bars 27–29, p. 9, Eulenburg edition, 1911 : octaves rising chromatically from A to B flat to B). The original theme reappears on the viola, followed by a statement on the violins. At this point a development begins, recalling the section which terminated in the last bar of Ex. 229, but with such differences that it actually becomes a new development altogether. Two bars used in the exposition (bars 17–18 from the beginning of the *Allegro*) :

Ex. 231.

thus provide a new and deeply appealing thematic episode, investing the passionate inspiration of the passage with melancholy. Again, at the point where the rhythmic animation loses its vigour beneath the sustained harmonic stretches on the upper parts, this time there appears an extended progression in the minor, slow and hushed, leading to the little *pianissimo* sighs on the 'cello, now joined by the viola and the second violin under a C sharp on the first violin held through five bars. This section is remarkable for its ingenious harmonies, and the development that ensues is a veritable mosaic of thematic design, fashioned out of the artist's fantasy, and yet moving with perfect balance and unerring logical sequence. Above all one must observe the return of the second theme, taken to a *crescendo* this time in a unison of all the instruments. This thematic flight is suddenly cut short, and fragments of the theme appear *fortissimo*, intersected by slow *piano* phrases; as it modulates to the minor, its last fluttering efforts die on the dominant, and finally come to an end on the final incomplete chord of D-F♯, where the omission of the dominant A heralds a new metamorphosis.

Nos. 3–4. Without any actual break, two energetic chords are struck in the key of B minor (tonic and seventh). The third section, *Allegro moderato–Adagio*, is in the key of B minor—although the signature indicates F sharp minor—in common time, and forms the introduction to a long slow movement which is the central point of the work. The introduction is eleven bars long, and the *Adagio* passage begins at the seventh, a recitative emerging from light figures of transition in B minor, modulating through F sharp minor to E major; a rippling semiquaver phrase on the first violin, *più vivace*, culminates in a fine declamatory phrase in the manner of Handel. Then the *Andante, ma non troppo e molto cantabile* opens, the fourth section in A major, 2/4. R. Wagner spoke of this poetic movement as a magic work in which Beethoven ‘cast a spell over a vision of loveliness for his own endless delight; the incarnation of perfect innocence, this ideal figure is revealed in countless different aspects, transformed in the brilliance shed upon her by the artist’s genius’. Here is found the climax of the ‘grand variation’. Up to this point Beethoven had made an extended use of this form only in the *Adagio* of the XIIth quartet, in E flat, Op. 127. But between these two movements, of equal technical skill, a fundamental difference appears beneath the apparently similar exterior form. In the *Adagio* of Op. 127 the variation is used primarily to develop the expressive resources of a given theme, and to present this theme, purely contemplative in character, in every possible aspect that the imagination could reveal.

The variations of the *Andante* of Op. 131, on the other hand, are much more than the medium by which a single idea finds more complete expression. They demonstrate the continual changing of this idea, as it follows the changing fantasy of the artist, as it is moulded afresh by the influence of his inner vitality, which was never fuller and richer than in the twilight of his life. To this continual changing of imaginative idea is bound the change of musical idea, constantly

Ex. 232.

charged with new thought (not merely technical variations of the same thought); and these new thoughts in their turn give rise to flexible thematic combinations that express their most delicate shades of meaning. It follows inevitably that these shades of meaning are expressed in a form that seems on the surface to be far removed from the original imaginative idea that gave them birth. But they all spring from the

same root, and the tiniest shoots reproduce in miniature
the growth of the giant branches that bear them. There
is, on a grand scale, a formal and psychological unity in
this work that is nothing short of a miracle.

The theme stretches over thirty-two bars, and is really
based on two underlying eight-bar phrases (Examples
232 and 233). The atmosphere is full of a shining

Ex. 233.

clarity, ' the incarnation of innocence,' as Wagner put
it ; above rhythmic quaver *pizzicati* in the bass, the two
violins share the elements of the theme in an interlacing
melody, taking in turn the upper and lower voice in
a combination that demands a double re-exposition,
also very much varied, of each eight-bar sentence. The

second sentence finishes in a cadence of deep and intimate feeling.

The first variation presents at first the theme with altered accent and rhythm, alternating with a figure of chromatic semiquavers :

Ex. 234.

Immediately after the last bar of the example, the polyphony thickens, by added movement in the inner parts. Long-drawn *crescendi* alternate with passages of unruffled calm. Alteration in the note values of the theme, specially noticeable in the last bars of the variation, imparts to the developments a quality of bubbling life.

Ex. 235.

The second variation (*più mosso*, in common time) opens in an atmosphere of pastoral freshness (Ex. 236) and soon acquires an energetic character, by the persistent drum rhythm marked by regular quavers which

continue to the end, and by the extension of the *motif* of
slurred quavers (second and fourth bars of Ex. 236),
which finally becomes an unbroken melodic line on the
firstviolin and 'cello, with varied imitative figures on the

Ex. 236.

inner voices. An even heroic effect is obtained when
the *motif* is heard on all the voices in unison (a technical
device often found in the last quartets) with a *sforzando*
accent on the weak beat; the parts fall away from the
unison in a rushing figure, to unite and separate again:

Ex. 237.

The next variation is marked *Andante moderato e
lusinghiero*. *Lusinghiero*, coaxingly (some piano editions
leave out this important expression indication). There
is a striking contrast between the transports of excitement in the preceding variation and the simplicity of

this polished dialogue, as it unfolds in imitations in canon, at first on the basses, then on the violins:

Ex. 238.

The trill figure in the last bar is taken as the element of the development which follows this exposition, a development in canon which extends in an extraordinary way in the last two bars to introduce the fourth variation.

This opens (*Adagio* in 6/8) with all the voices at a high pitch (Ex. 239); the first violin unfolds a rounded melodic design interrupted by fierce *pizzicati* like the clash of kettledrums, on the second violin and the 'cello, *sforzato*. The first four notes of the *motif* on the first violin in the third bar of Ex. 239 are taken as the basis of the development that is to follow (Ex. 240).

Ex. 239.

Ex. 240.

This is in pure ' quartet form '. But its apparent ease
and grace make way for a broadening of the design,
a glistening web of sound in which voices and *motifs*
are blended to attain a brilliant dramatic effect in the
last bars. All this reveals an imaginative power and
charm that amazed the musical world of Beethoven's
generation, and astonishes us no less to-day. Listening
to this expression of an ecstatic inner vitality, we can
understand what the friends of the musician meant by
the phrase : ' The Master has a *raptus* again to-day ! '

In the fifth variation, *Allegretto* in 2/4, it seems as if
shadows fall over the scene. Through strange harmonies, the distorted theme, with only its bare outlines
left, is reclothed in the garb of a chorale sustained by
long organ notes :

Ex. 241.

At the beginning of the second section, a fragment of
melody recalling a *motif* of the Op. 101 sonata makes
a fugitive appearance, to slip away again at once into
the sustained harmonies (Ex. 242). At the end of the
variation it escapes again, to form on the 'cello, at a very
high pitch, the figure of the second phrase of the theme
almost in its original shape.

The contemplative character of this variation anticipates the prevailing atmosphere of earnest supplication that fills the sixth and last variation. This very
developed movement, *Adagio, ma non troppo e semplice*
in 9/4, and *Allegretto* in 2/4, is perhaps the climax of
the whole quartet. Few pages in musical literature
reach the depths of poignant introspection realized

here (Ex. 243). Of this luminous phrase Beethoven
might have said with Goethe: *Ich habe da viel
hinein geheimnisst* (Here have I hidden many secret

Ex. 242.

Ex. 243.

non troppo marcato

Ex. 244.

thoughts). . . . It is hard to realize that the germ of
this melody can be traced in the tender and pastoral
motif of Ex. 232. It is repeated an octave higher
after the first statement, above a curious 'cello figure
(Ex. 244).

Here all is brightness and light, but after the seventeenth bar the feeling of the movement is tinged with disquiet. The 'cello figure is heard *forte*, while the other voices, uneasy and fearful, give the original theme ; in the ensuing development the same figure reappears alternately *forte* and *piano*, passing to the first violin as a momentary link phrase, and ending as a ground bass on the 'cello. Through modulations struggling to establish B minor and B flat major the underlying tonality persists. The opening of this episode makes one think of R. Schumann's piano piece *Fürchten machen*. It creates the same impression of haunting anguish, but while Beethoven's emotion is profoundly felt, with Schumann the inspiration is whimsical, and conceived merely as a sort of childish terror.

Tinged with agonized entreaty, this heart-felt prayer finally reaches its conclusion in the appropriate concluding cadence, and from that point the variation is prolonged by a sort of *Coda*. It takes the shape of a romantic dialogue in recitative, ending on a trill under which the lower voices ebb away, *morendo*, in *arpeggio* chords (Ex. 245 gives the last phrase on the first violin and the first bars of the trill). The trill (on B, C sharp, C) brings a modulation to A minor and F major (subdominant of C) ; and without warning the original theme (*Allegretto* in 2/4) returns in C major, with its character much altered from the beginning, no longer tender and emotional, but vivacious and in the style of a country dance. This impression fades as the first violin, *sempre più allegro, crescendo*, repeats the melodic figure, first above cadence harmonies, then heard alone finishing on a design of trills as though to chase away all the disturbing reflections that have crept in before. Freed from the last traces of restraint, the original theme reappears in the key of A major on the second violin and viola, in a passage of solemn magnificence, above harp-like figures in the bass and wreathed in trills by the first violin. This episode lasts only seven bars (Ex. 246).

Ex. 245.

Ex. 246.

The design of trills is heard again on the first violin above the *arpeggio* movement on the lower voices, no longer in crotchets but in semiquaver triplets, *crescendo*. A fresh episode follows in F major, *Allegretto*. This time the return of the tonic key is also to mark the conclusion of the movement. The first violin unfolds a recitative phrase, punctuated by short angular chords on the lower voices. Heard at the octave above, the figure of the cadence returns (the last bar of Ex. 233), the signal for a series of farewell *motifs* which combine in a graceful melodic design ; the elements of the theme split up, disperse, and halt on the chord of the seventh, to disappear finally in two soft *pizzicato* chords of the tonic. Each note here has a peculiar significance, marked by that individual imaginative intensity found only in Beethoven's last manner. If one reviews the musical course travelled over, from the exposition of the original theme to these final chords, it seems as if the artist has moved through countless changing phases of spiritual experience on his way, scattering abroad the wealth of his imaginative resource as he passed.

No. 5. *Presto* in E major, *alla breve*. Although less homogeneous than the corresponding movements in the Op. 130 and Op. 135 quartets, this *presto*, really a *scherzo* in duple rhythm, is a movement of remarkable external brilliance. R. Wagner describes its psychological relation to the ' grand variation ' that precedes it, in the following paragraph :

There we saw the artist's profound inner happiness casting a reflection of ineffable peace upon the material world. Here again the world appears before him, as in the *Pastorale*; and his inward joy illuminates everything around him. It is as if he were listening for strains of unearthly music, as visions pass before his gaze in perfect harmony, once ethereal, now embodied in material form.

A fierce gaiety runs through the entire movement, filling it with riotous life from beginning to end. It is of crystal clarity in design and form : a principal sec-

tion, an *alternativo*, both repeated, followed by a return
of the principal section and a *Coda*. Flowing on without a break, it forms an unbroken stream of sound,
a single melodic sequence, built upon a little *motif*
that anybody could hum over as they left the concert,
a *motif* ' found in the street, but transformed into the
loveliest music imaginable '! Constant striving after
whimsical effect, *staccato*, *pizzicato* (used here in a
remarkable way), sudden accelerations, single notes
heavily accented and abruptly interrupting the melody,
unexpected modulations, and the sudden disappearance
of the theme, curious harmonic effects, every conceivable technical device is used to create the most
brilliant possible result.

It opens abruptly with the first notes of the theme
on the 'cello, *forte*, followed by a bar's rest; then the
first violin, *piano*, gives the entire theme of eight bars
accompanied by a light movement on the inner voices,
coming to an end as the dominant of C sharp minor
bursts in :

N⁰ 5. Presto.

Ex. 247.

This eight-bar phrase is repeated an octave higher.
Then (bars 3 and 4 of Ex. 247) a fragment of the
original theme is taken as the element of a transition
figure, modulating through C sharp major to E major
and halting on B, to initiate a design of airy echoing
figures, F♯-B, G-B, G♯-B (modulating from E minor
to E major). The last echo is marked : *Molto poco
adagio*, *un poco più adagio*, and *più piano*. In curious
G sharp minor harmonies the germ of the theme (first

and third bars of Ex. 247) is then evenly distributed among the four voices, *pianissimo*, taken up by the first violin and completed; it is arrested on the chord of the dominant of G sharp, *ritardando*; a pause, and the original theme returns in the unexpected key of E major. This leads on to a melodic design of calmer character :

Ex. 248.

The development makes further use of the elements of the original theme, and leads through a period of playful humour to a fine conclusion. An immediate modulation to C sharp minor leads back to the repeat of this second section. The second time, this modulation is replaced by a figure of echoes on the notes B-E, which introduces the *alternativo* section. The theme of the latter is played in unison at the octave on the two violins :

Ex. 249.

and recalls the days of the artist's youth and happiness,
being none other than the *motif* written about twenty-
eight years earlier for the first movement of the quartet
in G, Op. 18, No. 2 (*motif* C of Ex. 10, Chap. I, p. 13).
Yet with almost precise formal identity, there is a deep-
seated difference in inspiration. In the quartet in G the
melody was inspired with a sort of elaborate grace,
which had won for the work, it will be remembered, the
name of ' The Compliment Quartet '. In the Op. 131
quartet the theme has gained a certain air of pomp and
flourish, like a popular song or the tune of a village
fair ; this is a characteristic trait of Beethoven's lighter
melodies, especially in his later period. Consequently,
the *alternativo* section, built up on a droning bass that
one might hear from a village band, has a vitality and
an objective force that makes it a striking foil to the
Adagio and brings it closer in manner to the works of
the second period, or, within this same period, to the
scherzo of the IXth symphony, very similar in inspiration
to this piece.

The theme is heard at first above an accompaniment
of evenly distributed crotchets, two by two, on the
lower voices, and repeated with richer expression to
a full accompaniment on both bass instruments in
unison. An eight-bar episode follows, based on the
accompaniment figure alone, in a curious passage where
the figure is tossed to and fro, *pianissimo*, among the
four instruments ; then the theme appears again, this
time on the lower parts with the accompaniment first
divided, then in unison, on the violins. A modulation to
A major expresses a change of the principal theme (Ex.
250) both in technical form and in imaginative meaning.

The line of melody is next extended by the last two
bars of the theme alone, heard joyously on the first
violin and the bass ; the inner parts raise an argumentative accompaniment of springing crotchets. The
movement broadens, the tone fills out, and the air of
festivity reaches its height with the appearance of a new

Ex. 250.

theme of almost comic character on the first violin,
afterwards hammered out by the 'cello with amusing
insistence :

Ex. 251.

After a bar of rest suddenly appears a figure of *pizzicati forte* for eight bars, in each of which one note is
struck by one of the four instruments; on the last
pizzicato of the first violin the 'cello breaks in with its
original *motif* (first bar of Ex. 247). The *scherzo* and
alternativo then return as before until the entry of the
pizzicato episode, which is this time more emphatic,
with two notes to a bar. The second repeat of the
scherzo is heard with several changes. It is linked on
to a *Coda* of most original type, to which the theme of

the *alternativo* forms an overture, interrupted by the *motif* of Ex. 251, in the key of A major. To this *motif* is connected a bar of the *scherzo* theme (first bar of Ex. 247), and the *pizzicato* episode follows it. Then, in the key of E major and in a very high register (the 'cello uses the G clef), *sul ponticello*, the *scherzo* theme returns once more, ethereal and distant, rather in the manner of the last bars of the *scherzo* of the Op. 59, No. 1 quartet, or of the *Coda* of the finale of Op. 95. After sixteen bars the normal bowing is resumed, and the pace rapidly increases, *crescendo*, in a hasty descent and brilliant recovery (all in contrary motion) upon the dominant chord, struck *fortissimo* : and the *scherzo* is at an end. But after a bar's rest and a pause, three dominant chords resound in the same rhythm. Another long pause, and the finale opens without a break, as Beethoven insisted, though his wishes are not always respected in performance.

Nos. 6 and 7. *Finale* preceded by an Introduction, *Adagio quasi un poco andante* in G sharp minor, 3/4. R. Wagner has the following comment to make, in his study of the XIVth quartet :

He [Beethoven] is surveying the course of material existence (in the *presto* in E major) and seems to pause (*Adagio*, 3/4) to wonder whether he should not portray this material existence in the gaiety of the dance ; his contemplation is short-lived but profound, as if he were buried for the moment in the depths of his own soul. In a flash the world is again illuminated before him ; he awakes, and evokes from the violin music the like of which the world has never imagined (*Allegro finale*). This is the fury of the world's dance of fierce pleasure, agony, ecstasy of love, joy, anger, passion, and pain ; lightnings flash and thunder rolls ; and above the tumult the indomitable fiddler whirls us on to the abyss. Amid the clamour he smiles, for to him it is nothing but a mocking fantasy ; at the end the darkness beckons him away, and his task is done.

This incisive comment leads us on to the thematic analysis of the finale.

A short twenty-eight bar introduction provides a sombre contrast with the bewilderment of joy expressed in the *scherzo*. Nowhere in all the quartets is there expressed a resignation so deeply felt, an introspection so profound, as this, revealed in a moving phrase on the viola :

Adagio quasi un poco andante

Ex. 252.

The phrase is repeated by the first violin with a significant change of A sharp (in the fifth bar of the example) to A natural. The two instruments then engage in a dialogue in which the second violin also takes part, while the 'cello has a continuous accompaniment in a counterpoint formed of the elements of the melody. A modulation to B major brightens the scene with a ray of returning hope, but a relapse into the minor accentuates the prevailing sense of agonized entreaty,[1] especially in bars 14 and 22, where the voices seem to sing as though with trembling lips : and bars 16 and 24, where the *sforzati* resound like desperate appeals. The following example gives bars 22–4 :

Ex. 253.

[1] The twentieth prelude of Chopin, in C minor, recalls this construction and expression.

It finishes on a note of tender melancholy, and is linked by a recitative on the first violin to No. 7 (*Allegro, alla breve,* in C sharp minor).

Ex. 254.

This is ' the world's mad dance, led by the indomitable fiddler '. . . . It opens with a *motif* of stormy challenge, *fortissimo,* in unison on the four instruments ; then a song of defiance bursts from the first violin in a rugged rhythm marked on the basses (Ex. 254). The descending figure in bars 7–9 of this example is developed alone for several bars, and appears in a smooth *piano legato* ; the transition passage is based on a new theme of profound gloom (Ex. 255). In it one recognizes, in inversion, the opening theme of the

quartet (Ex. 225). The melancholy cast of the theme
and its thematic relation to the original *motif* become
still more marked a little later, when the upper voices
give the first three notes of the theme (Ex. 225), and
the design of the melody appears, inverted, on the
basses. A *crescendo* brings a more robust conclusion,
and the *motifs* of the opening bars of the *Allegro* follow,

Ex. 255.

heard *piano* above the hammering rhythm of the
basses.

Above a wild entry in canon on the four instruments,
the first violin lifts a melody of sublime purity, like
a glimpse of blue sky among storm-clouds, imposing a
sense of mysticism and spiritual vitality upon the essentially material texture of the movement (Ex. 256).
The viola and the second violin take up the love theme
(bars 5–7 of Ex. 256) beneath a delicate figure high
on the first violin; perfect peace hovers above this
vision of ecstasy, as the *motif* rises from voice to voice.
. . . Entering unheralded, the challenging *motif* of
Ex. 254 strikes a note of sullen vigour; and the
principal theme (Ex. 254) develops in the key of F
sharp minor (arising from the dominant C sharp), with
the addition of the figure of bars 7–9 of the example;
the development in its elements conforms to the logical
plan of sonata form in a perfectly progressive and

definite course, but moving very freely within itself.
Its individual characteristics can only be lightly touched
upon.

The design of bars 7–9 of Ex. 254 is divided among
the parts and accompanied by primitive counterpoint

Ex. 256.

in the shape of a semibreve scale figure, itself varied
by octaves in different registers; the passage occupies
twenty-four bars in which the keys of B minor, E
minor, and B minor again are successively heard. Then
the challenging *motif* returns, destined to become one
of the elements in the ensuing development, appearing
and disappearing in an impish caprice. A modulation

to D major brings a new figure combined with a fragment of the *motif*:

Ex. 257.

This new figure is at first simple and fluent, as it were a rippling accompaniment to the dancing rhythm of the other, but it broadens and grows in tonal brilliance, and is finally transformed into a vigorous *non legato* passage. The air is filled with the murmur of a distant storm (return of the key of C sharp minor), and the ominous beating *motif* of muffled seconds, *ritmo di tre battute*, works up from *pianissimo* to the maximum tonal capacity of all the instruments; at this point the challenge *motif*, now in its original form, now altered (Ex. 258), makes an impressive return.[1]

The development makes use of this *motif* in both aspects, the original theme, the elements of the countermelody in semibreves, and the melancholy theme of Ex. 255, in elaborately worked-out counterpoint. After a modulation to D major, the mystic episode (Ex. 256) reappears, at first in this tonality, then in C sharp major. It is here more developed than in its original exposition, being forty-six bars long instead of twenty-one, and extended by a minim figure in contemplative vein, which deepens its poetic significance. From this point

[1] R. Wagner, in the *Ride of the Valkyries*, used the same idea of a persistent figure of seconds as an accompaniment to a strongly marked theme.

to the last bar of the finale is a veritable orgy of wild
joy, a passage unparalleled in the literature of chamber
music. The only works that even anticipate this last movement of Op. 131 are the finales of the quartets in E minor,
Op. 59, No. 2, and in C, Op. 59, No. 3, and the *scherzi*
of the quartets in E flat, Op. 74, and in F minor,
Op. 95. Out of the inexhaustible fantasy of the ' indomitable fiddler ' *motifs* spring without ceasing, and
sweep ' the world ' along in a mad riot. At first the
motif of challenge, both in its simple and transformed

Ex. 258.

shape, accounts for ten bars of a *crescendo* development,
followed by a return of the melancholy theme (Ex. 255),
but this undergoes a change ; the Master bestows upon
it rhythm and movement of a heroic cast, and links it
now with the original melody (Ex. 259).

This provides a striking instance of Beethoven's skill
in extracting the likeness of one imaginative idea from
themes of totally different shape. The development
leads to a return of the challenging *motif* heard *crescendo*
above a heavy rumbling of the basses, and to a *fortissimo*
outburst of the rhythm of the principal theme, encircled
in an imposing semibreve counterpoint (Ex. 260). In
this passage, as in so many others in the quartets,
one seems to hear the sonorous tone of trombones,

Ex. 259.

Ex. 260.

trumpets and horns, declaiming these mighty themes. In a sudden *pianissimo* the first violin ascends a scale of D major, *non legato*, above an accompaniment of tremulous quavers on the tonic; a crotchet figure, *crescendo*, boldly stated in C sharp, is followed by the scale passage again, forming a strange episode without any thematic link with the main design, the last flickering ray of the mystic vision. Above the last notes of the crotchet figure, and in the final tonality of C sharp minor, the rhythm of the original theme re-enters *fortissimo*, accompanied by the quaver *motif* of Ex. 257, here transformed:

Ex. 261.

From this moment the spirit of the artist is wholly emancipated from all doubt and suffering. Even the melancholy *motif* is invested with an air of serene consolation, raised on the wings of the *motif* of challenge. This tender melody unfolds on the first violin and viola and gradually fades away into silence. *Pianissimo*, the original theme is heard again, divided among the instruments; it passes through a last episode, *poco adagio*, where it regains its elegiac character (*semplice espressivo*, the Master wrote against it): suddenly the *tempo* is re-established, and, *crescendo*, the rhythm of the first theme springs up from the 'cello, leaps to the second violin, and finally to all the voices in a Bacchic frenzy, *fortissimo*, to crash wildly upon two gigantic chords of C sharp minor, setting a massive seal to Beethoven's most powerful chamber-music work, the work, it is said, that he himself accounted the greatest of all.[1]

Quartet No. XV, Op. 132 (in A minor).

Beethoven composed this quartet in the spring of 1823, after a long illness. On page 60 of the manuscript (Royal Library, Berlin) are the following words, written in the hand of the artist: *Heiliger Dankgesang an die Gottheit eines Genesenen, in der Lydischen Tonart*[2] ('Song of thanksgiving to the Deity on recovery from an illness, written in the Lydian mode'). This circumstance, together with the indisputable fact of Beethoven's ill health at the time, led A.-B. Marx to find in the XVth quartet the 'musical expression of illness and recovery'. 'The scene of the entire work is laid in an atmosphere of suffering; the music is restless, morbid, and nervous: creating effects that the sinewy, wailing tone of the stringed instruments is peculiarly fitted to express.' This quotation from Marx typifies the mentality that insists on finding for every musical work an appropriate 'programme'. The assertion makes Beethoven responsible not only for a continuous imaginative 'programme' of this type, but for descriptive realism and even imitative harmonic effects. On the rare occasions where Beethoven does this he expressly marks the passages (in the Pastoral Symphony: the picturesque descriptions at the end of the *Scene am Bach*, the storm passage, &c.; [3] and the *Battle of*

---

[1] According to V. Wilder, pp. 480–1. The XIVth quartet was scored for orchestra by Karl Müller in 1886, under the title, incorrect on two counts, of the Xth symphony.

[2] Above the words is an Italian translation: *Canzona di ringraziamento offerta alla divinità da un guarito, in modo lidico*, written in a strange hand later, with or without Beethoven's approval.

[3] It is well known that apart from these episodes Beethoven deliber-

Vittoria). Here it is not the case. Admittedly, Beethoven was a composer of ' programme ' music, but
always in its highest and psychological sense. In this
respect the XVth quartet only translates through
the medium of sound the artist's permanent habit of
spiritual thought, like all the last works : the struggle
against destiny, and the triumph of happiness over sorrow. It is only a coincidence that the composition of
the Op. 132 stretched over a period in which health
for a time overcame disease. Apart from the effort that
this fact inspired Beethoven to make in the *Adagio* of
his quartet, it is apparent that the work as a whole
reveals a more morbid trend of imaginative inspiration
than the others ; the first movement, for example, conveys the effect of darkness lit by fitful gleams, and
crossed by shifting moods of passion. But in all this
there is an etherealized spiritual restlessness, by no
means an expression of pathological disorder. Whatever
it may be, the Op. 132 demonstrates a more coherent
unity than Op. 131. It also keeps more closely to
traditional forms, less daring than its predecessor. But it
contains passages of wonderful loveliness, and the *Adagio*
especially is one of the summits of achievement in
quartet-writing and indeed in all music.

I. *Assai sostenuto. Allegro*, in A minor (common time).
The slow eight-bar introduction is a mysterious procession of minims (in which Marx would see ' long-drawn
agony' !) rising from the lowest register like creeping
mists from a river. A sense of uneasiness is born with
these *pianissimo* harmonies, chords of the seventh of
A minor and E minor. The progression of parts,
especially of the viola, is remarkable (Ex. 262).

At the entry of the *Allegro* the first violin darts away
with a rapid phrase, halts for a second, assumes a
plaintive air, then reasserts itself with renewed vigour,
before fading away into space. . . . All these passing

ately represented only the imaginative impulse given him by association
with the country, and not the country sights and sounds themselves.

inflections fill the first twelve bars with poignant meaning (Ex. 263). These twelve bars are quoted entire, because they contain all the thematic elements of this first movement (indicated by letters). These elements unite to form one unified phrase, and it is this thematic coherence which gives the piece its psychological unity, in the expression of a concentrated and morbid inspiration. In the various *motifs* the form of a principal theme and secondary themes can easily be traced, and these melodies, dependent on each other,

Ex. 262.

are framed in a musical setting approximating to sonata form.

In Ex. 263, the plaintive *motif a* is at first given by the 'cello in a high register, and then taken up and worked out by the first violin, forming at once a dialogue with the other instruments in a tissue of sound more and more closely woven ; the effect is particularly pointed in this quartet, where the instruments convey the impression almost of the speaking voice. The tone swells and deepens into the lofty strains of *motif b*, and breaks abruptly into the chords of *motif c*. One bar of *adagio* interrupts the continuity and brings back phrase *a*, out of which the plaintive *motif* rises again and develops ; the unison figure *b* modulates to F minor, where *motif a* re-establishes itself with greater warmth and colour, as it passes from part to part. In

Allegro

Ex. 263.

a figure for the violin alone it is heard again in tender guise :

Ex. 264.

leading to a unison *motif d* (last bar of Ex. 264) in a hammering rhythm, recalling certain themes from the third Op. 59 quartet. This figure only stays for two bars, moving without transition to an unusual *motif e*, worked in canon for four bars (Ex. 265) and afterwards to a sweeping flight on the first violin, based on *motif b* and taking it up to a high altitude, while the lower voices move in contrary motion. Its bursting energy evaporates in a conclusion in F major, in which tonality the second violin introduces the second principal theme *f* in accordance with sonata form (Ex. 266).

Ex. 265.

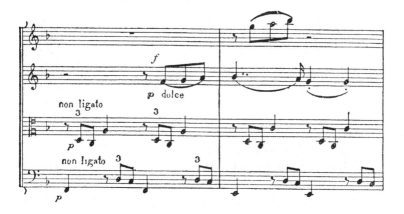

Ex. 266.

In this subtle, appealing melody, tinged with resignation, can be traced a close resemblance to the *motif* in canon (Ex. 265); its character of underlying uneasiness is revealed in the tonality and in the nervous accompaniment upon which it rests. A modulation to D major brings a less anxious note, but it is followed by a restless figure on the first violin which passes to all the parts, bringing back the key of F major through B flat, and filling the atmosphere with feverish anxiety (Marx even sees in the high altitude of the first violin an evidence of physical over-excitement!); this is a technical idiom common to the style of the later quartets. The *motif* imposes an energetic vitality upon the life of the work as a whole. The *motif b* is twice repeated in vigorous contrary movement—another favourite idiom of Beethoven's; the two statements are separated by an intervening bar of two slurred *piano* minims, and resolve into a graceful *ritardando* figure, poised and tentative, which constitutes the formal conclusion to the first section. Short quavers, *a tempo*, resembling the form of the *staccato* figure *c*—and anticipated in other instances in the earlier quartets of Op. 95, in F minor, and Op. 59, No. 1 (first movements)—form an episode leading to the second section. The F major tonality modulates to B flat (see the E flat of the second violin). Unexpectedly, the minims of the *Assai sostenuto* reappear on the 'cello, increased to semibreve length here to conform with the different *tempo*. They act as a firm counterpoint below the plaintive theme, now reappearing on the first violin in a modulation from B flat to G minor, by means of an F sharp in the bass. The theme modulates to C minor, supported by the other voices; the counterpoint in the bass creates a sense of heavy oppression, leading Marx again to suppose it to be a realistic description of bodily suffering. The impending uneasiness is curiously cut short by the *staccato motif c*, which now appears, bluntly vigorous, in a rhythmic bar on the dominant of C minor.

This is in turn followed by a new middle section, constructed on a *motif* based on *a* :

Ex. 267.

In brilliant unisons on variously combined voices the new design hovers between the keys of C major and A minor, as eloquent as recitative, extended in imitation and bringing the four voices together in a modified *motif b, piano*, and then *pianissimo*, like pale sunshine after rain. In the next three bars *motif a* on the 'cello is joined with the counter-melody of the introduction on the upper voices. One bar of the *staccato* theme, *forte*, in E minor, is followed by a return of the *motif* of the introduction in a *fortissimo* unison, as though to stress further the sense of oppression and the power of physical suffering. But these obstinate semibreves yield before the return of the plaintive theme, and a mood of quiet contemplation supervenes for four bars in E minor, a mood quickly banished, however, by the harsh *motif c* bringing the restless semiquaver figure A which opens the *Allegro* (in E minor), and consequently the third section of the movement in sonata form. The method of introducing this recapitulation section may be cited as one of the many instances in the last quartets of the fusion of the laws of logical formal construction with an unimpeded imaginative force. The third section here—that is to say, the first section repeated with modifications—is not presented as a concession to an inflexible tradition of form, which might be an alien influence in the psychological conception of the work, but as a means of consolidating the unity of the whole work from this very psychological aspect. Moreover, since Beethoven, there have been many instances of compositions of great freedom of form and thought, which have by no means on this account lacked strength of construction and logical coherence (Prelude to *Tristan*, *L'Apprenti Sorcier*, for instance).

The third section roughly corresponds with the first, with the advantage of normal changes of key. The transition *motif* derived from the *staccato* figure is now developed in a five-bar *crescendo* leading to a *Coda* in polyphonic style. Above the semibreves of the introduction the plaintive *motif* appears in a guise more appealing than ever :

Ex. 268.

An energetic episode combines the *staccato motif* with the plaintive theme, acquiring now a degree of pride and courage, and *motif b*, with its character of profound exaltation. It brings a return of the canon heard before, but this time lengthened and enlarged by combination with the *motif* of exaltation, now more and more impassioned. A return of the second section on the theme

of Ex. 266 follows, given by the viola in the new
tonality of A major. But the sense of regained peace is
troubled by a restless accompaniment and a modulation
to the minor; the plaintive theme *a* reappears, linked
in this way to the melody of appealing resignation as
an element of a single musical idea. From this point
the *motifs* are combined, through their points of resemblance, in an increasingly close relation. This combination, moreover, does not hesitate to alter the original
significance of the themes in order to express through
them a single thought, unifying apparently conflicting
elements into a whole. The statement can be verified
here by the examination of the combined themes of the
plaintive *motif a* with the heroic figure in the last bar
of Ex. 264, and then of the combination of this same
figure with the secondary theme of Ex. 266, which
receives from it a quite new impetus and meaning.
Out of the *motif* of appealing resignation grows a design
of proud defiance:

Ex. 269.

This development leads to a last return of the semibreves of the introduction, imposed upon *motif a* in
a *fortissimo* thematic clash. The plaintive theme loses
force, and the tone fades in falling chords. At this
moment a design of semiquaver seconds is established

in the bass, *sempre pp*, in a curious dissonance, D♯-E on the 'cello and F-E on the viola, above which are ranged the semibreves of the introduction :

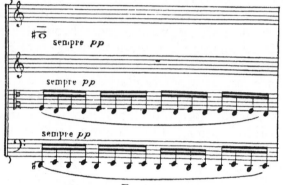

Ex. 270.

The entry of the violins brings a *crescendo* of the dissonant figure which lasts to the end. Then the first violin has a brilliant passage based on the same figure, and beneath it the second violin asserts a phrase of vigorous affirmation, of which the first three notes are those of the plaintive theme ; but here they resound like the cry of an indomitable will giving way to a momentary access of despair.[1]

II. *Allegro ma non tanto*, in A major (3/4). Following his ' programme ' at all costs, Marx describes this movement, in *intermezzo* form, as an illustration of ' the feeling born of approaching convalescence '.

' Inspired by the breath of renewed vitality, he takes

[1] The *Coda* recalls the *presto* of the finale of the Op. 57 sonata in F minor, and the end of the first movement of the IXth symphony. We can see here an imaginative affinity with these works. Again, the last lines of the *Allegro* of the XVth quartet can also be imagined to express a cry of despair from a lost soul, and it is by the combination of two *motifs*, similar to those of the first and second violins in the quartet, that Liszt gave a realistic description of supreme despair, in the ' Inferno ' of his symphonic poem *Dante*. This affords proof of the many imaginative interpretations possible, and of the inadvisability of ever making ' programmes '.

courage again. . . . But one feels that his state is still
precarious.'

Without giving this statement more credence than
it deserves, it cannot be gainsaid that from the very
first bars of this movement, with its simple four-voice
unison, its vivid dance rhythm, and its clear tone, an
impression is created of health regained, and of an
untroubled well-being following the feverish restlessness of the first movement. It is an entirely characteristic work, in which Beethoven extracts the last
ounce of development from each *motif*, sometimes in
whimsical fashion with a thematic transformation like
the following :

Ex. 271.

sometimes with added animation within the structure of
the theme (as in the modulation to C major in the second
section, where the lower voices give the original theme
in thirds. Marx sees here, with an extraordinarily distorted imagination, a physical shuddering !). There is
no need for any further comment upon this movement,
since the technical construction is perfectly clear. From
the imaginative aspect it can be compared with the
scherzo of the quartet in E flat, Op. 127 ; but as Marx
here acutely observes, the *scherzo* of Op. 127 grows in
conception bar by bar, with an ever-increasing range
of vision as the Master's inspiration deepens, whereas
this unity is lacking in the Op. 132, where, though the

motifs are separately repeated and developed with inexhaustible device of invention, their original thematic elements remain unaltered in form and scope (effects by unisons, imitations in canon, combinations of the principal theme, both in its initial form and split up into phrases, &c.).

This absence of unity is stressed by the addition of an *alternativo* in A major, which appears in the form of an elaborately worked-out *musette* of an unexpected and wholly alien character that breaks the logical sequence of the work.

Marx comments truly that after the rhythmic precision of the *scherzo* proper, which in this respect follows the rules of classical form, the broad outline of this new theme is surprising:

Ex. 272.

It stretches over eleven bars, at once repeated above
an entry of the basses, one after the other, on the sustained octave of A. But when Marx adds that in this
alternativo a resemblance can be traced to a development of the *adagio* bar of the first movement, he is
straining the limits of imagination, unless he is perhaps
referring to another part of the *alternativo*, to be considered later, and where Beethoven makes a curious
alteration in the normal rhythm.

Twenty-two bars from the beginning of this section
a new quaver figure is linked on without any bars of
transition :

Ex. 273.

stated by the viola, and followed in contrary movement
by the first violin. This new *motif* is a gay and lively
dance tune, forming brilliant arabesques on the four

instruments. The chief interest is mainly in the first
violin and viola parts. These two in turn unfold a
long-poised phrase of popular rustic character, a valse
with the *tempo* marked by *staccato* crotchets on the other
voices :

Ex. 274.

It calls to mind certain rather clumsy rhythms in
menuets of Haydn symphonies, or again, in Beethoven's
own work, the *Zusammensein der Landleute* in the
Pastorale. Notice the short *alla breve* passage, for
example, in the key of C sharp minor :

Ex. 275.

If for once we were to follow Marx's ' programme ',
let us suppose this passage to express the realistic

description of the invalid's first convalescence in the country, as he takes the fresh air while watching the country-folk making holiday ! It is this particular passage in which Marx tries awkwardly to trace a connexion with the troubled sadness of the opening of the quartet—perhaps because of the breaking of the rhythm and the return of a minim figure, and the entry of a *motif* that recalls the *adagio* bar of the opening. But his imagination carries him here beyond the bounds of reason.

The *alternativo* is followed by a repeat, note for note, of the first section without any modification. In this respect the *intermezzo* of Op. 132 shows a less advanced technique than that of the Op. 127, in which a less formal impression is conveyed by the unprepared return of the *alternativo* at the end of the movement.

III. *Molto adagio*, in C major (common time). *Andante*, in D major (3/8). This famous movement is the climax of the quartet and, in a way, the pivot upon which its spiritual inspiration turns. It is an ' act of grace' of matchless fervour, perhaps more deeply expressive of Beethoven's spirit of devotion than the Mass in D itself. It is conceived in so deeply religious a spirit that, as A. W. Ambros observes in his *Figures historiques*, it seems strange to listen to the strains of this *Adagio* in a brilliantly lighted room, before an audience expressing noisy approval, or even hissing disapproval, as often happened in the early years.

The impression is heightened by the fact that the artist has chosen to express his sense of gladness to the Almighty in the musical form of one of the ecclesiastical modes. It is a fact that he inscribed on the original manuscript : *in der lydischen Tonart* (in the Lydian mode). Marx claims that this mode was considered among the Greeks to have a morbid, flaccid character,[1] and that Beethoven, according to Marx's

---

[1] In Greece ' Lydian ' was a term implying effeminacy—an implication long obsolete. The ' Lydian mode' is here actually the plagal

supposed programme, deliberately chose this way to express the weakness of convalescence. This interpretation is too specious to be correct. It is simpler to suppose that Beethoven had considered only the liturgical aspect of what is here called the Lydian mode; and in the choice of an ecclesiastical tonality he had an effective setting for this melody, cast in the flat tints of plain-song.

The movement includes a principal section and an *alternativo* (*Andante*).

The principal section, *Adagio*, is strictly speaking the 'song of thanksgiving': a melody in minims with introductory bars and interludes in imitation, in crotchets; the key is F with a B natural (Lydian). The two phrases of each sentence of the theme stretch over six bars, and the theme recurs in regular succession five times; altogether, the first section of the *Adagio* is thirty bars in length. The theme itself:

Heiliger Dankgesang eines Genesenen an die Gottheit, in der lydischen Tonart.
(Canzona di ringraziamento offerta alla divinità da un guarito, in modo lidico.)

Ex. 276.

is given *sotto voce*, breathing gratitude for regained rest and peace, faith and conviction.

A bar of episode on the dominant of D leads to the *alternativo* (*andante*). The manuscript bears the words: *Neue Kraft fühlend*, and the score: *Sentendo nuova*

hypo-Lydian mode, with a scale of F with B natural; the authentic Lydian mode is in a scale of C.

forza. The change of rhythm and pace, the animation
of the theme, the technical character of accent, bowing,
and trills, all give a very real sense of the joy of the
convalescent on indeed 'regaining vitality':

Ex. 277.

Certainly there is here an effect almost of descriptive
realism. 'Intellectual power is wonderfully revealed in
this *andante*,' says Marx; 'this is no expression of
physical energy, but of a nervous force, a subtle sensi-
bility. The first violin, mingling with the melody of

the second, takes the theme and brings it to a conclusion that ravishes the ear; throbbing with a youthful
vitality and vigour that makes the pulse beat quicker
as one listens, it is nevertheless touched with a sense
of the continuous agony of deafness : the last passage
is marked *cantabile espressivo* :

Ex. 278.

The movement of the 'cello part seems to support this
interpretation.' The passage is rather an echo of the
Mass in D; it is a fifteen-bar melody growing in
fervour (see bars 6–8, after the last bar of Ex. 278) that
expresses the very spirit of the words of thanksgiving.
    The first entry of the *Andante* concludes in D major,
più piano; the *Adagio* is re-established by two *pianissimo* chords, the tonic chord of C major and the chord
of F-A-C (the B flat disappears to allow the logical
return of the Lydian mode). The two elements of the
theme acquire a larger aspect, and are divided between
the two violins; the minims of the plain-song theme
are heard on the first violin an octave higher than in
the exposition, giving a sense of ecstatic exaltation; the
other *motif*, transformed into a syncopated rhythm,
forms a florid species of counterpoint below the plain-
song. The following example gives the structure of the
two parts :

Ex. 279.

In this new form the *Adagio* extends as before over thirty bars, and admits of the same episodic transition, though a little modified. The *Andante* reappears in due course, enriched in thematic and rhythmic structure, and correspondingly deepened in imaginative power. One observes here the trend of development within the movement towards an increasingly intimate inspiration, characteristic of the last quartets and first felt in the *Adagio* of the Op. 127. It is also an example of the 'grand variation'.

The *Adagio* returns for the last time. Here again a new modification of the twofold theme is involved by the redoubled imaginative force of the artist, in whose hand is written on the manuscript: *Mit innigster Empfindung (Con intimissimo sentimento)*.

It is a passage of unspeakable beauty. Towards the end the plain-song theme, combined with the other thematic element, gains a new religious fervour; *sforzato* accentuations of each note seem to proclaim an unshakable conviction of belief (Ex. 280). The musician reaches so sublime a level of creative imagination that he is indifferent to passing harmonic harshnesses that a Fuchs or an Albrechtsberger would have undoubtedly condemned (see the ninths of the first two *sforzati*). These angularities only serve to stress the character of this rugged assertion of faith. In other respects the passage follows the same half-tone colour scheme as the rest of the movement; the *forte* and *sforzati* are the only high lights on the prevailing *piano*, and the continuous *diminuendo* is scarcely broken, except where thematic fluctuations are most pronounced. This veiled tone re-

Ex. 280.

sults in an atmosphere of another world; the radiance of the C major of Ex. 280 is almost imperceptibly dimmed, as the dual theme returns (evoking a memory of the clear serenity of Parsifal's prayer) for its last entry in the Lydian mode (F major without B flat); the last chord, prolonged to an infinite *pianissimo*, is that of F-A-C-A-F.

IV. This extraordinary movement is followed by a short march, *Alla marcia, assai vivace,* in A major (common time), in two parts of varying length. The first eight-bar phrase has the following theme:

Ex. 281.

and is repeated, modulating to a conclusion in the dominant E. The second:

Ex. 282.

is sixteen bars in length and is also repeated, finishing on the tonic.

Marx considers this movement to ' breathe an atmosphere of a speedy and certain recovery; there is revealed the return, not yet of perfect strength, but of definite vigour and assurance '. In defence of his interpretation he asserts the significance of the opening, in a *forte* that at once fades to a *piano*. . . . This theory can be dismissed on the ground that Beethoven constantly sets contrasting colours of *forte* and *piano* against each other, especially in the later works, when a movement is in a marked rhythm, whether march *tempo* or not. (See, for instance, the second movement of the Op. 101 Sonata.) In any case, this movement is full of vigour and freshness; the second section recalls the triumphal march of the *King Stephen* music. It is a relaxation of effort after the intense contemplation of the slow movement.

Immediately upon the conclusion of the second section of the march a *Più allegro* (in 4/4 time) opens, in a crotchet passage based on the second bar of Ex. 281, beginning in the key of A minor and gradually working into the key of C major. In this key the first violin unfolds an impassioned *recitativo* melody above a *tremolo* on the other voices. The passage rises to a climax, and *fortissimo*, from F in *altissimo*, the first violin falls in a rapidly descending quaver phrase to its lowest register (*presto, alla breve*); there it rises for a last languid flight of recitative (*Poco adagio, smorzando*), to be arrested finally on the dominant of A; after a momentary pause the last movement opens without a break.

The finale, *Allegro appassionato* in A minor, 3/4, is, according to Marx, ' the wonderful psychological outcome of the artist's trials and triumphs, suffering and consolation, bringing new vitality and new expressive effect. Yet this is no longer the fresh unimpaired vitality of youth; ill health is overcome, but the suffering it involved can never be forgotten, nor the old creative force be recaptured.' This interpretation may be correct for the opening bars of the movement only, where the minor tonality prevails and a sense of restless anxiety is felt; it may perhaps only be correct for the first few bars, where the accompaniment is alone. But the melody that enters at the third bar reflects marvellously, by its quality at once impassioned, proud, and appealing, the musician's bruised and weary spirit, his unsatisfied longing for peace:

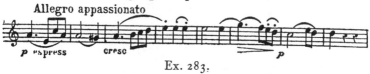

Ex. 283.

It is one of the most profoundly conceived melodies that Beethoven ever wrote, developed and used with such wonderful effect that it lifts the movement to a place among the finest quartet music in existence. The eight-bar example quoted contains the theme, immediately repeated an octave higher, and, where the emotion deepens in intensity, doubled by the viola. A secondary section follows this exposition:

Ex. 284.

Repeated as before to the length of sixteen bars alto-gether, it leads through a design where its last bars are combined with a link bar with a stressed weak beat (Ex. 285), to a cadence figure, where the movement gains a harsher, more incisive character (see the ninths on the violins).

The cadence figure is itself repeated in eight bars—a further evidence of the condensed form of the move-ment—in which the upper voices give the figure of the third bar of Ex. 285, while the 'cello takes the theme;

the harmonic and tonal richness increases. A modulation to G major in a bridge passage formed of short

Ex. 285.

quaver chords makes way for the secondary theme, brimming with fresh life, which recalls the ' *Sentendo nuova forza* ' of the *Adagio*, in more sprightly form :

Ex. 286.

This second section modulates to E minor and leads
to an episode of deeper intensity, where the four instruments are heard, *fortissimo*, in a harmonic effect whose
angularity reflects Beethoven's own inflexible determination :

Ex. 287.

This figure is twice presented, with three intervening
bars of a calmer melody on the first violin. Gradually
the atmosphere of repose returns ; a sustained *diminuendo* in crossing harmonies, a favourite idiom of Beethoven in his later works, and of Schumann after him,
is followed by a sudden modulation to A minor, and the
return in smooth sequence of the original theme. The
next thirty-two bars recapitulate the opening section of
the *Allegro*, but a new development section is shown,
in which the original theme on the first violin is at first
modified in the following way (Ex. 288).

By a change of rhythm in the basses, an effect of
breathless struggle ensues ; the forty-bar development,
much worked out, recalls in places the interweaving of
parts in the *Scherzo* of Op. 59, No. 1 ; this rugged
burst of melody is the outpouring of a liberated and
jubilant spirit, growing in ardour as the 'cello takes up
the melodic line at bar 21, in contrary movement with
the first violin. But a progression of episodic figures

leads back the principal section, repeated once more according to sonata form. To it is added an important extension based on the secondary theme (first bars of Ex. 286), and its final phrase (Ex. 289) is worked out in a long series of *pianissimo* imitations. Almost imper-

Ex. 288.

Ex. 289.

ceptibly, the theme of this strange episode merges into that of the principal theme; tone, movement and pace swell into a *Presto* of inimitable force (Beethoven's indication is: *Immer geschwinder—accelerando*), punctuated with *sforzandi*, where the 'cello cuts in with an eloquent statement of the original theme in its highest register, doubled at the octave by the first violin, while the inner parts resound in a quaver figure like a drum roll. For five bars after the end of this passage the first violin sustains the dominant E, as the 'cello takes the theme out of the dreary minor key and bursts into the long-expected tonality of A major. Full creative power and perfect health are now restored at last. When Marx saw in this finale a recovery still precarious, he forgot this *Coda* in A major, bubbling with renewed vigour and energy! A delightful *jeu d'esprit* slips out of the original theme, at first so feverish and uneasy, to be transformed into a tumult of wild rejoicing! The short *Coda* of the finale of Op. 95 employs the same device in transforming a sombre theme into a *motif* of sparkling gaiety. It is an idiom often found in the work of César Franck. The brilliant play of wit and humour here ends in a delightful canon, the passage marked in the score *colla punta d'arco*, a sort of idealization of the style of Haydn. The theme of the first bars of Ex. 286 sounds for a second, *forte*, in this forceful rhythm, and a design of broken chords of the A major triad finishes the movement. As Schumann said of the *scherzo* of Op. 59, No. 1, and of the *Allegretto* of the VIIIth Symphony, in B flat, one feels that the musician had taken up his pen probably in a mood of ill-humour, but now puts it down in the best of good spirits!

Quartet No. XVI, Op. 135 (in F major).

In actual dimension this work is much more concise than the quartets of Op. 127, 130, 131, and 132. It is not their inferior from the point of technique, but its imaginative significance is infinitely less; here can be traced no sequence of psychological meaning, as in the earlier works of Beethoven's later manner. The first, second, and fourth movements are, rather, a fluent play of brilliant but irresponsible wit. By way of contrast, the *Adagio*, in spite of its circumscribed form, is one of the most profound expressions of Beethoven's genius that his work can offer, and the quality of its inspiration shows that he wrote it with an instinctive foreboding of the end. Nevertheless, as has been pointed out, this quartet was not actually the last composition from the Master's pen; his last work of all was the finale of the XIIIth quartet, Op. 130, also written at Gneixendorff, in November, 1826.

I. *Allegretto*, in F major (2/4). This first movement is an example of pure 'quartet' technique, in the fluent polyphonic style proper to the genre, and obviously written at one effortless stroke. The little sprightly *motif* underlying the piece is developed with extra-ordinary fullness of inventive power, and the various thematic elements combined with striking ingenuity.

The viola ushers in the first *motif a*, echoed mockingly on the first violin, and revealing a glimpse of the minor in the D flat of the 'cello:

Ex. 290.

There is a sense of questioning in this theme; it is continued for the next two or three bars, and the *piano* echo of the first violin becomes a sudden *sforzando* on both the violins. The response to the question follows in the second *motif b*:

Ex. 291.

leaping from voice to voice to a conclusion in the following cadence :

Ex. 292.

in a unison on the upper parts, which at first introduced it in turn. A bridge passage, also in a unison of the three instruments in regular crotchets, leads through a triplet figure on the first violin, with a modulation to C, to a third *motif c*, derived from *a*, involving eight bars of imitation (Ex. 293). A monodic theme *d* follows in quick succession (Ex. 294), recalling the *Allegro* of the *Ruins of Athens* overture; it modulates through D minor to C and G major and finishes in a pleasant imitative design that might have come from

Ex. 293.

Ex. 294.

Ex. 295.

the pen of Haydn, except perhaps the last two bars,
which are characteristic of Beethoven (Ex. 295).
Immediately following these two bars an episode enters,
based on two combined figures *e* and *f* in contrary
effect, the one in ascending *staccato* quavers concluding
on a crotchet, and the other in descending semiquaver
triplets :

Ex. 296.

In the course of the eight bars of this episode the
triplet *motif f* overwhelms the other voices, *pianissimo*,
and moves through the keys of C, F major, A minor,
G major, to give place then to a unison melody *g* on
the upper voices, in E minor (D sharp in the bass) :

Ex. 297.

This four-bar melody also moves in varied tonalities, E minor, C, A minor. It is the same with the four following bars, which contain only rhythmic animation and an extension of the last melodic episode. The final section is in C major:

Ex. 298.

The four-bar theme is reminiscent of Haydn, but Beethoven is to give it an entirely original setting.

It must be pointed out that these half-dozen *motifs* presented in the first fifty-six bars of the quartet are interesting as thematic contrasts, and not as the development of one underlying idea, since all the themes have an equal significance.

The development section is not only concerned with the working out of *motif a* (Ex. 290) alone, perhaps because as a quartet theme this *motif* barely signifies. It opens with the unexpected halt of the concluding theme in Haydn's manner on the dominant of D. At once theme *b* (Ex. 291) appears on the first violin, then on the second, in a play of imitations concluding on the dominant of C (G major). In this key the 'cello gives, solo, the crotchet figure of the bridge passage; at the fourth bar this figure becomes the basis of *motif a* on the viola. The two *motifs* form a dialogue for two bars. Then the triplet figure *f* (Ex. 296) enters. These three themes are interwoven into a smooth polyphonic passage, modulating from G to B flat major through C major, C minor, A flat major. After several bars the bridge passage design disappears (in B flat minor); the triplet figure becomes the accompaniment of *motif a*, given vigorously by the first violin, and then by the second; at the point when it seems that this theme is to dominate the passage it is interrupted by a robust unison of *motif b* on all four voices. This *motif* continues to keep the ascendancy (in B flat and F) and the establishment of the principal tonality seems to point to the recapitulation of the first section. On the contrary, in a tentative modulation to A minor, the first violin leads the other voices after it in a triplet figure, heard above *staccato* quavers accentuated at random within the bar, and recognizable as elements of *motif a* by the grace-note that precedes the quaver. Modulations follow in quick sequence to A minor, D minor, G major, C major. *Forte*, the first violin soars to B flat in *altissimo*, and the viola, also *forte*, sounds the original *motif a*, acquiring here an energy reinforced by the beating triplets of the 'cello on D flat, and by the rich accompaniments on the upper voices. Immediately after the viola entry, and in the unprepared key of F minor established at this point, the two violins give the same *motif a*, *sforzando*, combined at once with the *motif b*. This curious re-entry of themes is quoted, opening the third section of the movement in sonata form:

Ex. 299.

This recapitulation varies in detail from the original exposition : the figure of Ex. 292, bar 3 and onwards, is given in slurred quavers in *cantabile* effect; this design returns in combination with *motif a* in the development of this section in a gracefully modified form.

The *Coda* employs a similar combination, where the *motif* of Ex. 292 is more flexible and vigorous. It breaks off into a unison descent of the four instruments, *crescendo*, on a transformed theme *a* :

Ex. 300.

The *motif* of the concluding figure (Ex. 298) follows in F major, and after it, instead of an energetic final exposition of theme *a*, the lower voices strike a robust E flat below the C in *altissimo* of the first violin ; the E flat becomes the harmonic foundation of the original theme, stated *piano* in G minor ; the theme reappears with its echo (the only re-entry of Ex. 290), in a moment of sombre energy. But the mood quickly passes. One does not expect from so slight a basic theme an impassioned built-up climax to conclude the work, like those of the quartets in A minor and in C minor. Sustaining the lively character of the movement the *motif b* is heard in response to the original theme, in B flat and F major ; the same *motif b*, after several imitative leaps, is arrested on a significant pause ; and from this point it falls in the cadence figure to a fluent conclusion in the principal tonality :

Ex. 301.

II. *Vivace*, in F major, 3/4. This movement is really a *scherzo*, although not so named.

At the outset an individual note is struck:

Ex. 302.

It is difficult to decide whether the principal theme is contained in the rhythmic *staccato* crotchets of the 'cello *a*, or in the syncopated minims of the first violin *b*; the parts move enclosed within the limits of the interval of a third, with distant veiled tone of a curiously poetical quality. After the conclusion of the design it is repeated with the parts inverted: the C of the second violin passes to the first, two octaves higher; the melody of the first violin moves to the second, one octave higher ; the 'cello lifts its theme an octave, and the viola gives out a figure of regular crotchets, sometimes *staccato*, sometimes slurred. The original *piano* becomes a *pianissimo*, increasing the ethereal remoteness of effect. It comes to an end on the tonic in unison. Suddenly a unison E flat resounds with full force on the weak beat of the same bar as the concluding chord ; it is repeated, *diminuendo*, in the bass parts alone, then by all the voices for six bars. Instead of the expected resolution upon B flat, at the seventh bar, the E flat changes to E natural, *pianissimo*, bringing back the key of F major and the original design. This time it forms a sustained *crescendo* throughout the double statement of the theme, of much richer and more varied texture than in its original exposition. The held C now falls to the 'cello, a long pedal point given before by the violins. The viola gives in double stopping a pedal C and above it a slurred version of the initial 'cello *motif*. In the repeated statement, *forte*, the melody *a* of the bass now appears in a fine unison on the two violins, above the *motif b* on the basses. This passage is a wonderful piece of musical structure. From this point the development is worked out on *motif a* with keen animation, in devices of imitation, contrary movement, &c., in the natural style of the genre, moving *pianissimo*, then *crescendo*, through elaborate harmonic modulations. The tone fades away to a whisper ; the mysterious E flat resounds in unison, and this second section of the *scherzo* begins its repeat.

The *Trio* opens with a statement of theme *c*, a quaver figure begun on the first violin, followed by theme *d*, a bold design of light *staccato* crotchets, rising through a long scale to a concluding figure *e* three bars in length (Ex. 303). The passage is repeated with an extension of the crotchet scale on the first violin to C in *altissimo*, and with thickened inner

harmonies. A design of imitations between the upper
and lower voices ensues, based on *motif c*, which merges
into a hesitating figure (Ex. 304). A modulation from
A minor to G major introduces the return of the original
Trio design. This time the first violin reaches B flat

Ex. 303.

Ex. 304.

in *altissimo*, and drops to low E and the concluding
motif e, repeated eight times in curiously individual
fashion. The viola then takes *motif c* and leads, *forte*,
to the key of A major, in which tonality the original
Trio design is repeated for eight bars, more or less
extended. At the ninth bar from the entry of A major,
a play of combined *motifs* begins, in which theme *c*

reappears in contrary motion. This twelve-bar episode, moving in a *crescendo*, leads to the strangest passage in the whole quartet. *Fortissimo* (for the first time in the work), the first violin carries all before it in a square, inflexible melody, based on *motif e* and interspersed with *sforzandi*; for forty-eight bars it persists, reiterated indefinitely above a unison accompaniment of *motif c* ranged at three levels:

Ex. 305.

Commenting upon this passage, Ulibishev transcribed it in its entirety, including the twenty bars following, in order to stigmatize it as ' nonsense '. He is notorious as a determined adverse critic of Beethoven. Marx gives the following commentary: ' Is the musical picture here obscured within the spirit by the throbbing auditory nerves of a sick man (this would be an extraordinary case of the influence of the physical state upon the imaginative in Beethoven's work), or is it merely meant to impress upon the mind some persistent idea? ' It seems that the second suggestion may be the true explanation of the passage, if one is to understand here the subjective working-out of a stubborn persistence, a veritable destructive force. What Beethoven does here, many great artists have done after him. It is similarly the case with Chopin—in the F sharp minor Polonaise for instance, and especially in the celebrated *staccato crescendo* of the E major section of the A flat Polonaise. The musical scene presented in this *trio* of the Polonaise in A, rather after the manner of Heine—the marching of thousands of troops, with lances and shields, and colours flying in the wind— might all be suggested by this passage from the quartet. It also evokes in the imagination the sound of bagpipes heard as the battalions pass by, growing fainter and fainter in the distance.

Again, it is the same with Wagner, who makes much of the repetition of a single persistent musical figure, especially in his later works, using it for dramatic effect in the same way as it is used in the purely instrumental conceptions of Chopin and Beethoven. (Opening bars and end of the *Walküre*, the tune of the shepherd in *Tristan*, development of the Bells theme in *Parsifal*, Assembly of the *Mastersingers*, &c.)

This episode concludes in a distant shadowy *diminuendo*, out of which emerges the *motif c*, played *ppp* in a unison of the four instruments, charming the first violin away from the stubborn *motif e*; it modulates from A to F major and brings back the syncopated figure *b*, still *ppp*, and played this time in unison. This is not the return of the *scherzo*, only its preparation. The passage is quoted below (Ex. 306). The first section of the *scherzo* now returns in the ordinary way with its repeated second section.

The conclusion is formed from nine chords of F major, at first in the low register, then in all the parts in a constant *diminuendo*, ending *pianissimo*, except for the abrupt *forte* of the last chord.

III. *Lento assai, cantante e tranquillo*, in D flat major, 6/8. This very short slow movement, in the form of very free variations, gives expression to a poignant and concentrated nobility of feeling. In the harmonic introduction of held notes in the tonic key a sense of mysterious suspense is at once felt. The use of this idiom is often found in the artist's later period (*Adagio* of the Op. 106 sonata, of the Op. 127 quartet, and of the IXth symphony), and it is one that has suffered much imitation since, especially at the hands of the moderns.

Ex. 306.

A sublime melody moves like a spoken prayer [1] above this harmonic basis for ten bars (Ex. 307). The concluding phrase of the tenth bar is taken up and repeated in imitation on the 'cello and first violin, during the next two bars. Then follows for the next ten bars a new melodic period of the same type. The atmosphere gradually changes with the appearance of a *crescendo* and an emphatic statement of the *motif*. Mournful phrases, long drawn out, and harsh harmonic leaps give the theme an air of angularity; it settles down again into a phase of calm repose, and culminates in an unexpected episode in C sharp minor, effected by means of the chromatic alteration of F, in the viola

[1] In a note-book of sketches for Op. 135 there are the following words set against the slow movement: ' *Süsser Ruhegesang oder Friedensgesang* ' (Song of rest or peace).

part, to F flat. The episodic theme has a tentative air, punctuated as it were by intermittent patches of light

Ex. 307.

Ex. 308.

(Ex. 308). The prevailing mood of distress seems to linger indefinitely, and though a modulation to E major would dissipate it at once, trailing chromatic harmonies maintain the melancholy tinge of C sharp minor. The passage lasts for nine and a half bars; a thin enharmonic change brings back the original key and the opening theme, now undergoing considerable alteration in method of treatment:

Ex. 309.

and it assumes a chorale-like effect by the use of canonic and contrary movement.

A graceful twelve-bar *Coda*:

Ex. 310 *a*.

leads to a *pianissimo* conclusion, throbbing with hidden intensity (Ex. 310 *b*).

This whole section is marked to be played *semplice*, in a mezzo-tint hardly lighted at all by *crescendo*, and effects a miracle of delicate subtlety. The example above gives two bars of the opening and the final bar.

IV. *Finale*. This movement is famous, at least for the musical problem it presents, an enigma that has never found a satisfactory solution. The following epi-

graph is actually written against it in the manuscript
in Beethoven's own hand (Ex. 311). The two *motifs*
quoted in this line of music form the thematic basis of
the finale ; the first is used in a twelve-bar introduction
which reappears later in the course of the movement ;
the second is the fundamental melody of the *Allegro*,
the principal section.

Ex. 310 *b*.

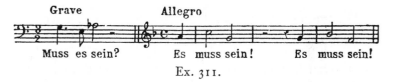

Muss es sein?   Es muss sein!   Es muss sein!

Ex. 311.

Various interpretations have been given to this extraordinary musical dialogue, among which the following
are the most important :—

Beethoven's friend and first biographer, Schindler,
furnishes a very prosaic explanation. The musician's
housekeeper asks him for money, and—' Muss es
sein ? ' (Must it be ?), asks Beethoven. ' Es muss
sein ! ' (It must be !) is the inexorable reply. Schindler,
who is rather doubtful about the authenticity of his
anecdote, adds that it might be related in another
context as a request for money from Beethoven to a
publisher.

In the second edition of his biography of Beethoven,

Marx, not without justification, sets aside the half-humorous anecdotes of Schindler, and quotes a letter of Herr Moritz Schlesinger, dated February 27th, 1859,[1] from which the following extract is taken :

Regarding the enigmatic phrase *Muss es sein?* that arises in the last quartet, I think I can explain its significance better than most people, as I possess the original manuscript with the words written in his (Beethoven's) own hand, and when he sent them he wrote as follows: 'You can translate the *Muss es sein* as showing that I have been unlucky, not only because it has been extremely difficult to write this when I had something much bigger in my mind, and because I have only written this in accordance with my promise to you, and because I am in dire need of money, which is hard to come by; it has also happened that I was anxious to send the work to you in parts, to facilitate engraving, and in all Mödlingen (he was living there then) I could not find a single copyist, and so have had to copy it out myself, and you can imagine what a business it has been! . . .' I remember the letter (continues Schlesinger) very clearly, and without possibility of doubt; unfortunately it disappeared in 1826, when my house was burnt down.

We cannot regret this loss acutely ; nor can we be sure that Herr Schlesinger remembered the exact words as clearly as he says, since it would have been odd for Beethoven to lament the shortage of copyists in Mödlingen (Mödling), seeing that the Op. 135 was not written at Mödling at all, but, as we know, at Gneixendorff near Krems in Lower Austria, where his brother lived ; after finishing the Mass in D at Mödling in 1822, a work of three years, he never went back there at all during the last two years of his life, according to Dr. Gerard von Breuning's explicit statement, and he should know, as his father was one of Beethoven's most intimate friends. Again, the original manuscript of Op. 135, lent by Herr Schlesinger to Marx to reproduce

[1] Herr Moritz Schlesinger, founder of the *Gazette musicale de Paris*, had taken part with his father, Ad. Martin Schlesinger, the famous music publisher of Berlin, in the publication of the Op. 135 Quartet, which appeared in September, 1827.

in facsimile in his biography, bears the following words in distinct script in Beethoven's hand : *Dernier quatuor de Beethoven. Gneixendorff, le 30 octobre 1826.* This discrepancy between Herr Schlesinger's statements and the evidence in the manuscript that he must have known perfectly well makes it impossible to attach any importance to the statement.

Moreover, as Marx points out, labouring the obvious, the themes of the epigraph cannot relate to the question of copyists, since they had already been used in the construction of the finale before the question arose !

It seems that the best explanation of the anecdote is as a momentary feeling of annoyance on the part of the artist, who was already seriously ill,[1] at the necessity of having to write this finale at all, the necessary fourth movement of the quartet, especially after the intense effort of spiritual revelation expressed in the *Adagio*.

After relieving his boredom by a musical caprice, he at once saw the use to which these themes could be put, and built upon them a movement of striking vigour and rhythmic force. But the mysterious preface was enough to intrigue the curiosity of listeners and critics, who see in it as a result a meaning that it does not possess. The argument shares the defects of all such attempts to set a ' programme ' to absolute music.

A. *Grave, ma non troppo tratto*, 3/2, in A flat major. The basses give a solemn statement of the theme *Muss es sein ?* in two bars separated and followed by a bar of transition (Ex. 312).

These four bars are followed by seven bars of chords of the dominant seventh of E flat major, and of the diminished seventh of F minor, in a 3/2 rhythm : (3/2) ♪♪♩ _ _. From the third bar the basses take up the interrogatory theme, *crescendo*, swelling from *piano* to *fortissimo*. The tone dies away, and an eighth bar of

---

[1] Yet several days later (November 1826) Beethoven was writing the wonderful finale of the Op. 130 quartet, to replace the Op. 133 Fugue.

chords, *adagio* and *pianissimo*, arrests the question on the unison of C.

The reply appears in the theme *Es muss sein!* (*Allegro* in F major, *alla breve*), vigorously attacked and reinforced by an emphatic accompaniment of *staccato*

Grave, ma non troppo tratto.

Ex. 312.

crotchets. These crotchets themselves form a new slurred figure, *piano*, which assumes an air of explanation of the reply, and gives place, above a long bass pedal, to a series of contrary figures on the other instruments:

Ex. 313.

As it works out the elements of the themes, the polyphony thickens, and, after a long period of the *staccato* crotchet design, modulates to E major, culminating in one of those expressive bars of rest that Wagner found such a marked feature of the latter Beethoven. The slurred crotchet figure (Ex. 313) is now burdened with a new development in A major. This design presently merges into a figure which passes

alternately between the first violin and the second, and
forms an accompaniment to a new theme on the 'cello:

Ex. 314.

This attractive melody, like a popular march tune, is
repeated by the first violin with sweeter, more delicate
tone, and towards the end of the phrase the ' *Es muss
sein !* ' *motif* reappears *crescendo*, robustly affirmed by
the inner parts and answered by the first violin.

This theme, in a *fortissimo* on all the instruments,
forms an imposing conclusion in A major to the first
section of the movement. The repeat is introduced
through a return of the *motif* in F major, contrasting
vividly with the preceding tonality.

The second section opens with a unison of three bars
on the theme *Es muss sein !* worked out in the following way:

Ex. 315.

The section is developed on the lines of a polyphonic treatment of this theme and the slurred crotchet design, moving from voice to voice through A minor and C major, with various modifications in the different entries which give rise to beautiful contrapuntal effects. The following figure appears on the second violin, for instance :

Ex. 316.

which is to reappear later in the course of the development; the march tune then enters again in the bright tonality of E major, marking an even rhythm in all the parts. Beethoven links this *motif* to the slurred crotchet figure in a bewildering succession of fresh imaginative ideas; a long passage ensues in which various themes are worked out in a riot of harmonic crudities. Sustained semibreves on the first violin (the first trilled, *ritardando*) open a transition passage leading to the return of the *Grave* 3/2 rhythm. *Fortissimo*, the basses declaim the ' *Muss es sein ?* ' *motif* in highly dramatic style, beneath heavy *tremoli* on the violins. The passage vividly suggests the preludes of Liszt, even as far as its details are concerned (note the linking phrase in the viola quaver figure). It is one of the earliest examples known, and perhaps even the first of all in quartet music, of this device, used and abused times without number from the beginning of the Romantic period to our own, i. e. the *fortissimo* statement of some massive theme under a *tremolo* of the upper voices. The phrase must be quoted on account of its historic importance (Ex. 317.)   One can imagine the theme played on the brass and bass strings, and the *tremolo* on the woodwind and violins.   A dialogue follows between the two *motifs* of question and answer (Ex. 318). Its sombre character resolves into the gaiety of the

Allegro, returning in F major (common time), with a new theme directly derived from the melancholy figure of the second violin quoted earlier (Ex. 316), but now transformed into an expression of joyous animation in a passage where the violins have the theme in succession. The *motif* of response reappears immediately after this

Grave, ma non troppo tratto.

Ex. 317.

Ex. 318.

episode, with its original energy unimpaired, and linked as before to the figure of ascending *staccato* crotchets. Then, in free recapitulation, the first and second principal sections return with Beethoven's inevitable modifications and modulations in 'wild' harmonies (Ex. 319). After the last chord of this passage (Ex. 319) which seems on the point of modulating to F sharp (G flat), the artist, riding rough-shod over classical tradition,

resumes the little march theme in F major. This time
it appears *pianissimo* in *pizzicato* form, raised to a high
pitch in all the parts. At the end of this eight-bar

Si repete la seconda parte al suo piacere.

Ex. 319.

episode, while the basses continue the *pizzicato motif*,
the first violin, *arco*, plays a strange little *pianissimo*
accompaniment like a trumpet-call:

Ex. 320.

Later, the second violin resumes its *arco* with the other
voices and gives out the answer *motif*; it forms the
centre of a rhythmic ensemble which gives it the air
of a dance:

Ex. 321.

This entire passage is played *pianissimo*; finally, on the last notes of the repeated theme of the second violin, all the instruments burst into a *fortissimo* unison for the four concluding bars of the quartet. An almost humorous effect is created by the contrast between these last bars and the twenty-seven bars of *pianissimo* immediately before; it is as though Beethoven is laughing at himself and at his audience for taking this little *motif* seriously, and making such a mystery out of his whimsical *Muss es sein?* which was no enigma at all!

A CATALOG OF SELECTED

DOVER BOOKS

IN ALL FIELDS OF INTEREST

A CATALOG OF SELECTED DOVER
BOOKS IN ALL FIELDS OF INTEREST

CONCERNING THE SPIRITUAL IN ART, Wassily Kandinsky. Pioneering work by father of abstract art. Thoughts on color theory, nature of art. Analysis of earlier masters. 12 illustrations. 80pp. of text. 5⅜ x 8½. 23411-8

ANIMALS: 1,419 Copyright-Free Illustrations of Mammals, Birds, Fish, Insects, etc., Jim Harter (ed.). Clear wood engravings present, in extremely lifelike poses, over 1,000 species of animals. One of the most extensive pictorial sourcebooks of its kind. Captions. Index. 284pp. 9 x 12. 23766-4

CELTIC ART: The Methods of Construction, George Bain. Simple geometric techniques for making Celtic interlacements, spirals, Kells-type initials, animals, humans, etc. Over 500 illustrations. 160pp. 9 x 12. (Available in U.S. only.) 22923-8

AN ATLAS OF ANATOMY FOR ARTISTS, Fritz Schider. Most thorough reference work on art anatomy in the world. Hundreds of illustrations, including selections from works by Vesalius, Leonardo, Goya, Ingres, Michelangelo, others. 593 illustrations. 192pp. 7⅛ x 10¼. 20241-0

CELTIC HAND STROKE-BY-STROKE (Irish Half-Uncial from "The Book of Kells"): An Arthur Baker Calligraphy Manual, Arthur Baker. Complete guide to creating each letter of the alphabet in distinctive Celtic manner. Covers hand position, strokes, pens, inks, paper, more. Illustrated. 48pp. 8¼ x 11. 24336-2

EASY ORIGAMI, John Montroll. Charming collection of 32 projects (hat, cup, pelican, piano, swan, many more) specially designed for the novice origami hobbyist. Clearly illustrated easy-to-follow instructions insure that even beginning papercrafters will achieve successful results. 48pp. 8¼ x 11. 27298-2

THE COMPLETE BOOK OF BIRDHOUSE CONSTRUCTION FOR WOODWORKERS, Scott D. Campbell. Detailed instructions, illustrations, tables. Also data on bird habitat and instinct patterns. Bibliography. 3 tables. 63 illustrations in 15 figures. 48pp. 5¼ x 8½. 24407-5

BLOOMINGDALE'S ILLUSTRATED 1886 CATALOG: Fashions, Dry Goods and Housewares, Bloomingdale Brothers. Famed merchants' extremely rare catalog depicting about 1,700 products: clothing, housewares, firearms, dry goods, jewelry, more. Invaluable for dating, identifying vintage items. Also, copyright-free graphics for artists, designers. Co-published with Henry Ford Museum & Greenfield Village. 160pp. 8¼ x 11. 25780-0

HISTORIC COSTUME IN PICTURES, Braun & Schneider. Over 1,450 costumed figures in clearly detailed engravings–from dawn of civilization to end of 19th century. Captions. Many folk costumes. 256pp. 8⅜ x 11¾. 23150-X

CATALOG OF DOVER BOOKS

STICKLEY CRAFTSMAN FURNITURE CATALOGS, Gustav Stickley and L. & J. G. Stickley. Beautiful, functional furniture in two authentic catalogs from 1910. 594 illustrations, including 277 photos, show settles, rockers, armchairs, reclining chairs, bookcases, desks, tables. 183pp. 6½ x 9¼. 23838-5

AMERICAN LOCOMOTIVES IN HISTORIC PHOTOGRAPHS: 1858 to 1949, Ron Ziel (ed.). A rare collection of 126 meticulously detailed official photographs, called "builder portraits," of American locomotives that majestically chronicle the rise of steam locomotive power in America. Introduction. Detailed captions. xi+ 129pp. 9 x 12. 27393-8

AMERICA'S LIGHTHOUSES: An Illustrated History, Francis Ross Holland, Jr. Delightfully written, profusely illustrated fact-filled survey of over 200 American light-houses since 1716. History, anecdotes, technological advances, more. 240pp. 8 x 10¾. 25576-X

TOWARDS A NEW ARCHITECTURE, Le Corbusier. Pioneering manifesto by founder of "International School." Technical and aesthetic theories, views of industry, eco-nomics, relation of form to function, "mass-production split" and much more. Profusely illustrated. 320pp. 6⅛ x 9¼. (Available in U.S. only.) 25023-7

HOW THE OTHER HALF LIVES, Jacob Riis. Famous journalistic record, expos-ing poverty and degradation of New York slums around 1900, by major social reformer. 100 striking and influential photographs. 233pp. 10 x 7⅞. 22012-5

FRUIT KEY AND TWIG KEY TO TREES AND SHRUBS, William M. Harlow. One of the handiest and most widely used identification aids. Fruit key covers 120 deciduous and evergreen species; twig key 160 deciduous species. Easily used. Over 300 photographs. 126pp. 5⅜ x 8½. 20511-8

COMMON BIRD SONGS, Dr. Donald J. Borror. Songs of 60 most common U.S. birds: robins, sparrows, cardinals, bluejays, finches, more–arranged in order of increasing complexity. Up to 9 variations of songs of each species.
Cassette and manual 99911-4

ORCHIDS AS HOUSE PLANTS, Rebecca Tyson Northen. Grow cattleyas and many other kinds of orchids–in a window, in a case, or under artificial light. 63 illus-trations. 148pp. 5⅜ x 8½. 23261-1

MONSTER MAZES, Dave Phillips. Masterful mazes at four levels of difficulty. Avoid deadly perils and evil creatures to find magical treasures. Solutions for all 32 exciting illustrated puzzles. 48pp. 8¼ x 11. 26005-4

MOZART'S DON GIOVANNI (DOVER OPERA LIBRETTO SERIES), Wolfgang Amadeus Mozart. Introduced and translated by Ellen H. Bleiler. Standard Italian libretto, with complete English translation. Convenient and thoroughly portable–an ideal companion for reading along with a recording or the performance itself. Introduction. List of characters. Plot summary. 121pp. 5¼ x 8½. 24944-1

TECHNICAL MANUAL AND DICTIONARY OF CLASSICAL BALLET, Gail Grant. Defines, explains, comments on steps, movements, poses and concepts. 15-page pictorial section. Basic book for student, viewer. 127pp. 5⅜ x 8½. 21843-0

THE CLARINET AND CLARINET PLAYING, David Pino. Lively, comprehensive work features suggestions about technique, musicianship, and musical interpretation, as well as guidelines for teaching, making your own reeds, and preparing for public performance. Includes an intriguing look at clarinet history. "A godsend," *The Clarinet,* Journal of the International Clarinet Society. Appendixes. 7 illus. 320pp. 5⅜ x 8½. 40270-3

HOLLYWOOD GLAMOR PORTRAITS, John Kobal (ed.). 145 photos from 1926-49. Harlow, Gable, Bogart, Bacall; 94 stars in all. Full background on photographers, technical aspects. 160pp. 8⅜ x 11¼. 23352-9

THE ANNOTATED CASEY AT THE BAT: A Collection of Ballads about the Mighty Casey/Third, Revised Edition, Martin Gardner (ed.). Amusing sequels and parodies of one of America's best-loved poems: Casey's Revenge, Why Casey Whiffed, Casey's Sister at the Bat, others. 256pp. 5⅜ x 8½. 28598-7

THE RAVEN AND OTHER FAVORITE POEMS, Edgar Allan Poe. Over 40 of the author's most memorable poems: "The Bells," "Ulalume," "Israfel," "To Helen," "The Conqueror Worm," "Eldorado," "Annabel Lee," many more. Alphabetic lists of titles and first lines. 64pp. 5³⁄₁₆ x 8¼. 26685-0

PERSONAL MEMOIRS OF U. S. GRANT, Ulysses Simpson Grant. Intelligent, deeply moving firsthand account of Civil War campaigns, considered by many the finest military memoirs ever written. Includes letters, historic photographs, maps and more. 528pp. 6⅛ x 9¼. 28587-1

ANCIENT EGYPTIAN MATERIALS AND INDUSTRIES, A. Lucas and J. Harris. Fascinating, comprehensive, thoroughly documented text describes this ancient civilization's vast resources and the processes that incorporated them in daily life, including the use of animal products, building materials, cosmetics, perfumes and incense, fibers, glazed ware, glass and its manufacture, materials used in the mummification process, and much more. 544pp. 6⅛ x 9¼. (Available in U.S. only.) 40446-3

RUSSIAN STORIES/RUSSKIE RASSKAZY: A Dual-Language Book, edited by Gleb Struve. Twelve tales by such masters as Chekhov, Tolstoy, Dostoevsky, Pushkin, others. Excellent word-for-word English translations on facing pages, plus teaching and study aids, Russian/English vocabulary, biographical/critical introductions, more. 416pp. 5⅜ x 8½. 26244-8

PHILADELPHIA THEN AND NOW: 60 Sites Photographed in the Past and Present, Kenneth Finkel and Susan Oyama. Rare photographs of City Hall, Logan Square, Independence Hall, Betsy Ross House, other landmarks juxtaposed with contemporary views. Captures changing face of historic city. Introduction. Captions. 128pp. 8¼ x 11. 25790-8

AIA ARCHITECTURAL GUIDE TO NASSAU AND SUFFOLK COUNTIES, LONG ISLAND, The American Institute of Architects, Long Island Chapter, and the Society for the Preservation of Long Island Antiquities. Comprehensive, well-researched and generously illustrated volume brings to life over three centuries of Long Island's great architectural heritage. More than 240 photographs with authoritative, extensively detailed captions. 176pp. 8¼ x 11. 26946-9

NORTH AMERICAN INDIAN LIFE: Customs and Traditions of 23 Tribes, Elsie Clews Parsons (ed.). 27 fictionalized essays by noted anthropologists examine religion, customs, government, additional facets of life among the Winnebago, Crow, Zuni, Eskimo, other tribes. 480pp. 6⅛ x 9¼. 27377-6

CATALOG OF DOVER BOOKS

FRANK LLOYD WRIGHT'S DANA HOUSE, Donald Hoffmann. Pictorial essay of residential masterpiece with over 160 interior and exterior photos, plans, elevations, sketches and studies. 128pp. 9¼ x 10¾.   29120-0

THE MALE AND FEMALE FIGURE IN MOTION: 60 Classic Photographic Sequences, Eadweard Muybridge. 60 true-action photographs of men and women walking, running, climbing, bending, turning, etc., reproduced from rare 19th-century masterpiece. vi + 121pp. 9 x 12.   24745-7

1001 QUESTIONS ANSWERED ABOUT THE SEASHORE, N. J. Berrill and Jacquelyn Berrill. Queries answered about dolphins, sea snails, sponges, starfish, fishes, shore birds, many others. Covers appearance, breeding, growth, feeding, much more. 305pp. 5¼ x 8¼.   23366-9

ATTRACTING BIRDS TO YOUR YARD, William J. Weber. Easy-to-follow guide offers advice on how to attract the greatest diversity of birds: birdhouses, feeders, water and waterers, much more. 96pp. 5³⁄₁₆ x 8¼.   28927-3

MEDICINAL AND OTHER USES OF NORTH AMERICAN PLANTS: A Historical Survey with Special Reference to the Eastern Indian Tribes, Charlotte Erichsen-Brown. Chronological historical citations document 500 years of usage of plants, trees, shrubs native to eastern Canada, northeastern U.S. Also complete identifying information. 343 illustrations. 544pp. 6½ x 9¼.   25951-X

STORYBOOK MAZES, Dave Phillips. 23 stories and mazes on two-page spreads: Wizard of Oz, Treasure Island, Robin Hood, etc. Solutions. 64pp. 8¼ x 11. 23628-5

AMERICAN NEGRO SONGS: 230 Folk Songs and Spirituals, Religious and Secular, John W. Work. This authoritative study traces the African influences of songs sung and played by black Americans at work, in church, and as entertainment. The author discusses the lyric significance of such songs as "Swing Low, Sweet Chariot," "John Henry," and others and offers the words and music for 230 songs. Bibliography. Index of Song Titles. 272pp. 6½ x 9¼.   40271-1

MOVIE-STAR PORTRAITS OF THE FORTIES, John Kobal (ed.). 163 glamor, studio photos of 106 stars of the 1940s: Rita Hayworth, Ava Gardner, Marlon Brando, Clark Gable, many more. 176pp. 8⅜ x 11¼.   23546-7

BENCHLEY LOST AND FOUND, Robert Benchley. Finest humor from early 30s, about pet peeves, child psychologists, post office and others. Mostly unavailable elsewhere. 73 illustrations by Peter Arno and others. 183pp. 5⅜ x 8½.   22410-4

YEKL and THE IMPORTED BRIDEGROOM AND OTHER STORIES OF YIDDISH NEW YORK, Abraham Cahan. Film Hester Street based on *Yekl* (1896). Novel, other stories among first about Jewish immigrants on N.Y.'s East Side. 240pp. 5⅜ x 8½.   22427-9

SELECTED POEMS, Walt Whitman. Generous sampling from *Leaves of Grass*. Twenty-four poems include "I Hear America Singing," "Song of the Open Road," "I Sing the Body Electric," "When Lilacs Last in the Dooryard Bloom'd," "O Captain! My Captain!"–all reprinted from an authoritative edition. Lists of titles and first lines. 128pp. 5³⁄₁₆ x 8¼.   26878-0

THE BEST TALES OF HOFFMANN, E. T. A. Hoffmann. 10 of Hoffmann's most important stories: "Nutcracker and the King of Mice," "The Golden Flowerpot," etc. 458pp. 5⅜ x 8½. 21793-0

FROM FETISH TO GOD IN ANCIENT EGYPT, E. A. Wallis Budge. Rich detailed survey of Egyptian conception of "God" and gods, magic, cult of animals, Osiris, more. Also, superb English translations of hymns and legends. 240 illustrations. 545pp. 5⅜ x 8½. 25803-3

FRENCH STORIES/CONTES FRANÇAIS: A Dual-Language Book, Wallace Fowlie. Ten stories by French masters, Voltaire to Camus: "Micromegas" by Voltaire; "The Atheist's Mass" by Balzac; "Minuet" by de Maupassant; "The Guest" by Camus, six more. Excellent English translations on facing pages. Also French-English vocabulary list, exercises, more. 352pp. 5⅜ x 8½. 26443-2

CHICAGO AT THE TURN OF THE CENTURY IN PHOTOGRAPHS: 122 Historic Views from the Collections of the Chicago Historical Society, Larry A. Viskochil. Rare large-format prints offer detailed views of City Hall, State Street, the Loop, Hull House, Union Station, many other landmarks, circa 1904-1913. Introduction. Captions. Maps. 144pp. 9⅜ x 12¼. 24656-6

OLD BROOKLYN IN EARLY PHOTOGRAPHS, 1865-1929, William Lee Younger. Luna Park, Gravesend race track, construction of Grand Army Plaza, moving of Hotel Brighton, etc. 157 previously unpublished photographs. 165pp. 8⅞ x 11¾. 23587-4

THE MYTHS OF THE NORTH AMERICAN INDIANS, Lewis Spence. Rich anthology of the myths and legends of the Algonquins, Iroquois, Pawnees and Sioux, prefaced by an extensive historical and ethnological commentary. 36 illustrations. 480pp. 5⅜ x 8½. 25967-6

AN ENCYCLOPEDIA OF BATTLES: Accounts of Over 1,560 Battles from 1479 B.C. to the Present, David Eggenberger. Essential details of every major battle in recorded history from the first battle of Megiddo in 1479 B.C. to Grenada in 1984. List of Battle Maps. New Appendix covering the years 1967-1984. Index. 99 illustrations. 544pp. 6½ x 9¼. 24913-1

SAILING ALONE AROUND THE WORLD, Captain Joshua Slocum. First man to sail around the world, alone, in small boat. One of great feats of seamanship told in delightful manner. 67 illustrations. 294pp. 5⅜ x 8½. 20326-3

ANARCHISM AND OTHER ESSAYS, Emma Goldman. Powerful, penetrating, prophetic essays on direct action, role of minorities, prison reform, puritan hypocrisy, violence, etc. 271pp. 5⅜ x 8½. 22484-8

MYTHS OF THE HINDUS AND BUDDHISTS, Ananda K. Coomaraswamy and Sister Nivedita. Great stories of the epics; deeds of Krishna, Shiva, taken from puranas, Vedas, folk tales; etc. 32 illustrations. 400pp. 5⅜ x 8½. 21759-0

THE TRAUMA OF BIRTH, Otto Rank. Rank's controversial thesis that anxiety neurosis is caused by profound psychological trauma which occurs at birth. 256pp. 5⅜ x 8½. 27974-X

A THEOLOGICO-POLITICAL TREATISE, Benedict Spinoza. Also contains unfinished Political Treatise. Great classic on religious liberty, theory of government on common consent. R. Elwes translation. Total of 421pp. 5⅜ x 8½. 20249-6

MY BONDAGE AND MY FREEDOM, Frederick Douglass. Born a slave, Douglass became outspoken force in antislavery movement. The best of Douglass' autobiographies. Graphic description of slave life. 464pp. 5⅜ x 8½.   22457-0

FOLLOWING THE EQUATOR: A Journey Around the World, Mark Twain. Fascinating humorous account of 1897 voyage to Hawaii, Australia, India, New Zealand, etc. Ironic, bemused reports on peoples, customs, climate, flora and fauna, politics, much more. 197 illustrations. 720pp. 5⅜ x 8½.   26113-1

THE PEOPLE CALLED SHAKERS, Edward D. Andrews. Definitive study of Shakers: origins, beliefs, practices, dances, social organization, furniture and crafts, etc. 33 illustrations. 351pp. 5⅜ x 8½.   21081-2

THE MYTHS OF GREECE AND ROME, H. A. Guerber. A classic of mythology, generously illustrated, long prized for its simple, graphic, accurate retelling of the principal myths of Greece and Rome, and for its commentary on their origins and significance. With 64 illustrations by Michelangelo, Raphael, Titian, Rubens, Canova, Bernini and others. 480pp. 5⅜ x 8½.   27584-1

PSYCHOLOGY OF MUSIC, Carl E. Seashore. Classic work discusses music as a medium from psychological viewpoint. Clear treatment of physical acoustics, auditory apparatus, sound perception, development of musical skills, nature of musical feeling, host of other topics. 88 figures. 408pp. 5⅜ x 8½.   21851-1

THE PHILOSOPHY OF HISTORY, Georg W. Hegel. Great classic of Western thought develops concept that history is not chance but rational process, the evolution of freedom. 457pp. 5⅜ x 8½.   20112-0

THE BOOK OF TEA, Kakuzo Okakura. Minor classic of the Orient: entertaining, charming explanation, interpretation of traditional Japanese culture in terms of tea ceremony. 94pp. 5⅜ x 8½.   20070-1

LIFE IN ANCIENT EGYPT, Adolf Erman. Fullest, most thorough, detailed older account with much not in more recent books, domestic life, religion, magic, medicine, commerce, much more. Many illustrations reproduce tomb paintings, carvings, hieroglyphs, etc. 597pp. 5⅜ x 8½.   22632-8

SUNDIALS, Their Theory and Construction, Albert Waugh. Far and away the best, most thorough coverage of ideas, mathematics concerned, types, construction, adjusting anywhere. Simple, nontechnical treatment allows even children to build several of these dials. Over 100 illustrations. 230pp. 5⅜ x 8½.   22947-5

THEORETICAL HYDRODYNAMICS, L. M. Milne-Thomson. Classic exposition of the mathematical theory of fluid motion, applicable to both hydrodynamics and aerodynamics. Over 600 exercises. 768pp. 6⅛ x 9¼.   68970-0

SONGS OF EXPERIENCE: Facsimile Reproduction with 26 Plates in Full Color, William Blake. 26 full-color plates from a rare 1826 edition. Includes "The Tyger," "London," "Holy Thursday," and other poems. Printed text of poems. 48pp. 5¼ x 7.   24636-1

OLD-TIME VIGNETTES IN FULL COLOR, Carol Belanger Grafton (ed.). Over 390 charming, often sentimental illustrations, selected from archives of Victorian graphics—pretty women posing, children playing, food, flowers, kittens and puppies, smiling cherubs, birds and butterflies, much more. All copyright-free. 48pp. 9¼ x 12¼.   27269-9

CATALOG OF DOVER BOOKS

PERSPECTIVE FOR ARTISTS, Rex Vicat Cole. Depth, perspective of sky and sea, shadows, much more, not usually covered. 391 diagrams, 81 reproductions of drawings and paintings. 279pp. 5⅜ x 8½.   22487-2

DRAWING THE LIVING FIGURE, Joseph Sheppard. Innovative approach to artistic anatomy focuses on specifics of surface anatomy, rather than muscles and bones. Over 170 drawings of live models in front, back and side views, and in widely varying poses. Accompanying diagrams. 177 illustrations. Introduction. Index. 144pp. 8⅜ x11¼.   26723-7

GOTHIC AND OLD ENGLISH ALPHABETS: 100 Complete Fonts, Dan X. Solo. Add power, elegance to posters, signs, other graphics with 100 stunning copyright-free alphabets: Blackstone, Dolbey, Germania, 97 more—including many lower-case, numerals, punctuation marks. 104pp. 8⅛ x 11.   24695-7

HOW TO DO BEADWORK, Mary White. Fundamental book on craft from simple projects to five-bead chains and woven works. 106 illustrations. 142pp. 5⅜ x 8.
                                                                           20697-1

THE BOOK OF WOOD CARVING, Charles Marshall Sayers. Finest book for beginners discusses fundamentals and offers 34 designs. "Absolutely first rate . . . well thought out and well executed."–E. J. Tangerman. 118pp. 7¾ x 10⅝.   23654-4

ILLUSTRATED CATALOG OF CIVIL WAR MILITARY GOODS: Union Army Weapons, Insignia, Uniform Accessories, and Other Equipment, Schuyler, Hartley, and Graham. Rare, profusely illustrated 1846 catalog includes Union Army uniform and dress regulations, arms and ammunition, coats, insignia, flags, swords, rifles, etc. 226 illustrations. 160pp. 9 x 12.   24939-5

WOMEN'S FASHIONS OF THE EARLY 1900s: An Unabridged Republication of "New York Fashions, 1909," National Cloak & Suit Co. Rare catalog of mail-order fashions documents women's and children's clothing styles shortly after the turn of the century. Captions offer full descriptions, prices. Invaluable resource for fashion, costume historians. Approximately 725 illustrations. 128pp. 8⅜ x 11¼.   27276-1

THE 1912 AND 1915 GUSTAV STICKLEY FURNITURE CATALOGS, Gustav Stickley. With over 200 detailed illustrations and descriptions, these two catalogs are essential reading and reference materials and identification guides for Stickley furniture. Captions cite materials, dimensions and prices. 112pp. 6½ x 9¼.   26676-1

EARLY AMERICAN LOCOMOTIVES, John H. White, Jr. Finest locomotive engravings from early 19th century: historical (1804–74), main-line (after 1870), special, foreign, etc. 147 plates. 142pp. 11⅜ x 8¼.   22772-3

THE TALL SHIPS OF TODAY IN PHOTOGRAPHS, Frank O. Braynard. Lavishly illustrated tribute to nearly 100 majestic contemporary sailing vessels: Amerigo Vespucci, Clearwater, Constitution, Eagle, Mayflower, Sea Cloud, Victory, many more. Authoritative captions provide statistics, background on each ship. 190 black-and-white photographs and illustrations. Introduction. 128pp. 8⅞ x 11¾.
                                                                           27163-3

PIANO TUNING, J. Cree Fischer. Clearest, best book for beginner, amateur. Simple repairs, raising dropped notes, tuning by easy method of flattened fifths. No previous skills needed. 4 illustrations. 201pp. 5⅜ x 8½. 23267-0

HINTS TO SINGERS, Lillian Nordica. Selecting the right teacher, developing confidence, overcoming stage fright, and many other important skills receive thoughtful discussion in this indispensible guide, written by a world-famous diva of four decades' experience. 96pp. 5⅜ x 8½. 40094-8

THE COMPLETE NONSENSE OF EDWARD LEAR, Edward Lear. All nonsense limericks, zany alphabets, Owl and Pussycat, songs, nonsense botany, etc., illustrated by Lear. Total of 320pp. 5⅜ x 8½. (Available in U.S. only.) 20167-8

VICTORIAN PARLOUR POETRY: An Annotated Anthology, Michael R. Turner. 117 gems by Longfellow, Tennyson, Browning, many lesser-known poets. "The Village Blacksmith," "Curfew Must Not Ring Tonight," "Only a Baby Small," dozens more, often difficult to find elsewhere. Index of poets, titles, first lines. xxiii + 325pp. 5⅝ x 8¼. 27044-0

DUBLINERS, James Joyce. Fifteen stories offer vivid, tightly focused observations of the lives of Dublin's poorer classes. At least one, "The Dead," is considered a masterpiece. Reprinted complete and unabridged from standard edition. 160pp. 5³⁄₁₆ x 8¼. 26870-5

GREAT WEIRD TALES: 14 Stories by Lovecraft, Blackwood, Machen and Others, S. T. Joshi (ed.). 14 spellbinding tales, including "The Sin Eater," by Fiona McLeod, "The Eye Above the Mantel," by Frank Belknap Long, as well as renowned works by R. H. Barlow, Lord Dunsany, Arthur Machen, W. C. Morrow and eight other masters of the genre. 256pp. 5⅜ x 8½. (Available in U.S. only.) 40436-6

THE BOOK OF THE SACRED MAGIC OF ABRAMELIN THE MAGE, translated by S. MacGregor Mathers. Medieval manuscript of ceremonial magic. Basic document in Aleister Crowley, Golden Dawn groups. 268pp. 5⅜ x 8½. 23211-5

NEW RUSSIAN-ENGLISH AND ENGLISH-RUSSIAN DICTIONARY, M. A. O'Brien. This is a remarkably handy Russian dictionary, containing a surprising amount of information, including over 70,000 entries. 366pp. 4½ x 6⅛. 20208-9

HISTORIC HOMES OF THE AMERICAN PRESIDENTS, Second, Revised Edition, Irvin Haas. A traveler's guide to American Presidential homes, most open to the public, depicting and describing homes occupied by every American President from George Washington to George Bush. With visiting hours, admission charges, travel routes. 175 photographs. Index. 160pp. 8¼ x 11. 26751-2

NEW YORK IN THE FORTIES, Andreas Feininger. 162 brilliant photographs by the well-known photographer, formerly with *Life* magazine. Commuters, shoppers, Times Square at night, much else from city at its peak. Captions by John von Hartz. 181pp. 9¼ x 10¾. 23585-8

INDIAN SIGN LANGUAGE, William Tomkins. Over 525 signs developed by Sioux and other tribes. Written instructions and diagrams. Also 290 pictographs. 111pp. 6⅛ x 9¼. 22029-X

PHOTOGRAPHIC SKETCHBOOK OF THE CIVIL WAR, Alexander Gardner. 100 photos taken on field during the Civil War. Famous shots of Manassas Harper's Ferry, Lincoln, Richmond, slave pens, etc. 244pp. 10⅝ x 8¼. 22731-6

FIVE ACRES AND INDEPENDENCE, Maurice G. Kains. Great back-to-the-land classic explains basics of self-sufficient farming. The one book to get. 95 illustrations. 397pp. 5⅜ x 8½. 20974-1

SONGS OF EASTERN BIRDS, Dr. Donald J. Borror. Songs and calls of 60 species most common to eastern U.S.: warblers, woodpeckers, flycatchers, thrushes, larks, many more in high-quality recording. Cassette and manual 99912-2

A MODERN HERBAL, Margaret Grieve. Much the fullest, most exact, most useful compilation of herbal material. Gigantic alphabetical encyclopedia, from aconite to zedoary, gives botanical information, medical properties, folklore, economic uses, much else. Indispensable to serious reader. 161 illustrations. 888pp. 6½ x 9¼. 2-vol. set. (Available in U.S. only.) Vol. I: 22798-7
Vol. II: 22799-5

HIDDEN TREASURE MAZE BOOK, Dave Phillips. Solve 34 challenging mazes accompanied by heroic tales of adventure. Evil dragons, people-eating plants, blood-thirsty giants, many more dangerous adversaries lurk at every twist and turn. 34 mazes, stories, solutions. 48pp. 8¼ x 11. 24566-7

LETTERS OF W. A. MOZART, Wolfgang A. Mozart. Remarkable letters show bawdy wit, humor, imagination, musical insights, contemporary musical world; includes some letters from Leopold Mozart. 276pp. 5⅜ x 8½. 22859-2

BASIC PRINCIPLES OF CLASSICAL BALLET, Agrippina Vaganova. Great Russian theoretician, teacher explains methods for teaching classical ballet. 118 illus-trations. 175pp. 5⅜ x 8½. 22036-2

THE JUMPING FROG, Mark Twain. Revenge edition. The original story of The Celebrated Jumping Frog of Calaveras County, a hapless French translation, and Twain's hilarious "retranslation" from the French. 12 illustrations. 66pp. 5⅜ x 8½. 22686-7

BEST REMEMBERED POEMS, Martin Gardner (ed.). The 126 poems in this superb collection of 19th- and 20th-century British and American verse range from Shelley's "To a Skylark" to the impassioned "Renascence" of Edna St. Vincent Millay and to Edward Lear's whimsical "The Owl and the Pussycat." 224pp. 5⅜ x 8½. 27165-X

COMPLETE SONNETS, William Shakespeare. Over 150 exquisite poems deal with love, friendship, the tyranny of time, beauty's evanescence, death and other themes in language of remarkable power, precision and beauty. Glossary of archaic terms. 80pp. 5³⁄₁₆ x 8¼. 26686-9

THE BATTLES THAT CHANGED HISTORY, Fletcher Pratt. Eminent historian profiles 16 crucial conflicts, ancient to modern, that changed the course of civiliza-tion. 352pp. 5⅜ x 8½. 41129-X

CATALOG OF DOVER BOOKS

THE STORY OF THE TITANIC AS TOLD BY ITS SURVIVORS, Jack Winocour (ed.). What it was really like. Panic, despair, shocking inefficiency, and a little heroism. More thrilling than any fictional account. 26 illustrations. 320pp. 5⅜ x 8½.
20610-6

FAIRY AND FOLK TALES OF THE IRISH PEASANTRY, William Butler Yeats (ed.). Treasury of 64 tales from the twilight world of Celtic myth and legend: "The Soul Cages," "The Kildare Pooka," "King O'Toole and his Goose," many more. Introduction and Notes by W. B. Yeats. 352pp. 5⅜ x 8½.
26941-8

BUDDHIST MAHAYANA TEXTS, E. B. Cowell and others (eds.). Superb, accurate translations of basic documents in Mahayana Buddhism, highly important in history of religions. The Buddha-karita of Asvaghosha, Larger Sukhavativyuha, more. 448pp. 5⅜ x 8½.
25552-2

ONE TWO THREE . . . INFINITY: Facts and Speculations of Science, George Gamow. Great physicist's fascinating, readable overview of contemporary science: number theory, relativity, fourth dimension, entropy, genes, atomic structure, much more. 128 illustrations. Index. 352pp. 5⅜ x 8½.
25664-2

EXPERIMENTATION AND MEASUREMENT, W. J. Youden. Introductory manual explains laws of measurement in simple terms and offers tips for achieving accuracy and minimizing errors. Mathematics of measurement, use of instruments, experimenting with machines. 1994 edition. Foreword. Preface. Introduction. Epilogue. Selected Readings. Glossary. Index. Tables and figures. 128pp. 5⅜ x 8½.
40451-X

DALÍ ON MODERN ART: The Cuckolds of Antiquated Modern Art, Salvador Dalí. Influential painter skewers modern art and its practitioners. Outrageous evaluations of Picasso, Cézanne, Turner, more. 15 renderings of paintings discussed. 44 calligraphic decorations by Dalí. 96pp. 5⅜ x 8½. (Available in U.S. only.)
29220-7

ANTIQUE PLAYING CARDS: A Pictorial History, Henry René D'Allemagne. Over 900 elaborate, decorative images from rare playing cards (14th–20th centuries): Bacchus, death, dancing dogs, hunting scenes, royal coats of arms, players cheating, much more. 96pp. 9¼ x 12¼.
29265-7

MAKING FURNITURE MASTERPIECES: 30 Projects with Measured Drawings, Franklin H. Gottshall. Step-by-step instructions, illustrations for constructing handsome, useful pieces, among them a Sheraton desk, Chippendale chair, Spanish desk, Queen Anne table and a William and Mary dressing mirror. 224pp. 8⅛ x 11¼.
29338-6

THE FOSSIL BOOK: A Record of Prehistoric Life, Patricia V. Rich et al. Profusely illustrated definitive guide covers everything from single-celled organisms and dinosaurs to birds and mammals and the interplay between climate and man. Over 1,500 illustrations. 760pp. 7½ x 10⅛.
29371-8

Paperbound unless otherwise indicated. Available at your book dealer, online at www.doverpublications.com, or by writing to Dept. GI, Dover Publications, Inc., 31 East 2nd Street, Mineola, NY 11501. For current price information or for free catalogues (please indicate field of interest), write to Dover Publications or log on to www.doverpublications.com and see every Dover book in print. Dover publishes more than 500 books each year on science, elementary and advanced mathematics, biology, music, art, literary history, social sciences, and other areas.